GREAT DECISIONS 2018

W9-DET-992

FOREIGN POLICY ASSOCIATION
1918

GREAT DECISIONS IS A TRADEMARK OF THE FOREIGN POLICY ASSOCIATION.

© COPYRIGHT 2018 BY FOREIGN POLICY ASSOCIATION, INC., 470 PARK AVENUE SOUTH, NEW YORK, NEW YORK 10016.

All rights reserved.

No part of this book may be reproduced in any form, or by any means, without permission in writing from the publisher.

PRINTED IN THE UNITED STATES OF AMERICA BY DART-MOUTH PRINTING COMPANY, HANOVER, NH.

LIBRARY OF CONGRESS CONTROL NUMBER: 2017953170

ISBN: 978-0-87124-261-7

Researched as of November 26, 2017.

The authors are responsible for factual accuracy and for the views expressed.

FPA itself takes no position on issues of U.S. foreign policy.

BONDS BEYOND BORDERS.

At Citi, enabling growth and economic progress, while connecting culture, ideas and people, have always been our focus.

The World's Citi

American Foreign Policy: The Reckoning

A S THE FOREIGN POLICY ASSOCIATION (FPA) marks its centenary in 2018, it is appropriate to reflect on the mission of this old and honorable institution.

FPA's roots can be traced to an undergraduate at Princeton University, who went by the name of Tommy. He became a lawyer and, subsequently, returned to school to complete a doctorate in political science. Armed with this degree, he decided that the name Tommy lacked sufficient gravitas. So he assumed his middle name: Woodrow. In quick succession, he would become president of Princeton University, governor of New Jersey, the 28th president of the United States and an ardent advocate for the League of Nations.

President Wilson's worldview was steeped in high idealism. "We are spiritually superior," President Wilson would assert in his declaration of war against Germany in 1917—a declaration couched not in terms of safeguarding the national interests but to make the world "safe for democracy." Overturning the cautious instincts expressed in George Washington's Farewell Address, President Wilson would commit the United States to a posture of enthusiastic global engagement. "Shall we or any other free people hesitate to accept this great duty? Dare we reject it and break the heart of the world?" President Wilson would ask a divided Senate as he sought ratification of the Treaty of Versailles.

Sensing the need to rally public support for President Wilson's vision for a new world order, a distinguished group of academics and journalists came together to found the Foreign Policy Association. Their legacy is intertwined with the arc of the narrative of U.S. foreign policy from Woodrow Wilson to the present. It is a narrative that cleaves from idealism to realism, from elitism to populism. The protagonists are familiar: isolationists and internationalists, know-nothings and know-it-alls, threat-inflaters and threat-deflaters.

The current revival of realism in U.S. foreign policy evolved over time. Twenty years ago, the quadrennial *Report on Public Opinion on Foreign Policy,* published by the Chicago Council on Global Affairs, identified on the part of those surveyed "a narrower definition of American self-interest and sense of responsibility in world affairs." The direction of this trend of public opinion was clear in its tendency to favor limits on the scope of America's international concerns. The "worst problem," for a majority of those surveyed, was "getting involved in the affairs of other countries." Protecting jobs and wariness of immigrants were deemed by the publisher of the report to be at record levels of public concern.

While growing numbers of Americans were expressing reluctance to shoulder the burden of global leadership, Washington was waging endless wars in Afghanistan and Iraq. Indeed, the U.S. military has been deployed in 188 interventions around the world since the end of the Cold War.

The first rule of realism is prudence. American military might is at its zenith when it deters, not when it is deployed. It is difficult to achieve one's ends with the sword, which is a blunt instrument in international relations.

Public opinion sets the parameters of the possible for foreign policy in a democracy. From its inception, FPA has sought to engage the public at the grassroots level. For 100 years, FPA has been committed to elevating the foreign policy debate by providing Americans with scrupulously objective, non-partisan information about world affairs. This information is presented contextually, with careful analyses of realistic policy options. In this way, FPA seeks to ventilate the issues and to contribute to a national conversation on U.S. foreign policy.

International affairs literacy has never counted for more. One has to understand world events to understand the global economy. Why is it important to have a handle on the global economy? Because, increasingly, globalization affects many aspects of our lives. Today, 23 million jobs in the United States are tied to international trade. The *2017 Chicago Council on Global Affairs Survey* found that Americans strongly support international trade, with 78% saying international trade is good for U.S. consumers and 72% agreeing that it is good for the U.S. economy.

FPA's mission is inseparable from America's role in the world. At issue are some of the most far-reaching decisions a government can make. Should the war in Afghanistan, now in its 17th year, continue to be fought? After expending $3 trillion dollars in the Middle East, what should America's role be in that region? And, more broadly, can America continue to bear the burden of Pax Americana?

Warfare is no substitute for attacking problems. The growing national security implications of climate change, the apocalyptic threats posed by nuclear proliferation, the risks presented by global pandemics, are just some of the challenges that argue for preventive engagement by the United States. A multilateral approach, where the U.S. takes a leadership role, will invariably be more effective than a unilateral approach. The United Nations, with its growing capabilities for conflict prevention, should not be marginalized. Indeed, President Franklin Delano Roosevelt could not have been more emphatic in his last speech to FPA on the importance of the United Nations to what he called "the enterprise of waging peace."

Domestic crises, however, cry for attention. A real sobriety about resources and capabilities deployed abroad is required. A central challenge is to reweave America's social fabric on the premise that the whole society advances together. This is what government of the people, by the people, for the people is about.

Alexis de Toqueville admired the democratic government devised by America's Founding Fathers. He stressed that: "the greatness of America lies not in being more enlightened than the other nations, but rather in her ability to repair her faults." Therein lies the genius of democracy. Democracy is what gives us the possibility of redemption.

This brings me back to FPA's mission. In the words of FPA Director Peter Krogh, "Educational institutions are fundamentally acts of faith." In our new century, our success at FPA will depend on how faithfully we pursue an inclusive dialogue on America's future in an interdependent world.

Noel V. Lateef
President and CEO
Foreign Policy Association

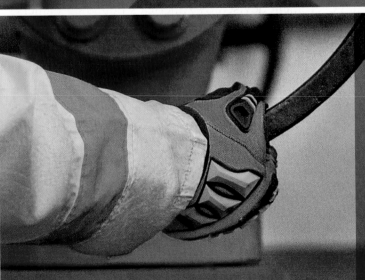

The energy to see and the energy to do.

Our energy has been traveling around 5 continents for over 60 years. Thanks to the work of all our hands.

eni

eni.com

Today we face risks
that didn't exist
20 years ago.

Some of them didn't
exist a week ago.

Whether it's from political upheaval impeding construction or hackers targeting servers, no successful company today can afford to ignore our world's emerging risks. We know you can't wait to let history play out, so we create insurance policies that reflect today's reality. When your company's goals can't wait for the world to settle down, reach out to Starr.

STARRCOMPANIES.COM

Property / Casualty / Accident / Aviation / Marine

STARR
COMPANIES

The Great War, Woodrow Wilson and the FPA

On April 2, 1917, President Woodrow Wilson addressed a joint session of Congress and called for a declaration of war against Germany. The resulting congressional vote brought the United States into World War I. (LIBRARY OF CONGRESS PRINTS AND PHOTOGRAPHS DIVISION, WASHINGTON, DC)

The three parts of my remarks—each of which is worthy of a lecture in itself—are intimately interrelated. The Great War set the scene for Woodrow Wilson to step onto the world stage and, having done so, he served as the inspiration for the founding of the FPA. The FPA essentially emerged from the crucible of the Great War and the mind of Woodrow Wilson.

With respect to the Great War, (which the United States entered 100 years ago, in 1917), memory of it has, in the words of historian Niall Ferguson, fallen into the historical void between the American Civil War and World War II. This is unfortunate inasmuch as the Great War spawned a chaotic and bloody 20th century and continues to condition the world we live in today.

PETER F. KROGH *is Dean Emeritus and Distinguished Professor of International Affairs at Georgetown University. He is the longest serving Dean of the Edmund A. Walsh School of Foreign Service at Georgetown University and the long-time moderator of the Foreign Policy Association's Great Decisions Television Series on PBS. He has served as a Director of the Foreign Policy Association since 1977.*

In his book *The Pity of War,* Ferguson calls World War I "the greatest error in modern history." It was cataclysmic across-the-board. It first buried and mutilated vast numbers of soldiers and civilians. Ten million soldiers were killed (sometimes upwards of 100,000 in a single battle and on average 6,000 a day for four and a quarter years), another 21 million seriously wounded, 8 million of whom returned home permanently disabled. Twenty-two million civilians were killed or maimed. Eight million horses were killed. The war from hell (fought with new, terrible weapons—the machine gun, poisonous gas, the submarine—and from within 60,000 miles of trenches with the "unknown killing the unseen") decimated a generation (France lost a quarter of its male population between the ages of 18 and 30), wrecked entire countries and empires, threw the Middle East into disorder and then spawned an early 20th century featuring communism, facism, totalitarianism, revanchism, civic and social violence, class conflict and yet another world war.

One looks back on all the pain and finds absolutely no gain. The world was infinitely better off before the war than in its aftermath. One searches almost in vain to find anything positive issuing from what George Kennan called "the great seminal catastrophe of the 20th century."

Perhaps one positive is that the history of the Great War might yield insight into how wars start and thus how they might be avoided in the future. A second positive is that the war ground on for so long and was so horrendous that it stirred up a public demand for the democratization of the conduct of foreign policy. And, finally a third positive is that, as Europe lay in ruins, a clarion call for a new world order was issued by Woodrow Wilson. As beleaguered as that call became, it still stands as a lofty goal summoning the conduct of international affairs to a higher standard. Let me now briefly address these three points of light.

When Woodrow Wilson was asked what started the Great War, he is alleged to have responded "everything in general and nothing in particular." The general factors he was referring to included: militarism, balance-of-power politics and their accompanying alliances (as transmission belts for war) and imperialism. But particulars also fed into the war-starting equation. One prominent particular was the condition of the Austro-Hungarian empire in 1914.

I think the start of the Great War leads us to the weakness of a major actor on the world stage in 1914; namely, the Austro-Hungarian empire. It was at the time a once great empire coming apart at the seams and on the way out as a self-styled great power. It felt compelled to prove that it was still in business as a great power by thrashing Serbia, the country it held responsible for the assassination in Sarajevo of its archduke, Franz Ferdinand. It was the bellicosity of a weakened player in the international system bent on proving its manhood that laid a basis, provided the tinder, for the Great War.

In reflecting on this explanation, it may help us understand the behavior of Russia today. Russia, like Austria-Hungary once a great empire, is a weakened great power, trying to reassert itself on the world stage. We see this in frictions across the board as Russia uses Syria as a stage for its comeback as a great regional and international power, reclaims the Crimea, aggressively protects its interests in Ukraine and reacts neuralgically to the mission creep, or expansion, of the North Atlantic Treaty Organization (NATO).

With respect to the democratization of the formation and conduct of foreign policy, the Great War brought forth demands that this be done. While the citizenry of the combatants entered the war quite enthusiastically, as the carnage and war weariness spread, so too did demands that the public be brought into the take offs, and not just the crash landings, of national security policies. The FPA emerged from these demands. It was born in the crucible of the Great War.

The earliest expression of demands for the social control of foreign policy emanated from Great Britain, but it was Woodrow Wilson who articulated them on the world stage and stood for them to wide acclaim right into his final hours.

Before turning to Woodrow Wilson's role, let me say a few things about the man himself and his conduct of foreign policy.

Woodrow Wilson is often seen as a noble figure. And in many ways he was. He can even be seen as a prophet. But he was also in some respects a strange and problematical person. To illustrate this observation—and to have some fun—I will proceed to do something that may astonish you. I am going to compare Woodrow Wilson to our current president without in any way intending to equate the two. So fasten your seat belts for a few minutes.

◼ Woodrow Wilson, like Donald Trump, was an outsider. He had very little political experience and no foreign policy experience before being elected to the presidency of the United States. His prior experience consisted of having served as an ultimately failed president of Princeton (Wilson once quipped that he left Princeton for government service to get out of politics. Henry Kissinger once quipped that academic politics were so intense because the stakes were so low!) Wilson was just a one-term, two-year, 658-day governor of New Jersey before being elected president by a minority of the popular vote.

This introduction is taken from one of a series of "Centennial Lectures" being given in 2017 and 2018 to celebrate the Foreign Policy Association's 100th anniversary. Peter Krogh gave this lecture on November 7, 2017.

A recent sympathetic biographer of Woodrow Wilson conceded that he was "quick tempered and impulsive." Now who does that sound like?

I don't think Donald Trump has any real friends. Neither did Woodrow Wilson. An early supporter of his, Oklahoma Senator Thomas Gore, said of Wilson that "he has no friends, only slaves and enemies." His ambassador in London, Walter Page, observed that "Wilson has no real companions. Nobody talks to him freely and frankly." Woodrow Wilson could not keep friends because once they disagreed with him, he "dropped them abruptly and angrily." His longstanding friendship with Colonel House ended in "absolute estrangement." For his part, Wilson ended his life practically in isolation, refusing even to see those former friends who reached out to him but whom he believed had wronged him.

Woodrow Wilson, like Donald Trump, felt most comfortable when surrounded by members of his family: his wife, his three daughters, his sons-in-law and brothers-in-law. When news of the archduke's assassination arrived in Washington, Wilson was having lunch with his daughter and son-in-law. At the end, his sole companions in his home on S Street were his domineering second wife, Edith Gault, and a brother-in-law from his first marriage who served as his private secretary.

Woodrow Wilson, like Donald Trump, was extraordinarily thin-skinned. He was quick to take offense—even petty— and just as quick to insult his detractors and act in vindictive ways. As one of Wilson's senior officials observed, "Wilson is a good hater."

Finally, Woodrow Wilson took his cherished cause—the League of Nations—directly to the American people, appealing for their support under and over the heads of elected politicians. Trump's constant road trips are a mirror image of the rallies Wilson orchestrated toward the end of his life on a transcontinental train trip designed to sell his League of Nations to the isolationist-oriented American voters in the mid-western and western states

And now on to some salient differences.

Woodrow Wilson was a gifted intellectual and public speaker. No one would attribute these qualities to Donald Trump.

Woodrow Wilson played golf almost every day and was a lousy golfer. Trump plays golf on occasional weekends and is apparently pretty good.

Woodrow Wilson apparently read books (even though he did not learn to read until he was 11 years old) and he went on to write books. Books do not seem to have intruded into Donald Trump's world.

Donald Trump is irritated when our American flag and anthem is disrespected and he condemns those involved. For his part, Woodrow Wilson crushed any dissent from his

President Woodrow Wilson in St. Louis, MO, on a speaking tour to promote the League of Nations. (BETTMANN/GETTY IMAGES)

decision to take the country into the Great War and presided over "a sweeping assault on established American liberties" which included jail time for those who disrespected the American flag.

Wilson was an extraordinarily effective domestic politician, dealing productively with the congress and seeing through to passage major pieces of legislation, including the establishment of the Federal Trade Commission, the Federal Reserve System and a graduated income tax. At least out of the starting gate, Trump has run into nothing but trouble on Capitol Hill.

While both men envisaged making America greater, their paths toward that objective differ dramatically. Woodrow Wilson wanted to lead America proudly—some would say arrogantly—onto the world stage, there to serve as the "world's overseer," the world's conscience if you will. Wilson sought to establish idealism at the core of American foreign policy. Trump favors a recessional from that now far-flung stage to concentrate on building up America from within, while dislodging idealism from its central place in our foreign policy.

Wilson felt that America had a responsibility and an opportunity to teach the world good governance. Trump feels that the U.S. has no such obligation and wants to get the U.S. out of the nation-building business that Wilsonianism had led us into.

And this brings us to Woodrow Wilson's conduct of foreign policy, for which he, like Donald Trump, had no prior experience. Prior to his election as president, Wilson's first-hand exposure to the world consisted of a couple of vacation trips to the Lake District of England. In fact, as he assumed the burdens of the presidency, he openly worried that it would be a cruel twist of fate if challenges would confront him from beyond the waters' edge.

But this they did, first issuing from the Western Hemisphere and then from across the pond. The former led him to order interventions in Mexico, the Caribbean and Central America. The latter led him to summon an intervention in the old world that abandoned the country's historic isolation from the travails of Europe, plunged his country into a world war and the peacemaking that followed it.

One is obliged to ask why he led his country into the Great War and whether it was wise for him to do so.

The conventional wisdom is that Wilson took the new world into an old world bloodbath to defend the rights of Americans to travel freely and safely on the high seas. After the German sinking of the passenger liners the *Lusitania* in 1915, with the loss of 123 American lives, and the *Sussex* in 1916 with five Americans injured, and then renewed German pursuit in February 1917 of unrestricted submarine warfare, Wilson decided that the upholding of American rights to safe passage on the high seas and America's honor were at stake and asked congress to authorize America to fight alongside Great Britain and France, not as an ally, but as an "associated power."

While the depredations of submarine warfare provided the proximate excuse to go to war, the declaration he presented to Congress involved much more than that. It essentially called for a new world order grounded in governments of, for and by the people. Woodrow Wilson was going to war to personally reengineer the world, liberating it from balance-of-power politics and militarism and reestablishing it upon liberal principles, to wit: freer trade, disarmament, the self-determination of peoples and a league to enforce peace. Justice would replace power as the foundation of a new world order.

Woodrow Wilson embarked on a crusade to, in his own words, make the world "safe for democracy," It was ironic and even hypocritical for him to do so inasmuch as he was not presiding over a democracy at his own home base. Women and blacks had no voting franchise in Wilson's America. But he believed that if people controlled their governments, rather than vice versa, the world would be made safe for peace. He could not pursue this crusade from the sidelines. He could only do it from a seat at the peacemaking table, and he could not get that seat unless his country, too, had spilled blood in the Great War.

So off the *doughboys* went—several million of them—their sheer numbers swinging the correlation of forces decisively in favor of the allied French and British forces. In consequence, the Germans—whose territory was still intact (but who were gradually being starved to death by a British naval blockade)—sought an armistice based on acceptance of Woodrow Wilson's liberal international order. That is the last anyone saw of that hoped-for international order, as vindictive terms of an armistice were shoved down the throats of the Germans with even more vindictive terms of a peace treaty to follow.

Woodrow Wilson got his seat at the table at the cost of 114,000 American lives; but all he got at the table was a covenant for what became a stillborn League of Nations. The other elements of his liberal international order were pretty thoroughly trashed in the treaty and, as Wilson once predicted, a second world war soon followed.

So should we have entered the war in the first place? Frankly, a very strong case can be made—and has been made—that we should have stayed out of the war, let the European combatants fight to a standstill, and leave it to them to, on the basis of equality, engineer a peace without victory (that Wilson had originally advocated!). Then maybe Germany, Italy and Japan would not have proceeded to tear up a peace treaty that they resented and the Middle East would not have been constructed along untenable lines, for which we are paying a heavy price today.

Before Woodrow Wilson's liberal international order was buried in 1919 at Versailles and immediately afterward in America, a group of Americans took up its cause at home. And this was, in 1918, the beginning of the FPA. Wilson believed in the democratization of foreign policy and so did groups initially formed under the banner of "the American Union Against Militarism" and "the League of Nations Association," later, in 1921, to be called the Foreign Policy Association.

The initial mission was to sell Woodrow Wilson's peace plan, including especially the League of Nations. In the words of one historian, the Association "carried the torch of internationalism," and of Wilsonianism itself. But, in the early 1920s, the FPA decided that it should not seek to directly influence foreign policy decisions, but to focus instead on public education "in the hope that a well-informed citizenry would push for enlightened policies." This was a hope—and still is a hope—that was inspired and instilled by Woodrow Wilson, who championed the right of the people's voice to be heard in the making of American foreign policy.

The waning of Pax Americana?
by Carla Norrlof

A boy wears a "Make America Great Again" hat at the Gettysburg National Military Park on July 1, 2017, in Gettysburg, PA. The U.S. Park Service issued protest permits for three groups, including Sons of Confederate Veterans and Real 3% Risen, on the 154th anniversary of the battle. (MARK MAKELA/GETTY IMAGES)

Until now, every U.S. president since the end of World War II (WWII) supported a liberal international order (LIO), promoting stable and peaceful interstate relations, open economic relations and individual freedoms, in a rules-based system backed by U.S. military power. Have we reached a turning point and the end of Pax Americana? Scholars have debated this question for decades, prompted in the 1970s and 1980s by apprehension about U.S. decline and in the post-Cold War era by the "rise of the rest" (that is, a post-American world defined by the rise of other countries, as opposed to the decline of the U.S.). But those debates were always "academic." Because the scales of world power change so slowly, no one expected the question to be put to the test anytime soon. When journalist Fareed Zakaria worried about the rise of illiberal democracies 20 years ago, he counted on the U.S.

to backstop liberal rules. The same was true ten years later, when military historian Azar Gat warned about the return of authoritarian great powers. Even Zakaria's more recent bestseller, *The Post-American World*, concerns incremental adjustments in a liberal order supported by the U.S. for decades to come.

Today, the U.S. confronts both external and internal challenges to foreign engagement. These tensions were already visible in the previous administration: War-weary President Barack Obama (2009–17) questioned the wisdom of expansive security commitments, advocating a new course in U.S. foreign policy based on selective engagement, with foreign

CARLA NORRLOF *is an associate professor at the University of Toronto. Her research interests are international political economy and great power politics.*

IS THAT ANY LONGER WORTH SHOULDERING?

(PARESH/THE KHALEEJ TIMES/DUBAI, UAE)

Cartoon Arts International: www.nytsyn.com/cartoons

commitments limited to areas of vital interest. President Donald Trump has not only cast doubt over U.S. security commitments, but more controversially has questioned U.S. economic commit- ments, proposing comprehensive disengagement. Can Pax Americana endure the twin challenges of deep-seated structural changes and the U.S.'s reduced willingness to uphold the system?

Before Pax Americana...

Pax, after the Roman goddess of peace, is often taken to mean a state of peace, but it more accurately describes a secure and stable political and economic order, backed by the principles of the prevailing military power. A Pax emerges after significant victory on the battlefield, and is maintained through foreign interventions, deterrent threats and economic and cultural exchange.

Pax Romana, also called Pax Augusta, was the first Pax. It lasted for two centuries, beginning with the reign of the first Roman emperor, Augustus, in 27 BC, and ending with the death of Emperor Marcus Aurelius in 180 AD. The philosopher, statesman and dramatist Seneca the Younger is credited with having made the first reference to the Roman peace in 55 AD. For Seneca, Pax Romana marked the end of civil war and the beginning of the Augus-

tan era following the defeat of Mark Antony and Cleopatra at the Battle of Actium in 31 BC. Subsequently, Pax Romana took on a broader meaning in the context of imperial conquests.

There nevertheless remained significant alterations between periods of war and peace. Even in Roman times, prominent thinkers were reluctant to equate Pax with peace. The senator and historian Tacitus drew attention to the brutality and devastation required to establish order after foreign subjugation, warning "where they make a desert, they call it peace" ("*ubi solitudinem faciunt, pacem appellant*"). Rather than establishing peace, Pax Romana ushered in a relatively stable order, securing cultural exchange and commerce across the Mediterranean and the Black Sea, covering an area stretching from Britain southward to North Africa and westward to the Middle East.

The Pax Mongolica, typically cited as between about 1270 and 1360 (also called Pax Tartarica), refers to the stability wrought by the Mongol conquests. Similar to Pax Romana, it paved the way for commercial, cultural and scientific exchange. The Mongols used brute

force to subdue challengers and secure sea lanes and trade routes. But by the time the Mongols had established the largest contiguous land "empire" in history, extending from the Pacific Ocean to Poland and from Russia to Pakistan, they had already dissolved into disparate warring khanates (the Yuan dynasty, the Golden Horde, the Chagatai and the Ilkhanate). In contrast to Pax Romana, Pax Mongolica was not enforced by a cohesive, political entity, but separate political entities (the khanates). Thus, it was not a prototypical empire since no single core, but rather multiple cores, ruled peripheral lands.

Pax Ottomana was essentially a Muslim Pax. It began after the fall of Constantinople, captured by the Ottomans, in 1453, and lasted until the very end of the 17th century (1683). At the height of the Ottoman Empire, a zone of political and economic stability was established over the Horn of Africa, the western and most eastern parts of the Middle East, Anatolia, Southern and Eastern Europe, and the Caucasus. During this period, several wars were fought, especially between Persia and the Ottoman Empire over the Caucasus, shifting control between them. The Ottoman sultans secured caravan routes so that commerce could flourish, and new developments in science and the arts spread throughout the region.

Pax Britannica lasted for a century, from the end of the Napoleonic Wars in 1815 to the outbreak of World War I (WWI) in 1914. Like Pax Romana, Pax Britannica was sponsored by an empire. Covering a quarter of the Earth's land mass, and nearly a quarter of the Earth's population, it was the largest non-contiguous empire that ever existed. Under Pax Britannica, the British Royal Navy did what the Romans, the Mongols and the Ottomans had done in the past when they secured sea passages to promote long-distance trade. Pax Britannica was not especially peaceful, but it marked a period largely absent of great power war. Apart from the Crimean War (1854–56), when the Ottoman Empire, Britain, France and Sardinia allied to overthrow Russia in the Balkans, the great powers did not fight each other until the eruption of WWI.

> Before you read, download the companion **Glossary** that includes definitions and a guide to acronyms and abbreviations used in the article. Go to **www.great decisions.org** and select a topic in the Resources section on the right-hand side of the page.

Origins of Pax Americana

The trajectory of Pax Americana is strikingly similar to that of Pax Romana. The first reference to Pax Americana described the peace within the U.S. at the end of the Civil War in 1865. From the time around the 1898 Spanish American War until WWII, Pax Americana referred to the promotion of stability and democracy in the Americas, achieved by supplanting European interference with U.S. interventions. This historic Pax was a logical extension of the 1823 Monroe Doctrine, which sought to protect the American hemisphere from European practices, such as collecting debt through military action, "gunboat diplomacy," and colonial administration as in Emperor Maximillian's reign over Mexico before his execution in 1867. In the post-WWII era—especially since 1949, when the Soviet Union acquired nuclear weapons, the People's Republic of China was proclaimed by Mao Zedong and the North Atlantic Treaty Organization (NATO) was created—Pax Americana has referred to an international order in which the U.S. provides relative security and stability, allowing states to interact peacefully for greater prosperity.

The complete destruction of economies and infrastructure caused by WWII weakened all great powers except the U.S., which was geographically isolated from Europe and entered the war late, emerging as the world's most potent economic power. The role that began for the U.S. when it intervened to end WWI was thus consolidated by its involvement in WWII and its aftermath. In providing economic assistance through food shipments to Europe and Japan—initiating the Marshall Plan to reconstruct Western Europe and providing grants and credits to Asia—the U.S. earned tremendous goodwill and loyal allies.

Unlike Pax Romana or Pax Britannica, Pax Americana was not secured by a formal empire that controlled the domestic or foreign policies of other countries. Rather, Pax Americana was "an empire by invitation." It used force to uphold international order and stability when necessary, and ruled through international institutions when sufficient. The U.S. played a major role in creating: the United Nations (UN) in 1945, with the mission of preventing wars and promoting cooperation based on international law; the General Agreement on Tariffs and Trade (GATT) in 1948, which was succeeded by the World Trade Organization in 1995; and the two 1944 Bretton Woods institutions for development and finance, the World Bank and the International Monetary Fund (IMF).

Similar to earlier historical examples, Pax Americana is based on U.S. values and principles. The liberal orientation of Pax Americana most clearly resembles Pax Britannica insofar as it is a system based on the liberal values of open seas, free trade and capital flows centered on the U.S. dollar, as well as respect for international law and human rights. However, significant differences exist in the respective interpretations by Pax Americana and Pax Britannica of liberal tenets such as free trade and human rights. Historically, the U.S. has delivered a relative peace by extending security guarantees backed by overwhelming military superiority, and by intervening to suppress conflicts that have the potential to spiral out of control and threaten core U.S. interests, values and system stability.

Bipolarity and Cold War rivalry

Quite immediately following WWII, relations between the U.S. and the Soviet Union started to decline. The wartime alliance between the Big Four (the Soviet Union, China, Britain and the U.S.) collapsed under mutual distrust, competing geopolitical designs and ideological differences. By 1946, the U.S. and Great Britain had grown increasingly wary of Soviet intentions, assuming expansionist motives. The mood was captured in George Kennan's "Long Telegram." As chargé d'affaires at the U.S. Embassy in Moscow, he sent an 8,000-word document to the Department of State that year, signaling concerns that the Soviet Union could not coexist peacefully with the U.S., and predicting Russia's communist expansionism.

British statesman Winston Churchill (L) preparing to speak at Westminster College, Fulton, MO, U.S., March 5, 1946. Known as his "Sinews of Peace" address, the speech is best remembered for Churchill's use of the term "Iron Curtain" in the context of Soviet-dominated Eastern Europe. On the right is U.S. President Harry Truman. (POPPERFOTO/GETTY IMAGES)

British Prime Minister Winston Churchill's (1940–45; 1951–55) imagery of an Iron Curtain separating the East from the West supported Kennan's telegram. Kennan and Churchill were right about the creation of a Soviet bloc in Eastern Europe, though some believe the Soviets created the bloc as a purely defensive buffer against a resurgent Germany and the emerging Western bloc. Kennan himself regretted the hardline approach of the Harry S. Truman administration (1945–53) to the Soviet Union, which left little room for negotiation. In 1947, the Truman Doctrine was established, pledging aid to countries that were at risk of falling to the Soviet Union's expansionism, and inaugurating the U.S. policy of containment that would remain in place throughout the Cold War. Containment promised economic and military aid to prevent leftist governments from taking hold in Europe, and later in Latin America, Asia and Africa. By 1949, NATO was formed between North American and West European countries that pledged collective defense, equivocating an attack on one member of the alliance with an attack on all.

The origins of the Cold War remain disputed. Traditional explanations mainly attribute blame to the Soviet Union, and revisionist accounts accuse the U.S. Laying all responsibility for the impasse on one side is too simplistic. Orthodox accounts that only stress Soviet liability overlook important facets of the brewing conflict. The Soviet Union could have reasonably felt a right to exercise power in Europe after having borne the brunt of the war. Meanwhile, the U.S. had its own hegemonic ambitions—specifically, the desire to create an open international economy antithetical to Soviet interests—which made it convenient for U.S. policymakers to exaggerate the Soviet threat. U.S. policymakers for their part were right to be suspicious of Soviet intentions since the Soviets had similar expansionist objectives. The great power confrontation between the U.S. and the Soviet Union was a Manichean ideological battle fought by states possessing unprecedented lethal capability.

The first Cold War crisis erupted over the Soviet Union's refusal to withdraw troops from Iran by the agreed deadline of March 2, 1946. Mutual mistrust botched the 1946 Baruch Plan, which stipulated that the U.S. would turn over its nuclear weapons on the conditions that other countries not produce their own nuclear weapons and also agree to UN inspection. A series of crises followed in quick succession over great power influence in Turkey and Greece, as well as the more critical crisis over Germany (i.e., the Berlin blockade and airlift in 1948, when Western powers delivered supplies to Berlin following a Soviet attempt to block access to Allied sectors of the divided city).

The Cold War never put the U.S. and the Soviet Union directly at war. Instead, they fought proxy wars involving overt and covert offensives. A system emerged based on spheres of influence. The U.S. spun a web of power and committed to defend more than 50 countries extending over Western Europe, Japan, South Korea, Australia, New Zealand and the Pacific Islands; whereas Eastern Europe, Cuba, Laos, Vietnam, North Korea and China (up until 1949), lay within the Soviet realm of defense. Latin America, Africa and the Middle East were divided between the superpowers, with allegiances shifting throughout the Cold War as liberation movements formed to fight oppression from authoritarian dictatorships sponsored by either side. Sometimes civil war erupted in the name of capitalism, other times in the name of communism. The U.S. had political goals in addition to economic ones and wanted to populate the world with like-minded liberal democracies. The country compromised along the way, sponsoring authoritarian regimes like those in Chile and Iraq. They believed pro-Western dictatorships could eventually be turned into democracies—a less likely future for totalitarian states—as elaborated in the Kirkpatrick Doctrine, named for UN Ambassador Jeane Kirkpatrick (1981–85) under President Ronald Reagan (1981–89).

Superpower rivalry created a bipolar order with two great powers balancing each other in a relatively stable system defined by the absence of great power war. The Cold War carried considerable risks, however: It brought the world to the brink of nuclear war in the 1962 Cuban Missile Crisis, and it claimed many lives—over a million in the Vietnam War (1955–75) alone. More than half a decade later, between 1969 and 1979, there followed a period of détente, in which superpower tensions were eased through negotiations, summits and treaties. This period ended with the Soviet intervention in Afghanistan. Overall, relations between the U.S. and the Soviet Union remained frosty up until the years immediately preceding the fall of the Berlin Wall in 1989, which marked the symbolic end of the 28-year-long division of East and West Germany, and was quickly followed by the collapse of the Soviet Union.

Unipolarity after the collapse of the Soviet Union

The Soviet Union started imploding in 1989 and dissolved in 1991. The West had won the Cold War, and the U.S. emerged as the sole superpower in the international system. Declinist thinkers of the 1970s and 1980s had misdiagnosed the U.S.'s relative power in the international system. Contrary to the predictions of the British historian Paul Kennedy's *The Rise and Fall of the Great Powers*, it was the Soviet Union—not the U.S.—that succumbed to "imperial overstretch," or the idea that a great power can extend its global commitments to the point where it can no longer sustain them.

In the last decade of the 20th century, the U.S. was *primus inter pares*—a first among equals—on all fronts, extending itself militarily, technologically, economically and culturally like no other state. The mood in the U.S. was effusive. "Not since Rome has one nation loomed so large above the others,"

A large group of customers in an unidentified store in CA gather in the electronics department to watch U.S. President John F. Kennedy as he delivers a televised address to the nation on the subject of the Cuban Missile Crisis, October 22, 1962. (RALPH CRANE/THE LIFE PICTURE COLLECTION/GETTY IMAGES)

wrote political scientist Joseph Nye in 2002. Drawing on large reservoirs of both hard and soft power (or the power to attract), the U.S. was, as Nye put it, "bound to lead." By the end of the century, French Foreign Minister Hubert Védrine (1997–2002) captured the less enthusiastic disposition to unipolarity in other parts of the world, labeling the U.S. a "hyperpower."

Bipolarity gave way to a "unipolar moment," presenting unique opportunities for U.S. power projection. In the course of the 20th century, liberal democracy superseded the ideological alternatives—fascism and communism—in a steady sociopolitical march toward what political philosopher Francis Fukuyama famously called the "end of history" (the idea that liberal, capitalist democracy was the inevitable final form of government). The new unipolar order was peaceful insofar as it made states more certain about the distribution of power, thus lowering

the probability of conflict. Unipolarity was also durable because no single state could defeat overwhelming U.S. military power, and any attempt to balance U.S. power would require substantial collective action.

Emboldened by the lack of systemic constraints, the U.S. embarked on an unusually activist foreign policy agenda, policing the world and promoting market freedoms, democracy and human rights. Controversial interventions in Haiti, Bosnia, Somalia and Kosovo had a mixed record of success. The secretary of state under the first Bill Clinton administration (1993–97), Warren Christopher, called the conflict in the former Yugoslavia "a problem from hell," an expression which took on broader meaning after the publication of Samantha Power's book by the same name. A former Harvard professor and U.S. ambassador to the UN under the second Obama administration (2013–17), Power

worked hard to shame the U.S. into recognizing a moral duty to act in the face of genocide.

Just how broadly the U.S. should define its interests remains the subject of intense debate. President Trump proposes that the U.S. should only act in a narrowly defined national interest based on sovereignty and issue-specific, short-term, cost-benefit analyses. Every previous U.S. president in the postwar era had interpreted the national interest more broadly as including long-term systemic interests aimed at preserving the U.S. as a global leader and the dominant international force. The 2016 Democratic presidential candidate, Hillary Clinton, and the contender for the Democratic party's presidential nomination, Bernie Sanders, defined the national interest in these broader terms as well, though Sanders was critical of the "Washington playbook" (excessive reliance on the use of force).

New threats to Pax Americana: terrorism and rising powers

A new national security phenomenon threatened Pax Americana starting in the early 1990s, as non-state actors wreaked havoc by targeting the U.S. at home and abroad (the 1993 attack on the World Trade Center in New York City; the 1996 explosion at a U.S. air base in Saudi Arabia; the twin attacks in 1998 on U.S. embassies in Tanzania and Kenya; the 2000 USS Cole bombing off the coast of Yemen). Washington's increasingly activist foreign policy, particularly in Iraq, dredged up old grievances in the Middle East and created unanticipated problems as militant Islamist fundamentalists used terror to avenge U.S. military installations in Saudi Arabia during the Gulf War (1990–91) and attack the spirit of Pax Americana.

On the morning of September 11, 2001, two commercial airline carriers blitzed the twin towers in Manhattan. A third crashed into the Pentagon. A fourth, aimed for the White House, was forced down by passengers and collapsed into the fields of Pennsylvania. For a nation that stood at the height of its power, and whose homeland had not been attacked by a foreign power since the Burning of Washington by British troops in 1814, the loss of life and security was cataclysmic. For the first time in history, NATO invoked Article 5 of its founding treaty, in which alliance members pledge that "an armed attack against one or more of them in Europe or North America shall be considered an attack against them all." On September 20, President Bush declared a "War on Terror." The administration blamed the militant Islamist organization al-Qaeda for the attacks and tried but failed to hunt down the organization's leader, Osama bin Laden, as well as the Taliban (the fundamentalist Islamist political movement that sheltered bin Laden in Afghanistan and then in Pakistan).

By 2002, the attention shifted to states sponsoring terrorism and to weapons of mass destruction (WMDs). President Bush characterized North Korea, Iran and Iraq as rogue states, who formed an "axis of evil." He asserted that the U.S. would exercise its "right of self-defense by acting pre-emptively against such terrorists." The prerogative to strike against threats before they emerged became a controversial element of the Bush Doctrine, which sought to maintain U.S. preeminence through unilateral policies "to bring the hope of democracy, development, free markets, and free trade to every corner of the world."

Neoconservative policymakers at the time—most prominently, Deputy Secretary of Defense Paul Wolfowitz (2001–05), Vice President Dick Cheney (2001–09) and Secretary of Defense Donald Rumsfeld (2001–06)—pushed for war with Iraq for multiple reasons. They wanted to stop Iraqi dictator Saddam Hussein's (1979–2003) alleged support of terrorism, to prevent him from acquiring WMDs and to bring democracy to Iraq in order to pacify the region. On September 8, 2002, National Security Adviser Condoleezza Rice (2001–05) pressed the case for war in Iraq on security grounds: "There will always be some uncertainty about how quickly [Hussein] can acquire nuclear weapons. But we don't want the smoking gun to be a mushroom cloud."

On October 16, 2002, Congress authorized the use of military force against Iraq. Presenting (false) evidence of Iraqi WMDs at the UN in 2003, the U.S. tried to pass a Security Council resolution authorizing war against Iraq, but failed and instead cobbled together a "coalition of the willing." The March 2003 invasion was still supported by some 40 countries, most of which contributed troops during the occupation. The Iraq War ended in 2011. Nearly half a million people died as a result of the conflict, which cost the U.S. about $2 trillion. Events like the 2003 UN debacle and subsequent human rights abuses against detainees at the Iraqi prison Abu Ghraib tarnished the U.S.'s reputation.

Many wondered whether the wars were in the national or international interest. The high price tag set off another round of declinist debate. The U.S. had undergone five previous rounds of declinism: in the late 1950s, amidst Soviet missile tests and the launch of the world's first artificial satellite, the Sputnik; in the late 1960s, during the period of Japan's economic miracle, known as the "golden sixties"; in the early 1970s, as Saudi Arabia's oil revenues skyrocketed; in the 1970s due to the Vietnam

President George W. Bush addresses his National Security Council, including Vice President Dick Cheney, Secretary of State Colin Powell, Secretary of Defense Donald Rumsfeld, and Deputy Secretary of Defense Paul Wolfowitz, in a meeting at Camp David, Thurmont MD, September 15, 2001. (SMITH COLLECTION/GADO/GETTY IMAGES)

War and perceived Soviet military superiority; and in the mid-1980s, due to unprecedented U.S. budget deficits and Japan's concurrent economic boom and asset price bubble.

The newfound pessimism regarding U.S. capabilities and leadership in the third millennium was not just about the costly wars on terror. Many felt the U.S. was destined to be outcompeted economically by rising challengers, especially China. Two years before the Iraq War, the chairman of Goldman Sachs, Jim O'Neill, captured the downbeat sentiment when he coined the acronym BRIC, which predicted Brazil, Russia, India and China as the dominant economies of 2050 (the leaders of these nations held their first formal summit under the BRIC acronym in 2009; in 2010, South Africa joined the group, resulting in the amended acronym BRICS). Even before the 2008 U.S. financial crisis was in full swing, Fareed Zakaria declared the end of Pax Americana due to the "rise of the rest" in a post-American world.

A new world order and the demise of Pax Americana

Arriving at 'America First'

The power shift from West to East awakened old concerns about whether the U.S. had the means to fund the globetrotting military presence necessary to uphold Pax Americana. Paul Kennedy's 1987 "imperial overstretch" hypothesis resonated with a growing chorus of scholars on both the right and the left of the political spectrum. On the right, those who sympathized with this line of thinking saw excessive military spending as resulting in fiscal profligacy that compromised U.S. prosperity. On the left, high military spending was seen as crowding out socially productive spending and signaling imperialist impulses.

By the time President Obama had stepped into his second term in 2013, it was clear that his foreign policy stance was not just a reaction to the global financial crisis, but that a more restrained foreign policy was in the making. "Leading from behind" was the epithet critics used to characterize the Obama administration's shift away from full-scale military intervention toward more limited covert interventions. Drawing lessons from the Bush wars, Obama eschewed foreign interventions in situations where the endgame looked like military occupation. While he authorized a troop surge in Afghanistan, committing some additional 60,000 boots on the ground, he otherwise favored launching missiles from warships or aircraft—especially from unmanned air vehicles (drones)— or using special operations forces to combat terrorism in Pakistan, Syria, Somalia and Yemen. In a 2014 commencement speech at the U.S. Military

U.S. President Barack Obama arrives at the U.S. Military Academy at West Point on May 28, 2014, in West Point, NY. In a highly anticipated speech on foreign policy, the president provided details on his plans for winding down America's military commitment in Afghanistan. (SPENCER PLATT/GETTY IMAGES)

Academy at West Point, Obama openly resisted the inclination to solve international problems through the use of force: "Just because we have the best hammer does not mean every problem is a nail."

As advocated in the 2015 National Security Strategy (NSS), exercising "strategic patience" was sometimes seen as a better option. In 2016, the president doubled down on the risks of overextension, distancing himself from the prevailing foreign policy consensus: "When it comes to the use of military power...[t]here's a playbook in Washington that presidents are supposed to follow...[Responses] tend to be militarized responses. Where America is directly threatened, the playbook works. But the playbook can also be a trap that can lead to bad decisions."

Obama's criticism of U.S. security policy did not, however, extend to the economic realm. In trade, he pushed for the Trans-Pacific Partnership (TPP), a massive pact between the U.S. and 11 other Pacific Rim countries, and supported the North American Free Trade Agreement (NAFTA) and the World Trade Organization (WTO). In the monetary realm, he exuded confidence that the dollar's role as the number one currency would continue to be determined by both governments and private investors, even as China, Russia, France and India called for a new order that would include a more diversified reserve currency system.

President Trump's "America First" policy extends Obama's turn toward restraint, opposing the U.S.'s self-proclaimed role as the world's "cop on the beat." But "America First" has a dark undercurrent that played no part

French far-right National Front (FN) political party leader Marine Le Pen, member of the European Parliament and candidate for the 2017 presidential elections, leaves after holding a press conference at the party headquarters on November 9, 2016, in Nanterre, France, after Donald Trump defeated Democratic presidential nominee Hillary Clinton to become the 45th president of the United States. (CHRISTOPHE MORIN/IP3/GETTY IMAGES)

in President Obama's rhetoric and policies. The slogan originates with the America First Committee (AFC), established to oppose U.S. entry into WWII. Charges of anti-Semitism and even pro-Nazism dogged several AFC members, notably Henry Ford and Charles Lindbergh. There is no evidence that Donald Trump is anti-Semitic, but he has been associated with discriminatory remarks and practices based on religion and race. For example, in the 1970s, his real estate company, Trump Management Company, was accused of racially profiling prospective tenants; in 2011, Trump questioned whether the U.S.'s first black president was born in the country, and in 2012, he offered a $5 million prize for President Obama's college application; as a presidential candidate, he called Mexican immigrants rapists, thugs and drug lords; as president, he issued an executive order banning Muslims from seven countries from entering the U.S.; in response to demonstrations in Charlottesville, Virginia, he made no moral distinction between white nationalist protesters and counter-protesters.

European far-right populist leaders applauded Trump's ascent to power. They shared common ground with him on issues pertaining to sovereignty, in-

cluding strong border protection, restrictions on immigration (particularly Muslim immigration) and discontent over globalization. Nigel Farage, former leader of the United Kingdom Independence Party (UKIP), who led Britain's vote to exit the European Union (Brexit) said Trump's electoral sweep was "one of two big revolutions" in 2016, Brexit being the first. Similarly, the leader of France's far-right National Front party, Marine Le Pen, said Trump's win represented "a great movement across the world." Authoritarian leaders, from Russian President Vladimir Putin (effectively in power since 1999–2000) to North Korean leader Kim Jong Un (2011–present) to Syrian dictator Bashar al-Assad (2000–present), also hailed Trump's victory. For them, a U.S. less inclined to intervene abroad meant greater latitude to pursue controversial domestic and foreign policies unpopular with previous U.S. administrations.

The 45th president is clearly not alone in his advocacy for a new world order based on more nationalist than internationalist principles. Like other nationalist politicians, President Trump wants to recalibrate U.S. policy to better reflect national interests, which he believes are not well served by the LIO.

He maintains that the U.S. ends up subsidizing other states' security, as well as their commerce and finances, as a result of the country's global leadership and involvement. "America First" aims to put U.S. interests above common interests with other states, thus threatening to pull the U.S. out of long-standing security treaties (e.g., NATO) and international agreements (NAFTA, WTO) while refusing to sign on to new ones regulating the environment (the Paris climate accord) and trade (TPP).

U.S. policymakers have raised similar concerns before, seeing stark tradeoffs between national and internationalist interests, and between military spending and economic prosperity. Before WWII, President Franklin D. Roosevelt (1933–45) struggled to explain why the U.S. had a stake in stopping the fascist advance in Europe. In his address to the University of Virginia in June 1940, he sought to impress upon the American people their interest in a free Europe: "[M]ilitary and naval victory for the gods of force and hate would endanger the institutions of democracy in the Western world." But it was not until Japan attacked Pearl Harbor and Nazi Germany declared war on the U.S. in December 1941 that bipartisan support for entering the war emerged.

After WWII, successor presidents signed on to an internationalist agenda, but other U.S. politicians certainly continued to harbor more nationalist inclinations. For example, Senator Robert Taft (R-OH) (1939–53) opposed the internationalist policies of President Truman and President Dwight D. Eisenhower (1953–61), and fought hard to isolate the U.S. from wars in Europe and Asia, while opposing NATO. In the 1970s, George McGovern, the Democratic presidential candidate in the 1972 elections against Richard Nixon, ran an anti-establishment campaign that sought to protect the interests of the middle class and put an end to profligate military spending in Vietnam. "Come home, America," he urged. Patrick J. Buchanan championed "America First" in seeking the Republican presidential nomination in 1992, asking very similar questions to the ones posed by President Trump: "Should the U.S. be required to carry indefinitely the full burden of defending rich and prosperous allies who take America's generosity for granted as they invade our markets?" Further, Buchanan pitted his opponent George H.W. Bush's globalist view against his own: "He believes in some pax universalis. We believe in the old republic. He would put America's wealth and power at the service of some vague new world order. We will put America first."

A multidimensional advantage

In stark contrast to this nationalist appeal is long-standing bipartisan support for sustaining liberal hegemony through U.S. security provision and leadership in international institutions. Different administrations have used different images to describe the U.S.'s special role in the world—the shining "city on a hill," "the power of our example," "the indispensable nation" and "American exceptionalism"—all of which converge on the idea that the U.S. has unique systemic responsibilities to promote an LIO in service of political freedoms and economic openness.

Central to this belief is the idea that the world is more peaceful and prosperous with the U.S. fully engaged, and that there is a risk of descending into turmoil if the U.S. turns isolationist, as was the case during the interwar years (1919–39). The unwillingness of the U.S. to assume a leadership role during these years—to pursue commercial openness and macroeconomic stabilization—sparked a tit-for-tat tariff war and created deflationary pressures that prolonged and deepened the economic downturn. The political repercussions were monumental, as the Great Depression (1929–39) contributed to the rise of Adolf Hitler in Germany and Benito Mussolini in Italy in the 1930s.

Before Trump took office, postwar presidents agreed that the U.S., as the preeminent economic and military power, was different than other great powers, and could not afford to define its interests narrowly using conventional criteria such as the preservation of territorial integrity, sovereignty or gains from specific economic bargains. In their eyes, the stability of Pax Americana resulted from the non-exploitative quality of the U.S.-backed LIO, which provided a context where all states could benefit. As long as the "rise of the rest" did not produce a regional hegemon, the diffusion of material gains was seen as an intended consequence of liberal economic exchange.

President Trump and other detractors of the LIO are correct that U.S. capabilities have declined relative to other states in the international system. Even though the U.S. remains by far the most powerful country in the world, it has lost ground in certain areas. Most controversially, and often taken as the ultimate sign of economic weakness, the U.S. is no longer the world's largest exporter (though it remains the world's largest importer). Declining export shares are, however, a misleading indicator of commercial retreat because global supply chains complicate the commercial scorecard. When calculating the balance of trade, the entire value of an imported good (e.g., an iPhone imported to the U.S.) is assigned to the exporting country (e.g., China), even if very little value was added in the exporting country as compared to the value added elsewhere (the U.S.) as a result of the component parts and technology embedded in the product. The WTO is currently developing a value-added methodology to better reflect the economic implications of global trade.

Concerns about the U.S. trade deficit also tend to obscure that it reflects the investment-savings imbalance in the U.S., and that the U.S. is structurally inclined to run a trade deficit as long as it remains the world's favorite investment destination. Whether U.S. trade deficits are a source of weakness or of strength, they are often seen as a threat to U.S. jobs. In reality, however, automation, not trade, accounts for the overwhelming portion of U.S. job loss in the manufacturing sector. But automation has not diminished U.S. employment more than trade in all bilateral relationships. During the period 1999–2013, economists estimate U.S. job loss due to imports from China to range between 2 and 2.4 million.

Looking at the broader picture, the U.S. remains the world's largest economy, largest trader (albeit with China close behind), and home to the world's most highly valued companies. It acts as "world banker," issuing the world's reserve currency. The U.S. dollar is also the number one currency for international business transactions, and the U.S. is home to the largest, most

This photo, taken on January 13, 2017, shows the foreign trade container terminal in Qingdao Port, east China's Shandong Province. (XINHUA/YU FANGPING/GETTY IMAGES)

liquid and deepest financial markets in the world.

Moreover, no other single state has so far been able to achieve the sort of multidimensional power base that the U.S. has maintained for more than 70 years. The Soviet Union and subsequently Russia have been militarily strong but economically weak. Germany and Japan have been economically strong but militarily weak. Even compared to China, whose military and economic power has been growing at a tremendous pace over the last several decades, the U.S. remains in a league of its own economically, while continuing to possess the most formidable military, air, naval and nuclear capability in the world. No challenger has ever gained a consistent advantage over the U.S., much less a multifaceted advantage.

The unraveling of the economic order

The Office of the U.S. Trade Representative has started to concretize an "America First" trade policy, which aims to use U.S. trade statutes to force other countries to adopt more market-friendly policies. In the 1980s, the U.S. also engaged in "fair trade" litigation when the WTO's predecessor, the GATT, did not have strong enforcement powers. These practices receded with the 1995 reform of the WTOs Dispute Settlement Body, which enhanced WTO enforcement powers by making Panel arbitration decisions binding.

The Trump administration has also raised the specter of replacing multilateral and regional trade agreements with bilateral agreements. "We're going to make trade deals, but we're going to do one-on-one," Trump said at the 2017 Conservative Political Action Conference. "And if they misbehave, we terminate the deal. And then they'll come back and we'll make a better deal. None of these big quagmire deals that are a disaster." The U.S.'s trade partners continue to pursue regional agreements, however. Despite the U.S. abandoning TPP in January 2017, other countries have moved ahead with an 11-member "TPP minus the U.S.," which includes large trading nations such as Japan, Canada, Mexico and Australia. If successfully concluded, it will reflect a desire to sustain free trade in spite of "America First." The agreement is especially important to Japan, which wants economic checks on China's growing influence in the region.

If the new pact does pass, it is questionable whether its members will want to negotiate bilateral agreements with the U.S., which provide greater opportunities for the U.S. to play hardball, making them attractive to Washington

and equally unattractive to other governments. NAFTA is currently being renegotiated under the threat of U.S. termination. Progress stalled during the November 2017 negotiations in Mexico. If NAFTA falls apart, the U.S. could still keep the 1989 Canada-U.S. Free Trade Agreement (currently superseded by NAFTA), but that all depends on whether Canada is willing to grant the concessions required to maintain the deal. During his November 2017 tour of Asia, President Trump confirmed that the U.S. would not be negotiating large trade deals that "tie our hands, surrender our sovereignty and make meaningful enforcement practically impossible."

If the U.S. renegotiates or repeals trade agreements, there is a risk other countries will retaliate, sparking a tariff war. If foreign goods are no longer welcome in the U.S. market, official investors may not want to support the dollar-centric international monetary system whereby central banks hold low interest-bearing U.S. dollar assets. If governments diversify into other currencies, private investors may follow suit. The U.S. dollar could lose its special place as the number one currency for reserves, trade and investment. The U.S. government's borrowing costs would rise as the significant perks associated with being the world's

first global currency started to erode. If U.S. dollar assets became less attractive, less capital would flow to the U.S., shrinking U.S. trade by reducing imports, including U.S. imports of intermediate inputs, upon which the U.S. export sector depends.

As U.S. economic power fades, so will U.S. authority within the institutions it created to regulate economic flows. If countries continue to pursue preferential trade agreements without the U.S., Washington may lose influence within the WTO as countries navigate towards other power centers—the EU or China. Further adjustments in IMF and World Bank voting rights may be necessary if the U.S. loses financial clout as a result of waning commercial influence. Changes are already underway, with all the BRIC countries gaining greater voting rights. As of 2016, China has the third largest IMF quota and voting share after the U.S. and Japan, while India, Brazil and Russia have increased their shares to become top ten members of the IMF. Power shifts within the Bretton Woods institutions may not, however, fully satisfy new great powers as the economic center of gravity moves away from the U.S. Alternatives to existing institutions, such as the China-sponsored Asian Development Bank, could gain a lot more traction.

The unraveling of the security order

In the security arena, "America First" means a preoccupation with sovereignty, acting upon immediate threats to the homeland, preventing the emergence of regional powers and viewing security bargains as quid pro quos. This turn in U.S. foreign policy poses

tremendous risks. Other states may interpret U.S. withdrawal as a license to pursue ambitious foreign policy goals, and the creation of power vacuums may lead the other great powers to fill the void. Indeed, we already see emboldened moves in many parts of the world by reclusive dictatorships such as Syria and North Korea, as well as aspiring regional hegemons Russia, Iran and China.

Russia, Iran and Syria have taken cover under the fight against terrorism to legitimize incursions in foreign lands and/or brutal repression at home. In 2013, Syrian President Bashar al-Assad attacked civilians with chemical weapons, crossing President Obama's "red line" (his 2012 warning that if Assad used chemical weapons, the U.S. military would intervene). The U.S. did not respond with intervention, thus exposing a reluctance to enforce the president's own ultimatum.

U.S. influence in the Middle East is fading despite the recent military defeat of the Islamic State (ISIS) terrorist organization. As an unintended beneficiary of the U.S.-led 2003 invasion of Iraq, Shi'a Iran is now in full-blown competition with its long-time Sunni rival Saudi Arabia for regional hegemony, fighting proxy conflicts in Syria, Iraq and Yemen.

Russia has also propped up the Syrian regime without serious rebuke from the U.S., and in Eastern Europe, Putin has pursued a new geopolitical blueprint as well, first invading and then annexing Crimea, and intervening in eastern Ukraine. By supporting separatist forces in eastern Ukraine, Russia has three strategic aims: to unite ethnic Russians; to create a buffer against NATO expansion onto Russia's doorstep; and to secure economic interests, especially the gas transit running through Ukraine to Western Europe. With activity steadily escalating since 2014, Putin may be testing the waters for a total invasion of Ukraine.

In the Pacific, the U.S. has a more serious problem. China is working hard to unseat the U.S. as East Asia's regional hegemon. Flexing considerable muscle, China is militarizing and building artificial islands in the disputed South China Sea, and increasing oil and gas exploration in the equally contested East China Sea, over which it has also introduced airspace restrictions (the Air Defense Identification Zone). Tensions between

the U.S. and North Korea continue to escalate, and President Trump has declared an end to the era of "strategic patience" with Pyongyang.

Today, the problem is not just that the world can no longer count on the U.S. to act as global policeman, but that the U.S. is seeking to shake down allies for better deals, using exceptionally tough negotiation tactics. The strategy could indeed produce better deals for the U.S., but it could also backfire. If all countries pursue nationalist goals using unbending tactics, international cooperation will become a zero-sum game, leaving no scope for agreement. We are already witnessing a drama of clashing nationalist hardliners. Two governments who praised Trump's rise to power and the new world order—Damascus and Pyongyang—are now on a collision course with Washington. Moscow is next in line.

By contrast, in a system of Pax Americana, U.S. security alliances are not ancillary to the liberal order; they are its very foundation. What separates the U.S. from other great powers is not only its material capabilities, but its unprecedented network of allies. If the U.S. loses these alliances, a long list of advantages will disappear. Historical allies have been willing to host and subsidize U.S. overseas bases, making

it easier for the U.S. to roll onshore when it wants to protect core interests. In addition, U.S. allies provide military support and legitimacy for U.S. missions, reducing the cost of U.S. operations. There are also critical economic interests at stake. A secure international system reduces the costs of international trade and investment. Many economists and political scientists believe that geopolitics shape reserve currency status and that U.S. allies hold dollar reserves as a quid pro quo for U.S. military protection. Slippage in the economic ranks will jeopardize U.S. security because commercial and financial exchange with the U.S. has worked as an economic containment strategy, reducing incentives to fight, and thereby contributing to a relative peace.

Inevitably, all Paxes come to an end. The success and longevity of Pax Americana has largely been due to the U.S.'s ability to strike a delicate balance between maintaining its privileged position, while at the same time ensuring sufficient global benefits to incentivize other countries to contribute to the system. If Pax Americana were to come to a close over the course of the next decade, it would not be by necessity, but as a result of deliberate U.S. choices.

United States Trade Representative Robert Lighthizer (R) and Mexican Secretary of Economy Ildefonso Guajardo Villarreal wait for the start of a press conference at the conclusion of the fourth round of negotiations for a new North American Free Trade Agreement (NAFTA) at the General Services Administration headquarters in Washington, DC, on October 17, 2017. (ANDREW CABALLERO-REYNOLDS/AFP/GETTY IMAGES)

discussion questions

1. Is Pax Americana over? What evidence supports your answer? Does the U.S. have a grand strategy informing foreign policy today? If so, what does it look like?

2. For decades, successive U.S. administrations promoted a liberal international order, championing individual freedoms and economic openness. Does this remain the best strategy to secure U.S. interests in the current international landscape? What is the international order likely to look like if the U.S. steps back from its global leadership role?

3. In the security domain, President Donald Trump's "America First" policy is in some ways an extension of the Barack Obama administration's aversion to military intervention abroad. Under what circumstances, if any, is U.S. military intervention expedient or imperative? What is at stake for both national security and global security if the U.S. retreats from intervening militarily to protect global interests? What guidelines or principles should U.S. policymakers use when distinguishing between national and global interests in an interdependent world?

4. How potent a threat is the "rise of the rest" to U.S. economic power? What about the BRICS economies (Brazil, Russia, India, China and South Africa), specifically? What are the security implications of ongoing shifts in economic power?

5. Nationalist and populist policies have been on the rise not just in the U.S., but also across the globe, a prominent example being the British vote to exit the European Union (Brexit). How might the nature of this political shift affect the international flow of people, goods, services and capital?

6. In Syria's ongoing civil war, both Iran and Russia have increased their involvement as power brokers to the detriment of U.S. goals in the region. In Syria and elsewhere, how might a reduced U.S. role and military presence impact U.S. power and interests?

suggested readings

Brooks, Stephen G. and Wohlforth, William C., **America Abroad: The United States' Global Role in the 21st Century**. 288 pp. Oxford: Oxford University Press, 2016. This book argues that the U.S. is and will remain the only global super power, that hegemonic benefits outweigh the costs, and that if the U.S. retrenches, core U.S. security and economic interests, as well as the liberal international order, will be jeopardized.

Fukuyama, Francis, **The End of History and the Last Man (Reissue ed.)**. 464 pp. London: Free Press, 2006. Writing at the end of the Cold War, Fukuyama, a political theorist, argued that history was an evolutionary process in which liberal democracy was the final form of goverment, and that although specific events would continue to unfold and even challenge liberal democracy, it would remain unassailable as a political idea.

Mearsheimer, John J. and Walt, Stephen M., "The Case for Offshore Balancing: A Superior U.S. Grand Strategy." **Foreign Affairs**, July/August 2016. The authors make the case that the U.S. should abandon liberal hegemony, and that because the costs of hegemony outstrip the benefits, the U.S. should drastically curtail its global military posture and focus on preserving the balance of power in Europe, East Asia and the Persian Gulf.

Norrlof, Carla. **America's Global Advantage: US Hegemony and International Cooperation**. 292 pp. Cambridge: Cambridge University Press, 2010. Norrlof maintains that U.S. hegemonic benefits exceed costs, and predicts that U.S. hegemony will remain stable due to the reinforcing logics between U.S. positional advantages as the largest economy, issuer of the global currency and the strongest military.

Nye, Joseph S., **The Paradox of American Power: Why the World's Only Superpower Can't Go it Alone (1st ed.)**. 240 pp. Oxford: Oxford University Press, 2003. This account builds an understanding of the U.S. as a world hegemon, but argues that to face the unique threats of terrorism, weapons of mass destruction and climate change, the nation must cooperate with the rest of the world.

Power, Samantha, **A Problem from Hell: America and the Age of Genocide (Reprint ed.)**. 656 pp. New York: Basic Books, 2013. Obama-era U.S. Ambassador to the United Nations Samantha Power unites history, political analysis, previously classified documents and interviews with top policymakers to reveal the U.S. government's failure to address modern genocide from Armenia and Kosovo to Darfur.

Don't forget: Ballots start on page 105!

To access web links to these readings, as well as links to additional, shorter readings and suggested web sites,

GO TO www.greatdecisions.org

and click on the topic under Resources, on the right-hand side of the page

Russia's foreign policy

by Allen C. Lynch

Russia's President Vladimir Putin (L) and U.S. President Donald Trump talk as they attend the Asia-Pacific Economic Cooperation (APEC) leaders' summit in the central Vietnamese city of Danang on November 11, 2017. (MIKHAIL KLIMENTYEV/AFP/GETTY IMAGES)

The year 2018 marks the 100th anniversary of Woodrow Wilson's Fourteen Points, the statement of principles for peace at the close of World War I (WWI) that signaled the advent of the U.S.' liberal internationalist vocation. Wilson's address was a direct response to the Russian Revolution, which removed Russia from the allied coalition fighting Germany. By highlighting U.S. ideals—such as the creation of a League of Nations—Wilson aimed to rally the allies to final victory and thereby establish the U.S. as the leader of the postwar international order. This initial encounter between communist Russia and liberal America would shape bilateral relations and the global order for the next seven decades, until the end of the Cold War in 1991.

In contrast to the Soviet regime, current Russian President Vladimir Putin's foreign policy has affirmed the Russian Federation's rejection of communist ideological elements; abjured global ambitions in favor of regional objectives that touch on strictly defined economic and security interests; and for a time even advanced the idea—expressed in Putin's speech to the lower house of German parliament on September 25, 2001—that Russia's cultural vocation, as far as international affairs were concerned, was *West* European in nature.

Since about 2003–04, Russia's relations with the Western world have been steadily deteriorating. There is probably less real dialogue going on now between Moscow and Washington than at any point since the Cold War. Given U.S. opposition to Russian influence along its historical borderlands, Putin has concluded that Russia can expect little compensation for any diplomatic concessions that it might

ALLEN C. LYNCH *is Professor of Politics at the University of Virginia and author of numerous books and articles on Russian foreign and domestic policy, including* Vladimir Putin and Russian Statecraft *(Potomac Books, 2011; Chinese translation, 2013).*

make. This conclusion is reinforced by an apparent consensus in Washington that there can be no true progress in the relationship as long as Putin remains in power. Broad bipartisan hostility toward Putin on the U.S. side raises an enormous domestic political barrier to executive branch flexibility in dealing with Moscow. Explosive charges about Russian interference in the 2016 U.S. presidential election have brought the relationship to a virtual standstill, making substantive progress on already difficult issues (like the Ukraine crisis or the Syrian civil war) almost impossible, while impeding efforts to simply avert further deterioration.

In order to understand how Moscow and Washington, and more broadly Moscow and the West, have reached this nadir, we need to reconstruct the dynamics of interaction between Russia and the outside world after the Cold War. To this end, we will analyze how Russia's experience of the early post-Soviet period (1992–99) at home and abroad has shaped Russian elites' assumptions about the country's international options. Then, we will address Putin's own worldview and the ways in which his twin fears of power vacuums and overcommitment have interacted to frame Russian national security and foreign policy choices. Finally, we will treat in detail three significant cases of recent Russian foreign policy: in Ukraine, in Syria and with the U.S., culminating in Russia's interference in the 2016 U.S. presidential election.

As we shall see, Putin's Russia—unlike Soviet Russia—pursues mainly pragmatic, regionally oriented foreign policy goals. Yet imbalances of power and values, as well as conflicts of interest with Washington, make it unlikely that there will be significant improvement in U.S.-Russia relations in the foreseeable future.

Before you read, download the companion **Glossary** that includes definitions and a guide to acronyms and abbreviations used in the article. Go to **www.great decisions.org** and select a topic in the Resources section on the right-hand side of the page.

The 1990s as crucible for Russia and the West

Russia's first post-Soviet president, Boris Yeltsin (1991–99), thought that Russia and the U.S. were natural allies. He told an enraptured joint session of U.S. Congress on June 17, 1992 that communism in Russia was dead, "never to rise again!" In his view, a Russia that aspired to become a market democracy was a natural ally of the leading market democracies, above all the U.S. Very quickly, however, Yeltsin discovered that there was a whole series of foreign policy and domestic challenges for which the premises of liberal internationalism provided little guidance.

These included the economic consequences of the collapse of the single, integrated Soviet economy; the general absence of geographically (and militarily) meaningful borders throughout Moscow's new and greatly reduced western and southern steppe borderlands; the presence of some 25 million ethnic Russians suddenly residing outside the confines of the Russian polity; and relatedly, the outbreak of ethnic tensions and conflicts throughout Russia's historical borderlands (those areas that were once part of the Soviet Union).

Post-communist Russia very quickly had to find a way to balance two overwhelming and potentially contradictory foreign policy challenges: It needed to establish the best possible relations with the U.S. and U.S. allies, but also to secure its varied and pressing interests along its border regions. In the best case, the U.S. would, while treating Moscow as a natural democratic ally, also understand that Russia occupied a unique position in central Eurasia and accept its privileged role in the management of regional relations. Over time, Russian leaders came to the reluctant conclusion that partnership with the West was unlikely, and perhaps even undesirable, if it meant abandoning the search for regional hegemony.

The discrediting of pro-Western factions within the Russian government and society, and the consequent turn from liberal idealism to raw realism in Russian foreign policy, had begun long before Putin assumed power in August 1999. One factor driving this disillusionment was the rapid and tumultuous transition from a command to a market economy. In the 1990s, the Russian industrial economy collapsed, near hyperinflation wiped out the life

Russian President Boris Yeltsin (C) greets members of the U.S. Congress June 17, 1992, after he spoke before a joint session of the House and Senate. Yeltsin, the first Russian leader ever invited to address the U.S. Congress, received a standing ovation of more than two minutes when he entered the chamber. (PAUL J. RICHARDS/AFP/GETTY IMAGES)

savings of most of the population and predatory holdover elites from Soviet days cornered stunning wealth in famously corrupt transactions implicating the Yeltsin government. All this occurred at the same time that Russia seemed constantly to be in retreat before a Western world—in the form of the North Atlantic Treaty Organization (NATO)—that was supposed to be its ally.

Throughout the first Bill Clinton administration (1993–97), the U.S. continued to back Yeltsin. In early October 1993, the Russian opposition began storming government buildings after Yeltsin extra-constitutionally disbanded the parliament. The U.S. government reaffirmed support for the Russian president should he choose to use force in response. Over 150 were killed in the ensuing battles between the opposition and the military, which remained loyal to Yeltsin. Parliamentary elections held two months later saw the victory of Yeltsin's opponents, with whom he refused to compromise. As a result, and with the continued backing of the U.S. government, Yeltsin increasingly governed by presidential decree. This, as well as subsequent U.S. intervention in the 1996 Russian presidential election, established critical authoritarian precedents years before Putin came to power.

The Clinton administration claimed to see Yeltsin as the only alternative to a communist backlash. In early 1996, when Yeltsin had just 6% support in the polls, the U.S. government brokered a major International Monetary Fund (IMF) loan to Russia in order to reinforce his financial and political standing at home. In addition, (unofficially but with the agreement of the Yeltsin administration) the U.S. sent four of Clinton's former campaign advisers from Arkansas days to Moscow to help with Yeltsin's reelection campaign. Both governments kept the news of U.S. involvement in the election secret until after Yeltsin was safely returned to power in July. The U.S. government was thus instrumental in helping to manage a campaign characterized by, for instance, massive corruption, cooptation of the media by the state, the invention of "false flag" candidates to draw votes away from the communist opposition candidate, and a successful cover-up of the actual condition of Yeltsin's health, especially the heart attack he suffered just before the decisive second round of the election.

Despite U.S. support for Yeltsin during these years, Russia's relationship with the West remained fraught. NATO's 1999 bombing of Yugoslavia during the Kosovo War triggered a massive anti-NATO and anti-American reaction in Moscow. NATO's three-month-long air war targeted Russian ally Serbia over human rights abuses in its province Kosovo. It was not just that the U.S.-led NATO had attacked and defeated a Russian client, occupying part of Serbia itself—and in circumvention of the United Nations (UN) Security Council (UNSC); rather, NATO's war against Serbia violated every assurance that had been given to Russia by U.S. leaders about the consequences of NATO expansion: that NATO would only act in self-defense (Serbia had threatened no NATO country); that NATO was limited by its charter to act only within the territories of member states (Serbia had no frontiers with any NATO member state at the time); and that Russia would be consulted beforehand on all matters related to European security (again, NATO's decision for war was advisedly taken outside the UNSC, where the Russians wielded veto authority).

The Kosovo operation ultimately succeeded in its objectives, but it also confirmed a growing Russian conviction that relations with Washington could only be conducted on the basis of raw power, not common values or interests. It also undermined Russia's dwindling band of liberal democrats, who felt that the U.S. had betrayed them domestically: The bombing made it impossible to argue in Russian politics that a pro-U.S. position was compatible with core Russian national interests. Permanent damage to the premises of U.S.-Russian partner-ship had been done. Russia remained outside the post-Cold War security system built by the U.S. and its NATO allies, and the U.S. believed Moscow was too weak and too dependent on Washington to do much about it. U.S. leaders would be disabused of this assumption soon enough.

Core Russian assumptions about foreign policy

We have dwelt on the years *before* Putin became Russia's leader because current Russian foreign policy beliefs about the U.S., NATO and the West were largely set by then. These assumptions may be characterized as follows:

1. Russia's aspiration to be accepted as a great international power can only be realized on the basis of sufficient economic and military power, not on the basis of alleged common values and interests with the Western world. As an old Tsarist-era adage has it, "Russia has just two allies: its army and its navy."

2. At the same time, today's Russia cannot be a global superpower in the manner of the Soviet Union. It needs to be wary of bankrupting itself through a tit-for-tat competition with Washington and its allies.

3. U.S. foreign policy is motivated by the desire to maximize power and influence, both absolutely and relatively, and at Russia's expense if need be. This reflects a broad bipartisan consensus in Washington and does not vary much depending on which party is in power.

4. Natural resources, especially oil and natural gas, will remain the foundation of Russia's domestic and foreign policies for the indefinite future. As European Union (EU) countries are Russia's largest customer for such fuels, Moscow needs to maintain stable economic relationships with them.

5. Therefore, while Russia has rejected the possibility, and even desirability, of political-economic integration with the Western world, it still seeks maximally profitable relations with it.

6. At the same time, Russia must strive for international primacy along its historical borderlands. This does not mean recreating formal empire, but rather obtaining recognition by regional and outside powers that Russian interests have to be taken into serious account in the region's international relationships. The Russia-Ukraine nexus is the most sensitive of these relationships.

7. The U.S. refuses to acknowledge such a role for Russia, dismissing it as an outmoded ambition for "spheres of influence." (From Washington's point of view, then, Moscow is a revisionist power seeking to transform the international system.)

8. Russia wants both profitable relations with the Western world and primacy throughout central Eurasia, but if it is forced to choose, it will choose the latter.

9. Finally, and as a precondition for advancing all of its international interests, Russia must possess a strong state at home. Inevitably, this will have to be done along authoritarian rather than liberal lines. Twice in the 20th century Russia experimented with liberal democracy: in 1917, under the provisional government that was in place for eight months in the wake of the Russian Revolution, and for a while in the 1990s. Each time, Russia virtually collapsed as a functioning society and international power.

These assumptions reflect above all the failure of the country's liberal experiment and the challenge that U.S. power poses for Russia's international position. To repeat: These beliefs had largely crystallized while Bill Clinton was president and *before* Putin came to power.

Enter Putin

Putin's consolidation of power and popularity in Russia is due in no small measure to the ways in which these assumptions have been embodied in his policies throughout his more than 18 years as Russia's leader (he became prime minister in August 1999 and then president on New Year's Day, 2000). At the same time, Putin has brought a very personal perspective to the management of Russian foreign policy. Two principles that are in implicit tension with each other appear to have shaped how Putin approaches crises.

On the one hand, Putin's experience as a witness of the Soviet collapse and its consequences convinced him of the dangers of what he refers to as "vacuums of power." According to Putin, such vacuums will eventually be filled, if not by your side, then by your enemy (in this case, the West). Many of his actions, including those in Ukraine and Syria, may be seen in this light.

A second and contradictory tendency is also at work in Putin's mind: fear of overextension. Putin has been keenly aware of Russia's relative weakness in the contemporary international system. He therefore believes that great care must be taken so as not to exhaust the country's relatively limited power resources. Take, for instance, his calculations in the following territorial disputes in Russia's historical border regions:

1. Chechnya: While destroying the capacity of Chechen guerillas to wage large-scale, organized warfare against Russia in the Second Chechen War (1999–2009) and establishing direct rule over Chechnya in 2000, Putin later abandoned efforts to rule there directly, and instead turned power over to local warlord Ramzan Kadyrov in 2004. Kadyrov rules Chechnya as a virtual satrap with a mainly personal bond of loyalty to Putin (who subsidizes more than 80% of Kadyrov's regional government). In this way, the economic and political costs to Russia that would be incurred by direct administration have (so far) been greatly reduced.

2. Georgia: After waging a brutal and effective weeklong war against

Georgia in August 2008, Putin withdrew troops to breakaway pro-Russian border provinces (Abkhazia and South Ossetia, whose independence he recognized later that month). The goal was not to occupy Georgia as a whole or to annex it to a new Russian empire, but rather to stop Georgia's progressive rapprochement with NATO. Putin sees formal empire as too costly in an era of mass-based nationalism, and has acted accordingly.

■ **3. Ukraine:** In February 2014, an international agreement to establish a ceasefire and a path to a transitional government in Ukraine collapsed overnight, and Putin's client, President Viktor Yanukovych (2010–14), fled the capital Kiev. The events triggered Putin's seizure of the Crimean peninsula. He then tried to repeat the operation throughout southeastern Ukraine, which he began calling "New Russia" (a name that dates back to Empress Catherine the Great in the late 18th century). Deadly uprisings broke out, with the clear support of Russian-sponsored armed forces. But Putin balked at escalating to all-out direct Russian military intervention. Such a war, given Ukraine's geographical size (roughly equal to that of France or Texas) and proximity to a series of NATO states, would have implied a commitment indefinite in time, space and ultimate outcome.

In all of these instances, Putin filled an emerging power vacuum, while at the same time minimizing the risks of overextension.

In terms of Russia's relations with the U.S., three issues in recent years have dominated American attention and served to propel bilateral ties between Washington and Moscow to their lowest point in the post-Cold War era. These are: the Ukraine crisis of 2013–14, culminating in the annexation of Crimea by Russia in March 2014; the Syrian civil war, culminating in direct Russian military intervention in fall 2015; and the collapse of the 2009 "reset" in bilateral relations by the Barack Obama administration (2009–17), culminating in Russia's interference in the 2016 U.S. presidential elections.

Ukraine, Russia and the West

Prior to the 2016 U.S. presidential election, it was the annexation of Crimea in March 2014 that, more than anything else, drove relations between Moscow and the West to their lowest point since before the denouement of the Cold War. Serious Western economic sanctions levied in response to that annexation and to Moscow's interventions in Ukrainian affairs remain in place. The U.S. has since been training Ukrainian troops on Ukrainian soil. U.S.-reinforced NATO maneuvers along Ukraine's borderlands have continued apace.

Why did Moscow seize Crimea in 2014 and not earlier? Powerful political voices in Russia (including President Yeltsin in August 1991, the Russian parliament since 1992, Moscow's influential Major Yuri Luzhkov throughout the 1990s) long threatened or explicitly called for the annexation of Crimea. Moreover, why would Russia be interested at all in seizing the area, which it recognized as part of Ukraine upon the dissolution of the Soviet Union in December 1991?

Origins of the current conflict

The Crimean peninsula is not only a matter of Russian strategic interests, but also of Russian historical and cultural narratives. Crimea became Russian in 1783, annexed by Catherine the Great after a series of successful wars against the Ottoman Empire. From then until 1954, Crimea was under Russian jurisdiction, either Imperial or Soviet. Russia maintained its Black Sea naval fleet there; fought bitter battles against the British and French (in the Crimean War) and Nazi Germany [in the Siege of Odessa and the Battle of Sevastopol in World War II (WWII)]; cultivated a rich literature involving Crimea in peace and war (including works by Leo Tolstoy and Anton Chekhov); and sponsored the historic Yalta Conference on Crimea's southern coast in February 1945, involving Soviet dictator Joseph Stalin (secretary-general of the Communist Party,1922–53; premier, 1941–53), U.S. President Franklin D. Roosevelt (1933–45) and British Prime Minister Winston Churchill (1940–45; 1951–55). In May 1944, Stalin ordered the deportation to Central Asia of the entire (Turkic Muslim) Tatar population of Crimea—nearly 200,000 individuals, accused collectively of collaboration with the Nazis. They were replaced by mainly Russian and Russified Ukrainians, to the point where, by the time of the Russian annexation in March 2014, some two

ETHNIC MAJORITIES IN UKRAINE
by Administrative Division

- MAJORITY RUSSIAN
- 50% TO <90% UKRAINIAN
- 90% TO 100% UKRAINIAN

0   100 Miles
0   100 Kilometers

SOURCE: 2001 UKRAINIAN CENSUS

LUCIDITY INFORMATION DESIGN, LLC

thirds of the Crimean population were ethnically Russian.

Then, in 1954, during a hasty meeting of the Soviet Presidium, Soviet leader Nikita Khrushchev (1953–64), for reasons that have yet to be fully understood, transferred Crimea from Russian to Ukrainian jurisdiction. Little publicity was given the event and it is certain that very few Russians in 1992 understood that Crimea was now part of Ukraine. After all, tens of millions of Russians had traveled over the decades from Russia proper to Crimea for summer holidays without ever realizing that they had left "Russia."

These facts help explain the emotional resonance of the Crimean issue in Russian politics, including the overwhelming public approval for its annexation. They do not, however, explain why Russian authorities waited 22 years to accomplish the deed. For that, we need to examine the interaction among Russia, Ukraine and the West in the preceding years.

Putin and Ukraine

Many Russians, Putin included, do not accept that Ukraine should be truly independent of Russia. In April 2008, Putin told then-President George W. Bush (2001–09), "Ukraine is not even a country." Time and again, Russian leaders have behaved as if Ukraine were more a province of Russia than a sovereign state under international law. Consider the following evidence:

1. There was massive (and ultimately unsuccessful) Russian economic and political intervention in the 2004 Ukrainian presidential election in order to promote Viktor Yanukovych (eventually elected in 2010), whose electoral base lay in strongly pro-Russian eastern Ukraine.

2. Twice—in January 2006 and January 2009—Russian authorities cut off the supply of natural gas to Ukraine in the dead of winter, claiming contractual violations, but in fact aiming to put political pressure on President Viktor Yushchenko (2005–

10). Yushchenko's electoral base lay in strongly anti-Russian western Ukraine, and he was committed to gaining membership for Ukraine in NATO and the EU.

3. In summer 2013, Russia, Ukraine's largest export market, imposed an embargo on the importation of many Ukrainian products: This was a clear signal to Ukraine not to sign the impending Association Agreement with the EU, which was to lay the foundation for a closer economic relationship between Brussels and Kiev short of actual EU membership.

In each of these instances of Russian interference in Ukrainian affairs, Russia's rulers tried to reconcile Ukraine's formal sovereignty with the country's continued economic, political and strategic dependence on Russia. Putin knows that he cannot simply annex all of Ukraine. Instead, he has been trying to leverage Russia's overwhelming power advantages and its territorial proximity in order to induce Kiev to accept Moscow's tutelage.

This has been no easy task. In 2010, for example, pro-Kremlin candidate, Viktor Yanukovych, was finally elected president. Yanukovych's government quickly renounced interest in NATO membership. It also renewed Russia's lease on the Black Sea fleet in Crimea (critical to Russia's international power projection) from 2017 to 2042, in effect removing the issue from the political calendar. Yet at the same time, Yanukovych refused to join Putin's recently established Eurasian Union and pledged to sign an Association Agreement with the EU. In so doing, he seemed to understand that any decision to commit Ukraine decisively to either Russia or the West risked splitting the country apart.

By November 2013, when the agreement with the EU was due to be signed, Yanukovych was faced with the choice that he had been trying to avoid: Russia or the West. He balked, postponing indefinitely the signing of the pact with the EU and instead accepting $15 billion in short-term Russian credits and a 30% discount for Russian deliveries of natural gas. This sparked widespread protests in Kiev and western Ukraine, which were reinforced in early December after the government's use of force against demonstrators. Within days, Yanukovych had lost control of the capital and much of the country. Government buildings throughout western Ukraine were now occupied by protestors, while an armed and increasingly radicalized resistance was building in Kiev. Putin had failed in his attempt to bring Ukraine under Russia's aegis while formally respecting its sovereignty.

Putin tried again. He feared that the sudden collapse of the Yanukovych government would bring to power a radically anti-Russian government committed to ushering Ukraine into NATO (as NATO had pledged in 2008). Putin therefore agreed in mid-February 2014 to cooperate with an international mediation effort to resolve the Ukraine crisis. Putin's envoy Vladimir Lukin attended negotiations in Kiev involving the Ukrainian government and the official opposition, as well as the foreign ministers of France, Germany and Poland. The parties agreed to (though only Russia did not sign) a pact providing for an immediate ceasefire and withdrawal of police and opposition from downtown Kiev, an amendment to the constitution substituting a parliamentary for a presidential republic, and accelerated presidential elections.

Once again, Putin failed. Within 24 hours, the armed street protestors in Kiev would not budge. They made it clear that they would accept no agreement that kept Yanukovych in power, however briefly. Yanukovych's own party quickly abandoned him, after which he fled, eventually finding refuge in Russia. Putin reacted quickly. He ordered the execution of contingency plans for the takeover of Crimea. Later, he exploited incendiary acts by the new government in Kiev (such as removing the status of Russian as an official language), and helped instigate armed resistance in the country's eastern provinces bordering Russia.

Since 2014, Crimea has been absorbed into Russia and Moscow has sustained a simmering stalemate in far eastern Ukraine. Two EU efforts to broker a settlement (Minsk I in September 2014 and Minsk II in February 2015) have yet to bear fruit. More than 10,000 have been killed while more than 2 million have been displaced. NATO has reinforced deployments and expanded exercises in nearby states such as Poland and Estonia. Western sanctions remain in place. Russia, too, has been conducting large-scale exercises along the Ukrainian borderlands, implying that it can match and even exceed any NATO escalation in the region. More broadly, Putin has tried to signal to the West throughout the crisis that Ukraine cannot be stabilized unless Russia agrees to it.

From one angle, this argument is uncontestable. So long as Russia retains the will to do so, it can ensure that Ukraine remains weak, divided, unstable and even ineligible for NATO membership. At the same time, Putin, and Russia more broadly, are politically toxic in U.S. politics. It is difficult to see how political capital in Washington could be mustered for a settlement that, to work, has to meet the Russians at least halfway.

People hold a rally on Maidan Square in Kiev on November 21, 2016, the third anniversary of the Euromaidan protests, which began on November 21, 2013, and led to the 2014 revolution and the downfall of President Viktor Yanukovych, who fled the country in February 2014. (JODI HILTON/NURPHOTO/SIPA USA/NEWSCOM)

Russian policy in Syria

A demonstration in Anjara, in the western Aleppo countryside. The demonstration was part of a series of rallies in opposition-controlled territories of Syria calling for the fall of the Syrian regime of Bashar al-Assad, to denounce what they describe as the massacres committed by Russian airstrikes in Syria, as well as to remember those who died and went to prison as they joined the Syrian revolution (JUMA MOHAMMED/ZUMA PRESS/NEWSCOM)

Since 2011, when Syria erupted into civil war following the series of uprisings across the Middle East known as the Arab Spring, Russia and the U.S. have opposed each other on nearly every aspect of the issue. Russia has vetoed every UNSC resolution proposed by Washington and its allies aimed at holding Syrian dictator Bashar al-Assad (2000–present) to account for the atrocities inflicted by his army on the civilian population. Moreover, Russia has supplied Assad's army with a steady stream of weapons—more than enough to maintain it in the field against a range of groups backed by the U.S. and Saudi Arabia, among others.

In 2013, Putin effectively parried President Obama's threat to attack Syria for use of chemical weapons by inducing Assad to give up his chemical stocks under UN inspection. Putin thereby thwarted impending U.S. airstrikes against his ally and also removed "regime change" in Syria as a realistic U.S. policy option. Most dramatically, on September 30, 2015, Russian air force units intervened directly in the Syrian conflict, thus saving the Assad regime from imminent collapse and rendering impossible any diplo-matic settlement that would not accord Russia a central role.

Why did Putin make such a dramatic move? First, Moscow's most vital interest in Syria involves the security of Russia's fragile southern borderlands. Northeastern Syria lies less than 500 miles from the old Soviet frontier in Armenia, where Russia maintains several military bases and has subsidized the Armenian government with hundreds of millions of dollars in weapons and economic assistance over the past two decades. Syria is too close for Russia to ignore.

Second, and more specifically, several thousand jihadists from the Russian North Caucasus and from post-Soviet Central Asia, have been fighting for the Islamic State terrorist organization (ISIS) and other anti-Assad groups inside Syria. Keep in mind too that over the past 20 years, thousands of jihadists from the broader Middle East, including Syria, have fought against Russia in its wars to keep Chechnya within the Russian Federation. For Russia, the security of Syria is connected to national security, internal as well as external.

Third, while Russia certainly has an interest in maintaining its base in the Syrian port city of Tartus (a legacy of the Soviet period), this is not its principal motive for intervening. It was Russia's commitment to the Syrian government that underscored the importance of the base, not vice versa. In 2013, the increased flow of Russian arms to Syria assured Assad that Russia would resupply his army with conventional weapons after he relinquished his chemical weapons: Russian port access in situ greatly eased that commitment. Likewise, that base was indispensable to Russia's direct intervention in 2015.

Fourth, Putin is adamantly opposed to what he sees as U.S.-sponsored regime change in the name of democratization. Putin has regarded such efforts as a cover for containment of Russia since at least 2004, when the U.S. played a role in internationally contested Ukrainian elections, funding pro-democracy youth groups and treating pro-West candidate Yushchenko for poisoning during his campaign. In addition, the recent record of U.S.-backed regime change in the Middle East and elsewhere (Kosovo since 1999; Iraq since 2003; Libya and Syria since 2011) has convinced Putin that such interventions tend to leave the country in question and its surrounding region worse off. The alternative to (often odious) strongmen in power has too often been a vacuum of authority that strengthens radicalized jihadist factions. The fact that the Obama administration spent $500 million in Syria trying to arm "moderate" rebels to fight ISIS and wound up at one point arming just "four or five" who met this standard, confirms Putin's view.

Such are the key background considerations that have shaped Putin's Syria policy. But what specifically triggered the momentous decision to send Russian air and naval units to Syria in fall 2015? That summer, Russian military intelligence concluded that, if left to its own devices, Assad's government was likely to fall before the year was out and that the consequence would be an enormous power vacuum that would almost certainly be filled by radical jihadist groups of one sort or another, including ISIS. The Israeli government shared this view and in late September 2015 Israeli Prime Minister Benjamin Netanyahu flew to Moscow to coordinate Israeli and Russian policies in the region.

The result was the ongoing military intervention, in which Russian airstrikes and military intelligence, rather than large-scale ground troops, have successfully defended Assad's government and even enabled it to recapture lost ground (Syria's largest city, Aleppo, fell to the government in December 2016). U.S. policy in the late Obama and early Donald Trump administrations has been limited to crisis-avoidance in the crowded skies over Syria, where both countries have been conducting separate air wars (with the U.S. attacking mainly ISIS targets). Whether that can be the basis of a broader collaboration to defeat ISIS and reestablish stability in Syria remains to be seen, especially given U.S. domestic political obstacles to cooperation with Russia. Even if those obstacles could be overcome, Putin has successfully secured Russia the head seat at any negotiating table on Syria.

Russia, the Obama/Clinton "reset" and the 2016 U.S. presidential election

Why would Putin have taken the decision, as the heads of the Central Intelligence Agency (CIA), Federal Bureau of Investigation (FBI) and National Security Agency (NSA) claimed in a January 6, 2017 report, to intervene in the 2016 U.S. presidential election by hacking servers belonging to the Democratic National Committee (DNC) and its staff and disseminating select e-mail traffic through third parties? Was it, as two of the three agency chiefs stated with "high confidence" (the third with "moderate confidence"), in order to help elect Donald Trump president?

Clearly, the Russian government (as well as many others) had the capacity to surveil DNC servers. The FBI warned the DNC in 2015 that it was likely being hacked (note: *before* Trump became a plausible candidate) and was ignored. The Russian government also had a strong motive to embarrass candidate Hillary Clinton, who by every measure seemed virtually assured of being the next president. Yet it seems clear that Putin's motive was *not* to help elect Trump. Putin assumed that Clinton would win. He intended to foment maximum possible international humiliation for the U.S. political system in order to neutralize efforts by a future Clinton administration to intervene in Russian politics and the politics of Russian client states in the name of democracy and human rights. The trajectory of U.S.-Russia relations since the Obama "reset" of July 2009, when Clinton was secretary of state, bears out this version of events.

The U.S.-Russia "reset" — broadly, an effort by President Obama to improve relations between the two countries — was based on the premise that the George W. Bush administration had seriously overextended U.S. foreign policy toward Russia, just as it had in the Middle East. The 2008 war between Russia and Georgia, in this view, exposed U.S. vulnerabilities in projecting influence along Russia's borders. In order to advance more important U.S. interests involving Russia, such as nuclear arms control and counter-terrorism, the U.S. would have to take into account (as a June 18, 2009 cable from the Moscow Embassy put it) Russia's "absolute" priority to: establish the country's great power status internationally; secure Russia's primacy throughout the post-Soviet region; and prevent further NATO expansion toward Russia. The results of this recalibration were impressive and included:

■ **1.** A treaty further reducing offensive nuclear weapons.

■ **2.** A U.S. commitment to accelerate Russia's entry into the World Trade Organization (WTO).

■ **3.** Russian agreement to cooperate with the U.S. on constraining Iran's nuclear weapons development through economic sanctions and deferment of major arms deliveries.

■ **4.** Renewal of the Megatons for Megawatts program, whereby the U.S.

U.S. Secretary of State Hillary Rodham Clinton (R) and Russian Foreign Minister Sergey Lavrov press a red button symbolizing the intention to "reset" U.S.-Russian relations during their meeting in Geneva, Switzerland, March 6, 2009. (AP PHOTO)

U.S. soldiers march through Red Square during the Victory Day parade in Moscow on May 9, 2010. Troops from four NATO states marched through Red Square for the first time as Russia marked victory in World War II with its biggest military parade since the collapse of the Soviet Union. (ALEXANDER NEMENOV/AFP/GETTY IMAGES)

paid Russia for delivery of weapons-grade uranium from decommissioned missiles and bombs.

■ **5.** U.S. deferral of the deployment of an anti-ballistic missile system in Eastern Europe to which the Russians objected.

■ **6.** Expansion of the Northern Distribution Network that allowed the U.S. and its NATO allies to transport military supplies to and from Afghanistan through rail networks traversing Russian territory via the Baltic Sea port of Riga, Latvia.

Russia saw real prospects for improvement in relations. In 2010, Moscow even invited the U.S. (and other NATO country) troops to march in the Victory Day Parade on Red Square marking the 65th anniversary of the Soviet victory over Nazi Germany. This was the first time in history that active duty U.S. troops had been invited to participate. Yet progress on specifics could not long mask the absence of an agreed overall conceptual and political framework for the bilateral relationship.

As important as the immediate results of the "reset" were, they represented less of a break with the past than most in the U.S. realized at the time. U.S. officials continued to treat Russia

as outside the NATO-based European security order. Moreover, American leaders continued to believe that U.S. power was so superior that Moscow had little choice but to acquiesce to Washington's policy. From Moscow's perspective, there was not much difference between Vice Presidents Joe Biden (of the Obama administration) and Dick Cheney (of the George W. Bush administration): Each was certain that the U.S. had the whip hand in the relationship and said so publicly. Finally, in contrast to Putin's government, the Obama administration was not in full control of its foreign policy. The U.S. Congress had an important say as well and would serve to complicate the administration's ability to manage its Russia policy.

By 2011 the relationship began to spiral. First, the U.S. and its NATO allies, having secured Russian neutrality in the UNSC, passed a resolution that authorized the use of force in Libya for humanitarian protection (against feared massacres in Benghazi). Within months, and contrary to explicit U.S. assurances to Russia, the government of Muammar Qaddafi (1969–2011) was overthrown and the dictator himself killed. Libya descended into virtual anarchy. Putin

concluded that Washington had simply lied to Moscow. Going forward, Putin would frequently point to this episode to warn about the dangers of the U.S. policy of regime change in the name of human rights and democracy.

Second, in December 2011, Russian parliamentary elections took place amidst a months-long decline in Putin's popularity. These were obviously manipulated by Putin's administration to give his United Russia party a much larger margin of victory than seemed plausible to careful observers. This fraud provoked large-scale protests in Moscow, St. Petersburg and several other major Russian cities. Then-U.S. Secretary of State Clinton publicly took the side of the protestors, criticizing the Putin government and Putin himself in ways that clearly angered him. The new U.S. ambassador to Russia, Michael McFaul (a self-described democracy activist), immediately reinforced this criticism as he engaged in positive exchanges with protestors on the social media platform Twitter, and invited them to the U.S. ambassador's residence just days after assuming his post in Moscow.

Moscow quickly took countermeasures to minimize U.S. interference in the future. In October 2012, Russia expelled the U.S. Agency for International Development (USAID) from the country. USAID had long been involved in funding and training Russian civil society initiatives, including election monitoring. The Russian parliament further tightened legal restrictions on Russian non-governmental organizations (NGOs). The restrictions hindered them from collaborating with foreign NGOs or governments, and in effect made them suspicious "foreign agents" in the eyes of the state.

On August 22, 2012, Russia finally entered the WTO. Ironically, this triggered a further deterioration in relations with Washington, as the U.S. Congress was forced to repeal a Cold War statute tying trade with Moscow to human rights concerns (illegal under WTO rules that require member states to promote normal trade relations). Congress moved instead to pass the Magnitsky Act, which sanctioned Russian human rights abusers. In response to this extraterritorial assertion of U.S. jurisdiction, the Russian parliament voted for a bill prohibiting the adoption of Russian children by U.S. citizens. It was in this atmosphere that Republican presidential candidate Mitt Romney declared Russia to be the "number one geopolitical threat" facing the U.S.

By summer 2013, then, U.S.-Russia relations already lay in a state of virtual ruin. Putin's refusal to extradite U.S. defector Edward Snowden (who wound up in a legal "no-man's land" in Moscow's Sheremetyevo Airport in summer 2013) reflected his belief that there was simply nothing to hope for in the relationship. In reply, President Obama cancelled a summit meeting with Putin planned for September 2013. Putin also sought to create a broad-based Eurasian Economic Union that would include Ukraine, further proving that he had abandoned any expectation that Russia could realize its primary global and regional objectives via partnership with the Western world. If Russia wished to staunch the loss of its power and influence, not to mention rebuild regional hegemony, it would have to do so on its own.

The denouement of the Ukraine crisis in late 2013–14, as well as Russia's involvement in the 2016 U.S. presidential election, cannot be separated from the overall decay in relations between Moscow and Washington since the "reset." While Putin bore a special animus toward Hillary Clinton, his core concern was the possibility that the U.S. and its allies—or indirectly, NGOs funded by their governments or affiliated foundations—would work with the Russian opposition to undermine his government at home and his allies abroad in the name of democratization.

The revelation by *The New York Times* in March 2015 that Clinton had been using a poorly secured private e-mail server as secretary of state had to alert the Russian government (and many others) to an improbable electronic vulnerability in her circle of close contacts. How could Putin— a self-styled realist and ever wary of overcommitment—have imagined a)

that Trump had a realistic chance of winning and b) that it was prudent to expose Russia to U.S. retaliation for *that* goal? Nothing in Putin's background suggests that he would have taken such a risk for such an unlikely outcome. Rather, undercutting the U.S. electoral process was expected to help undermine a future Clinton adminis-

tration by highlighting obvious double standards in U.S. foreign policy. Ironically, in the wake of Trump's improbable victory, the broad domestic reaction in the United States to revelations of Russian electoral interference has all but eliminated chances for a new "reset" in relations between Moscow and Washington for the foreseeable future.

U.S. policy options

The Obama administration's efforts to "reset" U.S.-Russia relations failed and, one year into the Trump administration, relations between Washington and Moscow remain at a post-Cold War low. Questions about Russia's role in the 2016 presidential election continue to dominate the U.S. domestic political conversation. In fall 2017, executives from the social media companies Facebook, Google and Twitter appeared in front of the Senate Intelligence Committee to testify about thousands of inflammatory political ads they sold throughout the campaign to Russian sources posing as Americans. Several House and Senate committees are conducting ongoing investigations into Russian interference in the election and into potential ties between Trump associates and the Russian government. Justice Department Special Counsel Robert Mueller is conducting a separate criminal investigation into Russia and the 2016 election, with the first indictments made in late October 2017 (though these were not directly linked to campaign issues).

Given the circumstances, it is difficult to foresee a political coalition emerging in Washington, not to mention in Moscow, that is in favor of taking risks, however small, on behalf of a new "reset" in relations. In March 2017, a confidential initiative by Putin's government to improve bilateral relations quickly died in the U.S. national security bureaucracy, and in July, Congress voted for new legislation that prevents President Trump from lifting sanctions against Russia without congressional assent.

As we have noted, Russians and Americans appear to have little interest in actually listening to each other. There-

fore, the U.S. should broaden confidential dialogue with Russia among both civilian and military officials, and maintain its tenuous bond with Russia in dealing with North Korea's nuclear ambitions. Collaboration between the U.S. and Russian air commands in Syria should be strengthened to avoid accidents in the air and on the ground, and the pattern of military deployments and exercises along the Russia-NATO borderlands, which have too frequently assumed hairtrigger dimensions in the past three years, should be reevaluated. If the overwhelming majority of U.S. leaders mean what they say—that is, that there can be no real improvement in U.S.-Russia relations while Putin is in power—openness to greater cooperation on military and security objectives is likely the best case scenario for the time being.

A demonstrator holds up a sign of Vladimir Putin during an anti-Trump rally on June 3, 2017, in New York City. Rallies and marches took place across the country to call for urgent investigation into possible Russian interference in the U.S. election and ties to U.S. President Donald Trump and his administration. (EDUARDO MUNOZ ALVAREZ/GETTY IMAGES)

discussion questions

1. In the 1990s, President Boris Yeltsin claimed that he wanted to lead a democratic Russia into the 21st century. His successor, Vladimir Putin, has repudiated the development of democracy in Russia and has worked to undermine foreign democracies, including by intervening in the 2016 U.S. presidential election. What are some reasons for the ideological shift between the Yeltsin and the Putin years? What historical experiences might have shaped Russian attitudes toward democracy?

2. The U.S. and Russia have clashed over the ongoing Ukraine crisis and the Syrian civil war. What are the ramifications of these disagreements for regional and/or global security? Where, if anywhere, might the two countries find common ground on these issues?

3. In the foreseeable future, could there be another "Russian reset" like the one attempted in 2009 under the Barack Obama administration? Why or why not?

4. Should the U.S. lift the economic sanctions imposed on Russia after the 2014 annexation of Crimea? How effective are sanctions in changing Russian behavior?

5. Since assuming office, Putin has directed military operations in Georgia, Chechnya and Ukraine, but, aside from the annexation of Crimea, has stopped short of assuming direct control over these satellite territories. How would you characterize Putin's regional policy and what are his goals?

6. The Cold War pit the U.S. and the Soviet Union against each other as adversaries, creating a bipolar world divided between capitalism and democracy in the West and communism in the East. How has the international order developed since the end of the Soviet Union in 1991? How do the Trump and Putin governments see the world and their respective roles in it?

suggested readings

Lynch, Allen C., **Vladimir Putin and Russian Statecraft**. 184 pp. Dulles, VA: Potomac Books, 2011. In his biography of Russian President Vladimir Putin, Lynch challenges American perspectives on the leader, which are often one-dimensional and stand in stark contrast to his reputation in Russia.

Marten, Kimberly, "Reducing Tensions Between Russia and NATO." 51 pp. New York: **The Council on Foreign Relations**, 2017. Available free online: <https://www.cfr.org/report/reducing-tensions-between-russia-and-nato>. In this report, Marten, a professor of political science at Barnard College, Columbia University, plays out several scenarios that could produce conflict between NATO and Russia and outlines a plan for how the Trump administration could work with Congress and NATO allies to prevent escalation.

Mosendz, Polly, "Read: The Full Transcript of Russian President Vladimir Putin's Speech at the United Nations General Assembly." **Newsweek**, September 28, 2015. Available free online: <http://www.newsweek.com/transcript-putin-speech-united-nations-377586>. This article includes the full transcript of Russian President Vladimir Putin's address at the 70th session of the UN General Assembly, made during a period of sharply deteriorating U.S.-Russian relations in the wake of the annexation of Crimea and Russia's military operations in Syria.

Plokhy, Serhii, **The Last Empire: The Final Days of the Soviet Union (Reprint ed.)**. 544 pp. New York: Basic Books, 2015. Plokhy reassesses the fall of the Soviet Union in order to interpret current conflicts and to decipher how the American narrative of the collapse has influenced the role of the U.S. on the world stage.

Putin, Vladimir, "Address by President of the Russian Federation." **Russian Federation Presidential Executive Office**, March 18, 2014. Available free online: <http://en.kremlin.ru/events/president/news/20603>. In this address to Russian federal, regional and civil representatives, President Vladimir Putin celebrates the annexation of Crimea, an event which precipitated a distinct rise in nationalist rhetoric on the official level.

Remnick, David, "Watching the Eclipse." **The New Yorker**, August 2014. Available free online: <https://www.newyorker.com/magazine/2014/08/11/watching-eclipse>. This article traces the erosion of U.S.-Russian relations and the hope for democracy in Russia, with insider commentary from Michael McFaul, U.S. ambassador to Russia from 2012 to 2014.

Don't forget: Ballots start on page 105!

To access web links to these readings, as well as links to additional, shorter readings and suggested web sites,

GO TO www.greatdecisions.org

and click on the topic under Resources, on the right-hand side of the page

China and America: the new geopolitical equation

by David M. Lampton

U.S. President Donald Trump (L) and Chinese President Xi Jinping shake hands at a joint news conference held after their meeting in Beijing on November 9, 2017. (ARTYOM IVANOV/TASS/GETTY IMAGES)

The U.S. and China were on an increasingly friction-laden path even before China's President Xi Jinping took office five years ago. Problems have grown since. Developments following the inauguration of U.S. President Donald Trump have compounded uncertainties and risks, though two presidential summits in 2017 had a patina of cooperation. For the last decade and a half, China has implemented an expansive strategy of economic outreach and growth of national capacities, including of military and diplomatic power. What are the challenges and opportunities for the U.S. in its relations with China? What can be done to improve prospects for productively managing differences, as the tectonic plates of global power shift?

During the 71 years spanning 1945–2016, the U.S. used its dominant economic, military and ideological power, along with that of its allies, to conceive of, build and support global institutions, alliances and regimes that have contributed to international growth and tolerable peace. Ironically, in so doing, the U.S. fostered the emergence of other power centers. Predictably, these increasingly capable countries now have growing ambitions and ability to pursue their interests. China is notable in this regard as a geopolitical, economic and security competitor with whom the U.S. will increasingly have to negotiate cooperation. Still, Beijing is not Washington's biggest threat, and there are many potential gains to be had from collaboration.

DAVID M. LAMPTON *is Hyman Professor and Director of China Studies at Johns Hopkins University—SAIS in Washington, DC. He is current Chairman of The Asia Foundation, and past President of the National Committee on U.S.-China Relations, and his most recent book is:* Following the Leader: Ruling China, from Deng Xiaoping to Xi Jinping *(University of California Press, 2014). With two colleagues, he is writing a book on Beijing's railway building effort aimed at connecting southern China to Southeast Asia. The views expressed are his own and he wishes to thank Jill Huang and Ji Zhaojin for their research assistance.*

Power is relative, not absolute. In 2013, China's global share of gross domestic product (GDP) exceeded that of the U.S. for the first time, as measured by the World Bank. As late as 1990, the U.S. could act more unilaterally than it can today. At that time, it commanded almost 21% of global GDP, compared to today's approximately 15.5%; China, by contrast, possessed less than 4% of global GDP compared to today's nearly 18% and growing.

External perceptions of power and strength are also germane, particularly in periods of crisis and transition. A spring 2017 poll by the Pew Research Center found that although more countries globally still name the U.S. as "the world's leading economic power" over China, the gap is narrowing. Meanwhile, perceptions of U.S. economic power have declined among most key allies and trading partners, and a majority of EU countries surveyed put the U.S. in second place after China. Australians believed that "China leads the U.S. by a two-to-one margin."

After years of protracted and costly entanglements all over the world, there is evidently a dwindling supply of political will in the U.S. for a global leadership role. Nonetheless, the U.S. possesses unique strengths, potential and resilience that many Chinese populists and nationalists underestimate. Considering the U.S.'s modestly sized population (about 323 million, compared to China's nearly 1.4 billion), the country controls a remarkably outsized share of global GDP. In per capita GDP terms (reflecting standard of living for average citizens) the U.S. leads China by a very considerable margin. Moreover, as Arthur Kroeber, managing director of the global economic research firm Gavekal Dragonomics, points out, "In terms of [technology] licensing value…the U.S. tech sector is 60 times stronger than China's."

Before you read, download the companion **Glossary** that includes definitions and a guide to acronyms and abbreviations used in the article. Go to **www.great decisions.org** and select a topic in the Resources section on the right-hand side of the page.

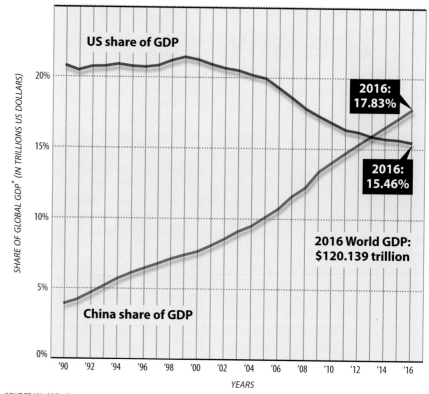

China vs. US Percentage of Global GDP

US share of GDP

China share of GDP

2016: 17.83%

2016: 15.46%

2016 World GDP: $120.139 trillion

SHARE OF GLOBAL GDP* (IN TRILLIONS US DOLLARS)

YEARS

'90 '92 '94 '96 '98 '00 '02 '04 '06 '08 '10 '12 '14 '16

SOURCE: World Bank, International Comparison Program database   *as measured in Purchasing Power Parity (PPP)

The image of China as an unstoppable leviathan is overstated, and Beijing's leaders run the risk of overestimating their own strength. Security anxieties among China's neighbors, engendered by Beijing's growing power, further diminish the country's economic influence. Washington's challenge now is to maintain its power share and play its cards shrewdly. The wisest path forward is for both countries to negotiate cooperation. The first step for the U.S. is to get its domestic house in order.

The state of play in Washington

Soon after taking office in January 2017, President Trump backed off several elements of his campaign rhetoric, at least temporarily, including: protectionism expressed as threats of dramatic tariff hikes; an inclination to alter the long-standing "One China" policy, by which the U.S. recognizes Beijing as the official government of China, rather than Taiwan's government, over which Beijing claims sovereignty; and impulses toward conflict in the South China Sea, where regional states maintain competing territorial claims. In addition, though Trump continues to call for greater security contributions from U.S. allies, he has conveyed reassurances to partners that Washington still values its alliances, in particular the North Atlantic Treaty Organization (NATO).

The first summit between President Trump and President Xi was held in April 2017 at Trump's private Mar-a-Lago resort in Florida. The two leaders rejiggered the Barack Obama-era (2009–17) Strategic and Economic Dialogue by agreeing to establish four parallel consultation mechanisms focusing on core economic, diplomatic, security, cyber, and cultural and human rights frictions. A 100-day negotiation period was initiated to address economic disputes in finance and trade under the framework of the U.S.-China Comprehensive Economic Dialogue, and the presidents made efforts to establish personal rapport and direct communication.

There were less positive developments as well. Trump's withdrawal from the Trans-Pacific Partnership (TPP) (the massive trade pact negotiations between the U.S. and 11 other Pacific Rim countries) three days after being sworn into office, and his stated intention to withdraw from the Paris Climate Agreement, frayed the U.S.'s mantle as leader on international institution-building and interdependence issues. Washington's partners in the TPP negotiations, notably Japan, were left high and dry, having made domestically painful concessions to meet U.S. demands that Washington then scuttled. Japan's Prime Minister Shinzō Abe (2006–07; 2012–present) soon sought to resurrect the TPP without Washington, and major progress in this direction was made in a meeting of trade ministers in November 2017 in Danang, Vietnam, at which the U.S. was not represented. In Germany, Chancellor Angela Merkel (2005–present) has sought to forge trade and other relationships not based in U.S. centrality. In May 2017, following a Group of Seven (G-7) summit, Merkel told one audience that: "The era in which we [Europeans] could fully rely on others is over to some extent."

In short, abundant chances to enhance China's international leadership have fallen into Beijing's lap. President Xi has already moved into the void to champion economic globalization and ecological responsibility. This was evident in a headline-grabbing speech at the World Economic Forum in January 2017, in which he emphasized commitment to "growing an open global economy," and noted that "no one will emerge as a winner in a trade war." In his lengthy speech to China's 19th National Party Congress of the Communist Party (hereafter, the Party Congress) in October, he reaffirmed dedication to environmental issues and a model of sustainable development guided by "harmonious co-existence between man and nature."

The North Korea problem

When he left office in January 2017, President Obama told President-elect Trump that the most pressing national security challenge he would face would be North Korea's efforts to advance its nuclear and missile programs and to threaten Asia-Pacific allies, U.S. regional bases and even the continental U.S. Moreover, this effort could energize a new round of nuclear proliferation in Asia, perhaps featuring the acquisition of nuclear weapons by Japan and South Korea. This would multiply the number of such weapons, foster an arms race and compound instabilities.

Pyongyang's nuclear effort became highly visible during the Bill Clinton administration (1993–2001), continued through the George W. Bush (2001–09) and Obama periods, and landed in the lap of President Trump. Not even a year into Trump's presidency, North Korea has already tested missiles over Japan and conducted its sixth nuclear test, in September 2017. Over the last two decades, there has been an unceasing stream of conferences, multilateral sanctions, interim deals, threats and joint military exercises involving various countries, but none of these efforts, including periodic shows of disapproval from Beijing, have deflected North

Korea from its chosen course. The ruling Kim dynasty has demonstrated an unshakeable commitment to acquiring weapons of mass destruction, believing that this is its "insurance policy" against forcible removal from power. There have been occasional glimmers of hope that some formula for denuclearization might be found and faithfully implemented, but these efforts have failed to get off the figurative launch pad, or have blown up shortly after lift-off.

President Trump has communicated that he believes his White House predecessors were right to press Beijing to ramp up pressure on North Korea, and correct in their assessment that Beijing had sufficient means to do so. However, Trump also came into office feeling strongly that past administrations had not taken a sufficiently transactional approach with Beijing. He therefore suggested that Washington would give Beijing concessions in other areas—trade and Taiwan among them—in exchange for cooperation on North Korea. In one post on the social media platform Twitter, he wrote: "The United States is considering, in addition to other options, stopping all trade with any country doing business with North Korea."

Presidents Trump and Xi initially labored to reach economic accommodations and cooperate on North Korean

(AMMER/WIENER ZEITUNG/VIENNA, AUSTRIA)

it will not put sufficient pressure on Pyongyang to risk North Korea's collapse. Beijing does not want unrest in North Korea spilling into northeast China. It wants a buffer state between itself and South Korea (and U.S. forces there), and leverage over Washington. Successive Chinese leaders have adhered to these priorities despite periodic slaps in the face by the Kim dynasty. Beijing sustained this posture during the November 2017 Trump-Xi summit: Vice Foreign Minister Zheng Zeguang told reporters that China wanted to "maintain [note: *not* increase] pressure regarding the nuclear activities" of North Korea and "promote peaceful resolution of the issue through dialogue and negotiation."

While Beijing did in fact interrupt North Korean currency-earning coal exports to China in the first quarter of 2017, its overall trade with Pyongyang grew 37.4% over the same period in 2016. Though Beijing joined the other four members of the UNSC in imposing new sanctions, it carefully avoided affecting its ongoing deals and exports to Pyongyang. China's northeastern provinces have interests in North Korea and resist shutting down their trade there. Shipping through Hong Kong to North Korea continues to be an important hole in the sanctions dike.

In short, China is doing just enough to avoid rupture with Washington, without doing so much as to endanger North Korea's survival. With the limits to China's will and capacity to change North Korea's behavior revealed, what will the White House do? What happens if Beijing comes to be seen by Washington as proactively undermining U.S. efforts?

In a remarkable June 2017 tweet, the U.S. president conceded that depending on China to bring North Korea to heel had not worked: "While I greatly appreciate the efforts of President Xi & China to help with North Korea," he wrote, "it has not worked out. At least I know China tried!" U.S. Secretary of State Rex Tillerson put a more hopeful cast on things, saying: "We have not given up hope" and expressing the intention of the U.S. to

denuclearization, but the burden of accumulating frictions soon weighed more heavily. In June 2017, Washington sold Taiwan weapons and equipment valued at $1.4 billion. The U.S. Department of State's 2017 *Trafficking in Persons Report* "downgraded" China (in human rights terms) and the U.S. slapped secondary economic sanctions on Chinese trading and certain financial entities (and individuals) for directly or indirectly aiding North Korean weapons programs. China's ambassador to the U.S., Cui Tiankai, responded: "[Attempts] to create leverage against China on the Korean nuclear issue by challenging China on Taiwan and the South China Sea are equally destructive." The ambassador went on to say that "secondary sanctions imposed by the U.S. on Chinese entities and individuals according to U.S. domestic laws are also not acceptable." In both Congress and the executive branch, moves were made and are now underway to subject Chinese foreign direct investment (FDI) in the U.S. to more scrutiny, to constrain

technology flows to China and to fight forced technology transfer provisions imposed on U.S. firms seeking market access in China. The White House has called on the U.S. Trade Representative to "investigate" China's practices in these regards. In August 2017, more secondary sanctions were imposed on Beijing with respect to North Korea. In early September, the United Nations (UN) Security Council (UNSC) imposed additional sanctions on North Korea with the backing of China and Russia, though they watered down U.S. proposals before agreeing.

One reason for this seesaw in relations with Beijing is that the Trump administration effectively attempted to outsource its North Korea policy to China. The fundamental obstacle to this approach remains that China opposes actions that would destabilize, much less topple, the regime in Pyongyang. Beijing has consistently shown that two principles govern its North Korea policy. First, it opposes North Korea becoming a nuclear weapons-capable country. Second, wage a "peaceful pressure campaign [on North Korea]." Shortly thereafter, the president ratcheted up pressure. "I am very disappointed in China," he tweeted. "Our foolish past leaders have allowed them to make hundreds of billions of dollars a year in trade, yet they do NOTHING for us with North Korea...We will no longer allow this to continue." During President Trump's first trip to China in November 2017, he took a more conciliatory tone, proclaiming the "mutual commitment" of the two presidents to the denuclearization of North Korea.

Of the numerous reasons that Trump's approach has not borne fruit, three are dominant. First, Pyongyang is able to resist potentially lethal pressure from China. Second, for Beijing, a nuclearized peace on the Korean Peninsula is preferable to war there. And third, while President Trump has gyrated on whether the U.S. approach to Pyongyang should rely on force or dialogue, the Chinese have never wavered in their aversion to the use of force to denuclearize North Korea.

Consequently, the current U.S. administration is left with the same stark choices as its predecessors, except that Trump has staked even more on the issue and North Korea is further down its deliverable nuclear weapons path. Washington has never attacked a nuclear-capable country. The U.S.'s options—none of them ideal—fall into three categories:

■ **1.** Implicitly or explicitly accept that North Korea has nuclear weapons and deter Pyongyang from using them, as was done with the Soviet Union and China. This approach has two variants: One is to seek to negotiate a freeze in North Korean warhead and missile levels and testing (with verification), and negotiate a peace agreement. The second option is simply to establish a deterrent relationship without official agreements—just the promise of certain destruction if weapons are used or proliferated.

■ **2.** Persist in a policy of tightening sanctions, knowing that there are limits to the pressure China will apply on North Korea and that North Korea has

(KAL/*THE ECONOMIST*/LONDON, ENGLAND)

a seemingly endless capacity to endure such punitive measures. In this scenario, Pyongyang continues to build more warheads and develop their means of delivery.

■ **3.** Use force to try to destroy North Korea's nuclear capacity (or the regime entirely), knowing that Pyongyang's death throes could take hundreds of thousands (possibly millions) of South Korean and other lives with it.

It is time for Washington, in close consultation with its South Korean and Japanese allies, to seriously consider either explicitly or implicitly acknowledging that North Korea has a modest nuclear deterrent, and to prevent North Korea's use of these capabilities (and proliferation) just as Washington did with the Soviet Union and China. The wisdom of such a policy partially hinges on whether or not one conceives of North Korean leaders as rational; that is, whether one believes that their instinct for survival outweighs their impulsiveness. A principal downside to adopting an overt approach of deterrence is that it would likely encourage others in Asia (not least South Korea and Japan) to obtain their own "deterrent," thereby multiplying regional nuclear actors and the attendant dangers. Of course this would also stimulate Beijing to further boost its capacities, thereby fueling a regional arms race.

In sum, President Trump initially put other contentious issues with China on the back burner, hoping to achieve his primary goal—North Korea's denuclearization. When that failed, the front burner of the U.S.-China relationship became crowded with previously repressed issues: U.S. freedom of navigation operations in the South China Sea, talk of steel and aluminum tariffs, weapons sales to Taiwan, the threat of tightened restrictions on technology and investment flows, and secondary sanctions on Chinese institutions and individuals. Some of these threats have been pursued, others downplayed or delayed, and still others seemingly abandoned, leaving Beijing, Washington's allies and many others confused. This brings us to executive branch decision-making.

Executive branch decision-making

White House personnel, not least those involved in national security, have been in continual flux since Inauguration Day. Deep divisions on trade policy persist among the president's senior advisors. Across all agencies, nomination and confirmation of officials has been painstakingly slow. As of mid-November 2017, only 469 out of over 600 key positions requiring Senate confirmation had been nominated—249 had been confirmed and 144 posts still had no nominee. In the State Department, only 56 out of 152 slots had been filled; at the Defense Department, 26 out of

54; and, at the Commerce Department, 10 out of 21. This leaves key agencies staffed with politically insecure ("acting") personnel. Although many of these individuals are very capable, foreign governments do not know with whom they can engage with confidence, and the risks of ill-considered policy, spotty implementation and inaction increase.

President Trump initially gave members of his own family notable roles in dealing with Beijing: His son-in-law Jared Kushner and daughter Ivanka liaised with the Chinese and advised the president. This blurred lines with the State Department and other agencies and dimmed what should have been a bright line between family and national interests. In the run-up to the president's November trip to Beijing, family members became less involved as far as China was concerned, at least publicly.

Looking ahead, the U.S. Congress is already moving into campaign mode for the pivotal 2018 midterm elections. The upcoming struggle for Capitol Hill is unlikely to improve the climate for dispassionate debate about China policy. Alternatively, Congress may become so preoccupied with domestic politics that it does not focus on China at all.

The state of play in Beijing

The driving consideration in Chinese political life for Xi Jinping's first term (2012–17) was the 19th Party Congress (October 18–24, 2017). The Party Congress is held only once every five years, and is used to set the party's foreign and domestic policy agendas and select its leadership. Prior to this conclave, President Xi—who also serves as general secretary of the Communist Party (CCP) and chairman of the Central Military Commission—had two desires, each in tension with the other. First, he sought to cultivate stable relations with the Obama administration and thereafter the Trump administration, looking to keep U.S.-China relations on an even keel. At home, however, he wanted to appear tough on the U.S: Xi remains determined to be seen domestically as a staunch guardian of China's equities: Taiwan, the South and East China Seas, North Korea, economic interests and "national dignity." He stated his driving aspiration succinctly when he first took office: "great rejuvenation of the Chinese nation."

In April 2017, at the Mar-a-Lago summit, Xi therefore held out to Trump the prospect of the aforementioned 100-day negotiation aimed at producing quick, politically satisfying and visible trade gains. Yet when the first Comprehensive Economic Dialogue discussions in Washington rolled around 100 days later, Beijing gave very little. Xi's principal concession was U.S. beef exports—dear to ranchers in the American West, but not a game changer. In short, Xi was preoccupied with consolidating power up until the conclusion of the 19th Party Congress. Being soft on the U.S. was inconsistent with the logic of building his nationalistic coalition at home.

Domestically, Xi has restored key aspects of strongman politics and moved the CCP to center stage in society and governance. The 19th Party Congress was less a pro forma reappointment than a coronation. Xi augmented his already considerable power by building a more pliable seven-person Standing Committee of the Politburo. He put a close confidant in charge of anti-corruption work (Li Zhanshu), disposed of opponents and potential competitors (Sun Zhengcai), weakened competitive factional networks (the Communist Youth League), embedded his "Thought on Socialism with Chinese Characteristics for a New Era" in the CCP Constitution—as only Chairman Mao Zedong, China's revolutionary communist leader (1949–76) and paramount leader Deng Xiaoping (1978–92) had done before—and made possible (though not inevitable) his retention of power beyond his second five-year term, heretofore an evolving retirement norm in Beijing. Even before the recent Party Congress, Xi had achieved the exalted status of "core leader."

Despite his political achievements, however, President Xi faces constraints and is deeply insecure about the forces roiling below the surface in Chinese society. Ministries, provinces, localities, corrupt individuals and interest groups cannot be counted on to comply with orders from the top. The sweeping anti-corruption campaign that Xi launched at the close of the 18th Party Congress in 2012 has won him popular support, but also created enemies among its actual and potential targets. Demographically, China's median age is increasing rapidly, as is the dependency ratio, meaning that health and retirement costs associated with an aging population will grow and the working-age population will decline.

The Chinese economy is awash in corporate debt (though it has huge financial assets), and there is a shadow banking and irregular financial sector creating enormous uncertainties. Economic efficiency (total factor productivity) in the state-owned enterprise sector has been declining for years. Excess production capacity in key sectors weakens the economy, requiring endless central subsidies. It also motivates dumping products abroad. All this, in combination with political uncertainties, periodically stimulates large-scale capital movements from China abroad. These are sometimes so large that Beijing imposes capital controls, as was done in 2015–16. Tightened capital controls, in turn, slow Chinese foreign investments. Most fundamentally, Xi must worry that the growing middle class and already disaffected intellectuals may not remain quiescent forever.

Xi's foreign policy

When it comes to national strategy and dealing with the U.S., President Xi is in charge. Washington will be dealing with him as the leader of an increasingly capable China for the foreseeable future. Some issues to consider include: What can we expect the contours of Xi's future foreign policy to be? How can Washington influence them and

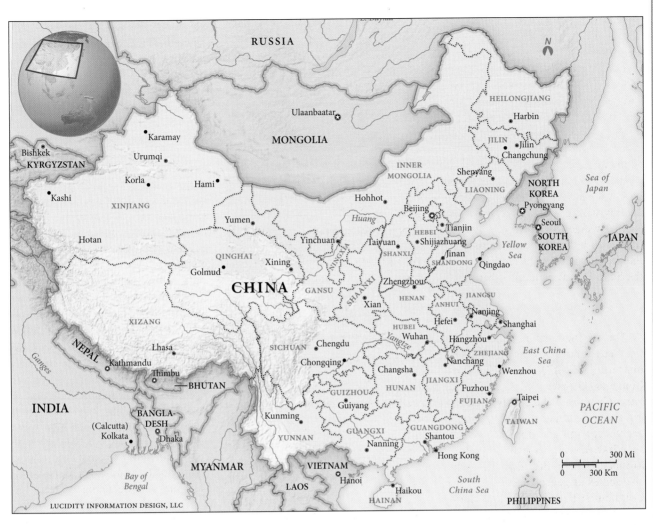

LUCIDITY INFORMATION DESIGN, LLC

how should it respond? And, most fundamentally, how can the U.S. increase its own comprehensive power?

Under Xi, Beijing has become progressively more assertive in safeguarding national interests and winning more say for China abroad. Beijing views Washington as simultaneously gridlocked at home and increasingly alienated from its traditional friends in the international arena. As a former Chinese vice-minister of foreign affairs wrote recently: "We have entered a `Post-American Era,' meaning that the so-called `Pax Americana' and the American century is over…The most obvious characteristic of a Post-American Era is a reconfiguration of the global power balance, with developing nations gaining strength year by year." This assessment reinforces Beijing's current course. Americans should be concerned when *People's Daily*, the official newspaper of the CCP, carries a

piece ridiculing Trump's Washington as "a bizarre soap opera," and saying that "U.S. foreign policy is in total disarray, and world regard for the U.S. has plummeted." The piece goes on to say, "China cannot afford to play such political games. As a country with 1.4 billion people, China must focus on economic development, and a strong central leadership is needed." Broadminded Chinese who see a progressive and successful U.S. as being advantageous to China's political reform and long-term interests are alarmed at developments in the U.S.

Xi has expansively asserted sovereignty in the South China Sea, pressured India on its shared border in the Himalayas, pushed along the median line separating Japan and China in the East China Sea and punished South Korea economically over defensive missile deployments. This muscular trend is also evident in Xi's July 2017

announcement of a "red line" for dissidents in Hong Kong who are pushing for more autonomy and electoral reform, as well as his warning to outsiders not to seek to "infiltrate" and "sabotage" the mainland from Hong Kong. Xi has ratcheted up political, economic and surveillance pressures on Taiwan since the independence-leaning Democratic Progressive Party formed a government there in May 2016.

Xi's muscularity is also a reflection of China's more than three-decade trend of modernization in its military structure, operations and equipment—particularly its naval, air force, missile, space and cyber components. A major reorganization of the military launched in 2015 signals accelerated efforts to boost capacities and Xi's personal control over the armed forces. China's civilian R&D and manufacturing industries are making increasing contributions to the People's Liberation

Chinese President Xi Jinping reviews the armed forces as part of the commemorations to mark the 90th founding anniversary of the People's Liberation Army at Zhurihe military training base in north China's Inner Mongolia Autonomous Region, July 30, 2017. (XINHUA/ LI GANG/GETTY IMAGES)

Army's (PLA) arsenal, and in the process growing the military-industrial complex. The Pentagon's 2017 report to Congress concluded that, "China's military modernization is targeting capabilities with the potential to degrade core U.S. military-technological advantages." In late July 2017, on the occasion of the 90th anniversary of the PLA founding, Xi reviewed a huge military parade in Inner Mongolia at which 40% of the weapons displayed had not been seen before. All of these were domestically produced.

Under Xi there has been progressively closer alignment with Putin's Russia, though important frictions remain between Moscow and Beijing. Growing cooperation is evident with respect to Syria and North Korea, and to UN voting. In July 2017, Beijing announced joint naval exercises in the Baltic Sea with Moscow—exercises focusing on "strengthening Sino-Russia naval combat and coordinating capabilities." *China Daily*, China's most widely circulated English-language newspaper, observed: "This is the first time the Chinese navy is conducting exercises at NATO's doorstep." En-

hanced sanctions imposed by the U.S. government on both Russian and Chinese entities and individuals may serve to drive the two countries even closer.

Geostrategically, Beijing is making very sizable international infrastructure investments in ports, transportation and power grids through the Belt and Road Initiative (BRI). This nominally $1 trillion effort aims to make China

a connectivity hub for the region and beyond. The BRI's projects combine the wish lists of almost every Chinese bureaucracy, locality and enterprise, as well as the aspirations of recipient countries. Beijing hopes BRI projects will absorb its substantial excess domestic production.

To be sure, there are enormous challenges facing Beijing in this effort. Some of these include: problematic financing and debt loads in developing countries; insufficient revenue flows for planned projects; inappropriate technology; substandard construction; corruption; and local backlash against Chinese intrusion and land acquisition. In addition, China's assertiveness with respect to sovereignty disputes makes some of its neighbors reluctant to participate in BRI, including Vietnam and India (the latter boycotted the May 2017 Belt and Road Forum). Even in Hong Kong, a special administrative region of China, the local populace is concerned about a planned high-speed railroad that would run directly from China into the heart of the city, because Chinese law enforcement would come with it.

Nonetheless, BRI represents the prospect of increased geo-economic and geostrategic clout. In 2016, China was the leading trade partner of 124 countries, compared to the U.S.'s 76— almost a complete reversal from just

Chinese company digging a tunnel in Laos for high-speed rail project, in June 2017. (DAVID M. LAMPTON)

ten years earlier. Washington would be making a strategic error in assuming that China's outward thrust is destined to fail. It is almost certain that a modern, high(er)-speed, Chinese-constructed rail line will be completed from Kunming in southwestern China to Bangkok, Thailand and beyond well before a decade has passed. This will orient 600 million emerging consumers in Southeast Asia with growing purchasing power toward China. Beijing is also developing several other economic corridors around its periphery. This connectivity push is a developmentally and strategically sound policy direction; indeed, BRI was even enshrined in the CCP Constitution at the 19th Party Congress.

Geopolitically, Beijing seeks to drive wedges between the U.S. and its allies and close friends [notably South Korea, the Philippines, Thailand, Australia, Europe and the Association of Southeast Asian Nations (ASEAN)], and to establish multilateral organizations that provide Beijing with new regional and global platforms for action and influence. Beijing hopes to diminish post-World War II (WWII) U.S. sway, without destroying the international structure that helped China get where it is today. This ambition is reflected in Beijing's central role in the formation of the Shanghai Cooperation Organization (SCO), a Eurasian security grouping involving Central Asia, Russia and others as observers; the BRICS grouping (of five major emerging economies: Brazil, Russia, India, China and South Africa) and BRICS Bank; and the Asian Infrastructure Investment Bank (AIIB), with an impressive list of 80 members, including China's neighbors and all G-7 members, except the U.S. and Japan. All this is occurring as Beijing boosts its clout in established organizations such as the World Bank and the International Monetary Fund (IMF).

Some of this is good news for a world order that has been deeply influenced by U.S. policies since WWII. Increasing China's role in the global trade system, boosting its voting share in multilateral institutions such as the

World Bank and the IMF, and encouraging China to provide international public goods have been features of U.S. policy for decades. However, China also uses its growing strength to press sensitive issues in its relations with the U.S. and with its neighbors—Hong Kong, Taiwan and countries with interests in the East and South China Seas. Moreover, Beijing no longer acquiesces to U.S. military domination of its periphery. Its disquiet with "close-in" U.S. maritime and air surveillance is apparent. The gradual placement of U.S. and allied anti-ballistic missile defenses in East Asia to guard against

North Korean intimidation is another raw spot. Consequently, there are periodic Chinese air and sea challenges to U.S. naval and air forces that elevate the risks of accidents and miscalculations. Beijing steadily builds cyber, space and strategic deterrent and defense capabilities, further energizing an action-reaction spiral among China, its neighbors and the U.S. Of course, looked at from Beijing's perspective, the U.S. is striving to maintain or increase its technological lead across the full range of military power. Gross U.S. military spending is about two and a half times that of China.

Issues and approaches

The above developments give rise to two key policy questions (setting aside the issue of North Korea, treated above): how to foster an economic balance of power in Asia and how to achieve more reciprocity in relations with China.

Fostering a balance of economic power

Comprehensive national power has three components: the capacities to coerce, materially induce and persuade. The U.S.'s regional and global role throughout the post-WWII period has been underpinned by its large and balanced portfolio of these three power instruments.

Moving into the new millennium, however, U.S. missteps, global developments and intelligent moves by others have combined to diminish the U.S.'s relative strength. Factors include: the combined weight of post-9/11 conflicts in Iraq and Afghanistan; the 2008–09 global financial crisis (which hit the U.S. harder than China); China's impressive economic growth combined with Beijing's "going global policy" initiated in the early 2000s to encourage domestic firms to invest abroad; the 2011 Obama administration "pivot to Asia," which sought to rebalance U.S. interests away from Europe and the Middle East and toward Asia, but over-emphasized U.S. mili-

tary power, alienating China to no positive effect; Washington's policy bias against infrastructure construction in its World Bank, Asian Development Bank, Export-Import Bank and U.S. Agency for International Development (USAID) programs; domestic governance problems in the U.S. itself; and counterproductive opposition to initiatives such as the AIIB and the TPP. The shortening economic leg of U.S. power in Asia weakens U.S. capacity to maintain balance.

How might Washington lengthen that leg, beyond getting back into the regional trade agreement game and concluding a bilateral investment agreement with Beijing? A central part of Xi Jinping's geo-economic vision is to expand regional links and promote urbanization and economic growth on China's periphery, making China the central node for the region. In East, Southeast and South Asia this means north-south connectivity; that is, creating goods and services supply chains that originate in China and extend to the Indian Ocean, the South China Sea, the Andaman Sea, the Bay of Bengal and beyond. In order to maintain influence, the U.S. will need to become more involved in the construction of regional infrastructure and collaborate to foster linkages that are not just north-south, but also east-west (which would involve links from In-

China's Global Trade Surplus

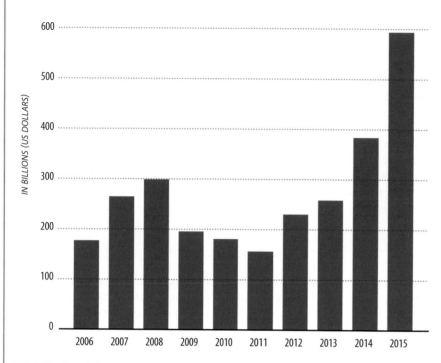

SOURCE: China General Administration of Customs; The Wall Street Journal

US – China Trade Deficit: from near zero to over $350 billion in nearly 20 years

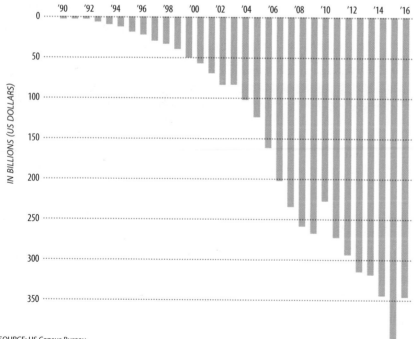

SOURCE: US Census Bureau

dia to Vietnam, through Burma, Thailand, Cambodia and on to Japan and the wider Pacific, including the U.S.). This would involve participation from U.S. companies, foreign aid and development agencies, allies, and multilateral development agencies. Balanced connectivity between China and the U.S. would help avoid spheres of influence that give rise to resentment and conflict.

Achieving more reciprocity

Prior to the 2000s, China was preoccupied with its own development, being neither a major exporter nor a significant source of outward investment. Once China joined the World Trade Organization (WTO) in 2001, its trade and investment abroad grew enormously, as did its global trade surplus and the U.S. bilateral trade deficit with China.

Beijing soon had the technology, capital and capacity to take advantage of opportunities abroad without simultaneously providing commensurate access to China for the U.S. and others, particularly in the services, IT and agriculture sectors. China's global trade surplus exploded, creating huge cash reserves that needed to be kept abroad in order to avoid generating domestic inflation. Beijing bought U.S. Treasury securities in enormous quantities to soak up the cash, but soon sought higher returns by buying tangible foreign assets. As has been widely reported, China has conspicuously expanded its outward FDI, purchasing factories, property, resources, R&D facilities, etc. China's outward foreign investment exceeded its inward FDI for the first time in 2014; its FDI in the U.S. grew rapidly.

Compounding all this, from about 2008 on, the pace of domestic economic, financial and foreign trade liberalization in China slowed. While Xi Jinping's accession to power in 2012–13 initially promised to energize market-based reforms, the ensuing years have revealed his determination to pursue a wide range of muscular industrial policies, known as "Made in China 2025." Consequently, the issues of "reciprocity" and "fairness" have moved front and center in U.S.-China relations. There is enough blame to go around, but some analysts in the U.S. believe that U.S. trade negotiators at the time of China's WTO entry "dropped the ball" on pushing for access to China for U.S. service providers.

It is one thing to identify inequities and another to find remedies that don't disproportionately hurt U.S. interests and innocent bystanders. Limiting Chinese investment into U.S. employment-generating firms diminishes domestic U.S. job opportunities. An example of

perverse results from retaliation can be found in the Trump administration's threatened tariffs on imported steel from China and other suppliers. That threat, made in 2017, led to a surge in U.S. steel imports in anticipation of price rises, while also raising the specter of higher costs for U.S. steel users and public consumers. So, while feelings of resentment mount in the U.S., finding ways to enhance reciprocity that don't injure everyone is hard. On the other hand, ignoring the problem invites extremist proposals at home and contempt from Beijing.

President Trump's November 2017 trip to China attempted to address inequities on the trade front. Beijing and Washington collaborated on bundling an assortment of already agreed-upon transactions, memoranda of understanding, letters of intent and new deals, to produce a huge headline figure ($253.5 billion) for benefits bestowed on the U.S. as a "result" of the president's trip. But the actual transactions in the package did little to address the fundamental issue of the tilted field on which U.S.-China trading and investment is played out.

Negotiating cooperation

The U.S. today faces policy choices in its relationship with China the magnitude of which it has not confronted in Asia since the earliest days of the Cold War. In terms of economic engagement with Asia and China, Americans must ask themselves how to proceed. The U.S. can continue to advance its interests through multilateral trade arrangements, or it can do so through bilateral trade arrangements, negotiated one by one between Washington and individual countries, as advocated thus far by the Trump administration. With respect to a more level playing field between China and the U.S., the U.S. must consider what points of leverage it has to extract reciprocity from Beijing without unduly hurting itself and innocent bystanders. What tools does the U.S. need to develop to be more effective in its economic engagement with Asia? For instance, should the Export-Import Bank be strengthened? And should U.S. infrastructure development and foreign assistance funds be increased or reduced?

Turning to security issues, the U.S. must consider a host of policy alternatives. Washington must decide whether to strive for balance in Asia or to seek to maintain its primacy in the region. In doing so, it must consider what primacy looks like in an age of interdependence. Relatedly, the U.S. might choose to prioritize its five security alliances in

Asia (with Japan, South Korea, the Philippines, Thailand and Australia), or alternatively to work gradually with Beijing and others to develop security structures that include both powers. In seeking to balance China's strength, would it be a feasible strategy to develop a coalition of China's neighbors, including India, or would this ignite a regional arms race? Finally, the U.S. faces difficult choices in North Korea. It can accept the fact that Pyongyang already has nuclear weapons and seek

to deter their use, proceed along the course of gradually tightening pressure on North Korea, or pursue a third path that involves the use of force.

Each one of these policy choices has ramifications throughout the regional and global systems. Beijing and Washington must manage the challenges and prioritize the key tasks that, if handled well, will lay the foundation for mutual benefit and peace. The U.S. is no longer in a position to compel cooperation; cooperation must be negotiated.

Vietnamese cheer as the convoy transporting U.S. President Donald Trump passes by on Nguyen Van Linh Road on November 10, 2017, in Danang, Vietnam. President Trump, who was on a 12-day Asia trip, took part in the Asia-Pacific Economic Cooperation (APEC) summit hosted by Vietnam. The APEC meeting aims to promote free trade throughout the Asia-Pacific region. (LINH PHAM/GETTY IMAGES)

discussion questions

1. Keeping in mind the Donald Trump administration's withdrawal from the Trans-Pacific Partnership (TPP) and its vow to pull out from the Paris Climate Agreement, what does China's pursuit of leadership roles in multilateral organizations like the Shanghai Cooperation Organization, the BRICS grouping and the Asian Infrastructure Investment Bank mean for U.S. influence in Asia and beyond? Do China's actions present any opportunities for the U.S.?

2. Considering China's recent 19th Party Congress, how might President Xi Jinping's consolidation of power domestically affect Beijing's dynamics with Washington? How do domestic concerns shape Xi's foreign policy? Likewise, how do President Trump's domestic considerations shape his policy approach to China and to Asia more broadly?

3. What are U.S. policy options with respect to deterring an increasingly belligerent North Korea? To what extent can the U.S. rely on China to put pressure on North Korea? What are the risks and benefits associated with theoretical military action by the U.S. against Kim Jong Un's regime?

4. How might a power balance that favors China over the U.S. in Asia impact regional security issues such as North Korean nuclear proliferation, South China Sea territorial disputes or Taiwan? How might the U.S. balance with China to avoid creating spheres of influence that could lead to conflict? Should the U.S. prioritize its existing security alliances in Asia, or should it work gradually with Beijing and others to develop security structures that include both powers?

5. In the years following its entry into the World Trade Organization, Beijing has taken advantage of market openness abroad, without simultaneously providing commensurate access to China for the U.S. and others. How might the U.S. push for greater reciprocity with China? What are the potential pitfalls of pursuing "fairer" policies?

6. What does China hope to achieve with its "Belt and Road Initiative" (BRI)? What are some of the challenges facing Beijing in this effort?

Don't forget: Ballots start on page 105!

suggested readings

Christensen, Thomas J., **The China Challenge: Shaping the Choices of a Rising Power (1st ed.)**. 400 pp. New York: W.W. Norton & Company, 2016. Christensen, the former U.S. deputy assistant secretary of state for East Asian and Pacific Affairs, argues that instead of working to hinder China's rise, the U.S. should instead seek to steer its trajectory away from regional aggression toward taking on a positive role in the international arena.

Garver, John W., **China's Quest: The History of Foreign Relations of the People's Republic of China (1st ed.)**. 888 pp. New York: Oxford University Press, 2016. A sweeping history of the People's Republic of China since its emergence in 1949, this book focuses on the country's foreign policy, emphasizing how the Chinese government has prioritized internal stability in the formulation of its international agenda.

Kroeber, Arthur R., **China's Economy: What Everyone Needs to Know (1st ed.)**. 336 pp. New York: Oxford University Press, 2016. Kroeber, an economist, employs a historical perspective to tell the story of China's economic development into the world's first or second biggest economy in the 21st century.

Lampton, David M., **Following the Leader: Ruling China, From Deng Xiaoping to Xi Jinping**. 312 pp. Berkeley, CA: University of California Press, 2014. Based on more than 500 interviews with high-level Chinese officials, Lampton presents an intimate look at China's last 40 years and the leaders propelling the country forward.

Pomfret, John, **The Beautiful Country and the Middle Kingdom: America and China, 1776 to the Present (Reprint ed.)**. 704 pp. New York: Picador, 2017. Long time foreign correspondent John Pomfret details the coevolution of the U.S. and China throughout history.

Shambaugh, David, **China's Future? (1st ed.)** 244 pp. Malden, MA: Polity Press, 2016. This book assesses various scenarios for China's future economy, society, politics, national security and foreign relations, as well as their potential effects.

Wu, Guoguang, **China's Party Congress (Reprint ed.)**. 384 pp. Cambridge, UK: Cambridge University Press, 2017. This book analyzes the composition and role of the Chinese Party Congress, outlining the ways in which informal politics and formal institutions in China interact with one another and legitimize authoritarianism.

Xi, Jinping, "Secure a Decisive Victory in Building a Moderately Prosperous Society in All Respects and Strive for the Great Success of Socialism with Chinese Characteristics for a New Era." **The Great Hall of the People of Beijing**, October 18, 2017. Available free online: <http://news.xinhuanet.com/english/special/2017-11/03/c_136725942.htm>. In this speech, delivered to over 2,000 Communist Party members at the 19th Party Congress, Chinese President Xi Jinping lays out plans for Chinese economic and political development by 2050.

To access web links to these readings, as well as links to additional, shorter readings and suggested web sites,

GO TO www.greatdecisions.org

and click on the topic under Resources, on the right-hand side of the page

Media and foreign policy

by Susan D. Moeller

Supporters gather to rally with Republican presidential nominee Donald Trump at Minneapolis-Saint Paul International Airport two days before the election. Raquel Rutledge, an investigative reporter at the Milwaukee Journal Sentinel, *noted, "T-shirts advocating our lynching are among the most disturbing displays of hatred toward journalists in the U.S. that I've seen in my lifetime."* (JONATHAN ERNST/REUTERS)

I t is well to recall that "media" is a plural noun. Perhaps when you hear the word "media" you think about the Sunday paper that still shows up on your doorstep, or the public radio station that you listen to in your car, or the news that you watch on your television. Or maybe when you say "media" you are thinking about your smart phone, and the photos you share with family members, the websites you go to for recipes, the online crossword that has made finding a pencil with a good eraser unnecessary. Maybe you think about the biased commentators you have heard, the "facts" that had to be corrected.

"Media" can be used to refer to something actual, but it is often used to reference an abstraction, and a negative one at that. In the U.S. today, the term "media" is regularly employed as an epithet. Yet the Founding Fathers understood that if there

was going to be such a thing as "American exceptionalism," it would be predicated on belief in a free press. A free press is a sentinel; it arms citizens with information so that they can make informed decisions in their own best interests. The press (or what we call the "news media") are a bulwark of democracy, and in the estimation of the Founding Fathers, an essential one—hence, the First Amendment. But in our time, the term "media" consists of more models, and more problematic models, than just the traditional press.

SUSAN D. MOELLER *is Professor of Media and International Affairs at the University of Maryland, College Park, and the director of the International Center for Media & the Public Agenda (ICMPA), a research center that bridges the Philip Merrill College of Journalism and the School of Public Policy.*

Media are a contested zone, a place where countries like China, Russia and Turkey play out authoritarian control of information by flooding the Internet with state-sponsored news, blocking external websites and apps, denying visas to international reporters and arresting and assassinating journalists. Media today thrive in virtual environments, including those shadowy places where Russian agents and non-state actors like the Islamic State (ISIS) terrorist organization can wage war for hearts and minds and bodies. ISIS used to openly network with its followers on platforms as well-known as YouTube and Twitter until such communication trails became more easily surveilled. They have since migrated to the dark web and end-to-end encrypted message services like WhatsApp and Telegram.

Media are our era's disruptive force. Both state and non-state actors view media not just as a propaganda arm, but as a battlefield on its own terms. From Russia's covert human agents and robot computer programs, to ISIS' calculated information technology (IT) specialists and Macedonia's teenage hackers, cyber is the new frontier. Banking, power and water grids can be hacked and entire regions can go dark. Personal data can be stolen to siphon off resources. Ads and fake news can be unleashed and micro-targeted to foment hate and racial and economic rage among undecided voters in a tight presidential campaign. Media attention can be both the means and the end: Sometimes the incentive is economic gain; on other occasions, media can be manipulated by groups committed to a particular political agenda. Meanwhile, wielding power today entails, at least in part, dominating the global conversation on social media.

Beginning with 9/11

"It is obvious that the media war in this century is one of the strongest methods [of waging jihad]; in fact, 90% of the preparation for war is effective use of the media." —Letter to Mullah Mohammed Omar, the Taliban supreme commander, from Osama bin Laden (undated)

Even before 9/11, the international news repertoire included coverage of terrorism. But part of what was so diabolical about September 11 was that al-Qaeda masterminded the attacks so that the whole world would be watching when the second plane hit the World Trade Center. The first plane prompted every news outlet in Manhattan to train its cameras on the Twin Towers. And the cameras were still running when the second plane struck, and when first one, and then the other tower imploded. Terrorism broadcast live—terrorism conducted with the explicit intention of having the whole world witness the deaths of thousands—was a new horror.

Today, when mainstream media cover terrorism or other crises in the international arena—from outbursts of extremism to hotly contested elections to distant natural disasters—they cover them with 24/7 reporting and on-the-scene interviews. They lead the news with dramatic images, break into regular programming with updates and, in short order, post the "best" photographs or videos of the event culled in part from Twitter or Facebook. The faces of stunned victims, tearful bystanders, solemn experts and grandstanding politicians shuffle across our screens. If the tragedy appears to be a terrorist attack, media outlets across platforms give airtime and space to claims of responsibility, even when the perpetrators and their motives are unknown. If no one has claimed responsibility for a given attack, cable shows are wont to fill their time with speculation. More thoughtful publications may opine about the context of an event: Where does this latest tragedy fit into larger patterns of violence? What are the implications for future policies? What are the ramifications for the current government?

Unfortunately, in almost all cases, terrorism coverage serves in part to publicize the tragedy, to further the notion that there is an ongoing threat and to perpetuate the mythos of terrorism. Terrorists rarely have sufficient human and financial capital to defeat their enemies on the ground. Wars have historically been about gaining territory; terrorism is asymmetric. As the terrorism expert Paul Wilkinson put it, one consequence of this is that terrorists thrive on the "oxygen of publicity." Therefore, "free media in an open society are particularly vulnerable to exploitation and manipulation by ruthless terrorist organisations." In this way, media coverage also assists terrorists' own efforts to attract recruits. That is why terrorists today almost always choose targets where there are lots of everyday citizens carrying cameras and where there is already a robust mainstream media presence. This is how terrorists weaponize media.

The U.S. military-industrial-tech complex is deep into researching ways to protect our country and our world from "bad actors" wielding cyberweapons, including via social media platforms. The future of threat assessment in foreign policy is cybersecurity and artificial intelligence (AI). On the frontier of war, AI systems are already being used to enable cyberattacks and to defend against them. As the Department of Homeland Security's "Preventing Terrorism Overview" webpage states: "Terrorist tactics continue to evolve, and we must keep pace. Terrorists seek sophisticated means of attack, including chemical, biological, radiological, nuclear and explosive weapons, and cyberattacks. Threats may come from abroad or be homegrown. We must be vigilant against new types of terrorist recruitment as well, by engaging communities at risk [of] being targeted by terrorist recruiters."

! Before you read, download the companion **Glossary** that includes definitions and a guide to acronyms and abbreviations used in the article. Go to **www.great decisions.org** and select a topic in the Resources section on the right-hand side of the page.

Social media and foreign policy

> **Social media is not the cause of violent extremism…but a powerful amplifier and accelerant. Digital platforms and increased access to smart phones and internet connectivity help facilitate radicalization and recruitment."** — Center for Strategic and International Studies Commission on Countering Violent Extremism, "A New Comprehensive Strategy for Countering Violent Extremism" (2017)

In late July 2017, Facebook, YouTube, Microsoft, Twitter (later joined by Google and Snap, Inc., the parent company of Snapchat) launched the Global Internet Forum to Counter Terrorism (GIFCT). In identical blog posts published on the websites of the partnering corporations, the GIFCT wrote "Our mission is to substantially disrupt terrorists' ability to use the Internet in furthering their causes, while also respecting human rights." The GIFCT project envisioned technological solutions to the cascading crises of extremism, violence and terrorism—crises aggravated by the tools and reach of social media platforms. As TechCrunch, an online publisher of technology industry news, described it: "The GIFCT started as an extension of the shared industry hash database that allows tech companies to share the digital fingerprints of extremist and terrorist content, such as photos and videos, so that once one identifies a piece of prohibited content, all the others can also block its upload."

The social media tools of political sabotage are sophisticated and effectively invisible. Those who deploy social media have the ability to set loose messages on the world—messages that can proliferate exponentially. Social media is also capable of micro-targeting literally anyone. Democracies rise and fall on the public opinions of their citizens. How many swing voters need to be swung before an election is lost or won? Just 79,646 votes in the swing states of Michigan, Pennsylvania and Wisconsin decided the outcome of the 2016 U.S. presidential election.

Consider only a few of the unfolding revelations about what took place in cyberspace during the 2016 presidential election: Russian intelligence agencies funded "troll farms" that spread paid ads across Facebook and invented "American" Facebook profiles to pass on fake news. Russian agents disseminated disinformation across Google as well, including via its subsidiary YouTube, and through advertising on Google search, Gmail, and the company's DoubleClick ad network. According to *The New York Times,* "one of the most powerful weapons that Russian agents used to reshape U.S. politics was the anger, passion and misinformation that real Americans were broadcasting across social media platforms." The Russians repurposed social media posts from real Americans to exacerbate existing anger about immigration, race, religion and patriotism. As *The Times* reported, "The Russian [Facebook] pages—with names like 'Being Patriotic,' 'Secured Borders' and 'Blacktivist'—cribbed complaints about federal agents from one conservative website, and a gauzy article about a veteran who became an entrepreneur from *People* magazine. They took descriptions and videos of police beatings from genuine YouTube and Facebook accounts and reposted them, sometimes lightly edited for maximum effect."

Then there were the botnet spamming operations unleashed by Russia that spread fake news on Twitter using accounts that appeared to be from undecided Midwestern Republican voters. Former FBI agent Clint Watts explained the Russian propaganda effort to the Senate Intelligence Committee in March 2017 testimony. During the 2016 campaign, Watts said, the Russians built on claims made by candidate Donald Trump, such as his false contention that the Obama administration had wiretapped Trump Tower in New York City. Once candidate Trump went public with that accusation, the Russians added "further conspiracy theories about that claim and that just amplifie[d] the message in the ecosystem."

Flooding U.S. information channels with false and fake news has terrifying implications for democracy, but the current threats facing the U.S. pale by comparison to the Russian government's domestic oppression of media and citizens' access to information. Russian journalists learned to avoid reporting on subjects that could anger the Kremlin after the 2006 assassination of *Novaya Gazeta* investigative reporter Anna Politkovskaya outside her apartment in Moscow. Since Politkovskaya's death, the Committee to Protect Journalists, a U.S.-based non-profit, estimates that

(PATRICK CHAPPATTE, COURTESY CAGLE CARTOONS)

at least 20 journalists in Russia have been killed; Freedom House counts over 60 violent attacks on reporters in the past decade; and internal observers watch as bloggers are sentenced to prison for their activities on social media. The only remaining media that independently cover the news in Russia are small operations, and even these are threatened with closure if their reporting dares to question Kremlin policies.

In Anna Politkovskaya's posthumously published book, *Putin's Russia: Life in a Failing Democracy,* she briefly related this World War II story: "When the Fascists entered Denmark, the Jews were ordered to sew yellow stars on their clothing so they could be easily recognized." But what happened next was a surprise: "ALL the Danes promptly sewed on yellow stars," and "their king joined with them." Why did the Danes do this? According to Politkovskaya, they wanted to save the Jews in Denmark from deportation and death. Moreover, they "wanted to save themselves from turning into Fascists."

Media, the First Amendment & the presidency

66**Congress shall make no law respecting an establishment of religion, or prohibiting the free exercise thereof; or abridging the freedom of speech, or of the press; or the right of the people peaceably to assemble, and to petition the Government for a redress of grievances."**—First Amendment to the United States Constitution (1791)

In the 21st century, American media have had extraordinary influence on international affairs and foreign policy, and social media's impact has been outsized. It wasn't long after the creation of the giants—Facebook (launched in 2004), YouTube (2005) and Twitter (2006)—that the U.S. foreign policy establishment understood it needed to divert resources to address the new realities of engagement. On November 15, 2007, Duncan MacInnes, principal deputy coordinator in the Bureau of International Information Programs (IIP) in the George W. Bush (2001–09) State Department, spoke before the House Armed Services Committee's Subcommittee on Terrorism. MacInnes laid out the argument for why the State Department needed to have a robust, outward-facing Internet presence:

Combating ideological support for terrorism poses a variety of daunting, new challenges for U.S. public diplomacy. Terrorists have shown themselves to be adept at exploiting the freedom of the Internet to spread their propaganda directly to young Muslims around the world. Our traditional communication tools are designed for mainstream media and have little impact in this new infor-

mation 'battlefield.' Our audience stretches beyond the traditional opinion leaders and political elites to include the general public and specifically the youth who are the target of extremist propaganda."

Three months later, the State Department declared that it was making an "exciting" foray into the online world with a new website, America. gov. As then-Secretary of State Condoleezza Rice (2005–09) noted, the site would encourage a "two-way conversation between America and people in other countries."

Three years later, in late March 2011, the Barack Obama (2009–17) State Department announced that it was "archiving" the rather static America.gov site. Money and personnel formerly directed to the site would be deployed instead into the department's "social media assets," such as Facebook, YouTube and Twitter. MacInnes, by then the deputy assistant secretary to the IIP, spelled out how the department would get its messages out in the contemporary social media landscape: "We'll produce an article, we'll reduce that to a 200-word piece that can be used for a Facebook page and three or four tweets that can be used on a Twitter feed and instant messaging." The State Department noted, too, that it would post on its social media platforms, using such already-familiar Facebook inducements as photo albums and snap polls, and that it would tap Silicon Valley experts to develop more targeted public diplomacy tools.

Already in the first Obama administration (2009–13), it had become evident to the foreign policy establish-

ment that social media were evolving into a critical instrument for disseminating policy information, evaluating public opinion, and surveillance. There was still recognition of the authority of the First Amendment, namely, its endowment of the "press" with a constitutional watchdog role, but the government's interest in using social media as a platform for person-to-person communication and for monitoring online conversations began to overshadow its traditional relationship with the news media.

President Obama's administration tried to intimidate and control the press. It used "intrusive measures" against reporters, spying on journalists by monitoring their phone records and issuing subpoenas to reporters to try to force them to reveal their sources—behavior that raised serious questions about the administration's respect for freedom of the press. Journalists—including *New York Times* reporter James Risen, whom the Obama administration had attempted to compel to reveal his confidential sources as part of a criminal leak investigation—criticized President Obama, together with the Justice Department and the FBI, for "waging a war on whistleblowers" and for using the 100-year-old Espionage Act "against suspected leakers." (The Espionage Act was signed into law by President Woodrow Wilson (1913–21) to deal with enemy spies during World War I.) Indeed, under President Obama, the White House used the Espionage Act to prosecute nine cases involving whistle-blowers and leakers, compared with only three prosecutions by all previous administrations. Prominent cases

A history lesson: the birth of the right to freedom of speech & of the press

> "Since the founding of this nation, freedom of the press has been a fundamental tenet of American life. There is no more essential ingredient than a free, strong and independent press to our continued success in what the Founding Fathers called our 'noble experiment' in self-government." —President Ronald Reagan (October 6, 1983)

Early in the American experiment, the Founding Fathers were outspoken in their support for free speech and a free press. They believed the American Revolution had begun because those rights had been trampled, and they believed it had survived because even in the darkest hours, when the Continental Army was poised to mutiny against the U.S. Congress of the Confederation, those ideals overcame self-interest.

On April 16, 1784, three months after the Confederation Congress ratified the Treaty of Paris ending the revolution, Thomas Jefferson wrote to General George Washington. Jefferson's letter praised the general, not just for leading the American Continental Army, but for saving the revolution itself. It was "the moderation and virtue of a single character [Washington]" Jefferson said, that "has probably prevented this revolution from being closed as most others have been by a subversion of that liberty it was intended to establish."

The pivotal moment of "moderation and virtue" to which Jefferson alluded occurred on March 15, 1783. The army was encamped at Newburgh, outside British-occupied New York City, awaiting diplomatic news from Paris that would end the armed hostilities. Washington delivered an address to his senior officers, some of whom had fought beside him for eight years. He had called the meeting in response to anonymous letters from "a fellow-soldier," letters that threatened violence if Congress did not pay the soldiers their promised enlistment bonuses and long-overdue pay. The messages warned the troops to "suspect the man"—clearly insinuating Washington—"who would advise to more moderation and longer forbearance."

The soldiers had survived the winter without pay, blankets or even much food. Yet the Confederation Congress could do little; it had no authority to collect taxes or funds from the loose confederation of states. Few in the camp believed its pledges that the soldiers would be paid "when funds became available" following the anticipated peace treaty. The men feared that when the war was over and the army disbanded, the government would forget their back pay. So that March morning, General Washington was the only force that stood between the dream of a civilian republican government in America and mutiny.

Washington addressed the crowd of men assembled before him. "I spurn," he said, "the advice given by the [anonymous] Author, to suspect the Man, who shall recommend moderate measures and longer forbearance…for if Men are to be precluded from offering their sentiments on a matter, which may involve the most serious and alarming consequences, that can invite the consideration of Mankind, reason is of no use to us—the freedom of Speech may be taken away—and, dumb & silent we may be led, like sheep, to the Slaughter." As he drew to a close, he wondered if perhaps another's voice might be more persuasive, and reached in his pocket for a letter from Congressman Joseph Jones of Virginia, who had promised his support for the back pay. But Washington couldn't read the congressman's small handwriting. He patted his regimentals, looking for his hidden bifocals as the noise in the room increased.

He glanced up, apologetically, with the new glasses settled on his nose. "Gentlemen," he said, "you must pardon me. I have grown gray in your service and now find myself growing blind." Those in the room later wrote of the watching officers rubbing their own weary faces, even some weeping. That morning they had seen Washington as he was: old beyond his years, grown tired along with them, but never faltering in his service to the army, to Congress and above all to the "national character of America." The men stood. They trusted him. There was no mutiny. Washington had upheld their freedom to speak out, their right to challenge authority. Further, he had upheld the "the liberties of [the] Country."

Eight years and nine months later, on December 15, 1791, the right to freedom of speech and freedom of the press were codified in the U.S. Constitution when Virginia became the tenth of 14 states to ratify the Bill of Rights, including the First Amendment.

This tweet from Donald Trump showed his support for free speech in 2013. Trump has since, as a candidate and now as president, backtracked on his support for First Amendment protections.

in the Obama years included Chelsea Manning, the former army private, and Edward Snowden, the former National Security Agency contractor.

Since Donald Trump's presidency, the Fourth Estate has come under a further barrage of direct attacks by the White House. Just one month into his term, Trump held a 77-minute press conference, much of which he spent criticizing the "dishonest media," because, as he tautologically explained, "the news is fake because so much of the news is fake." In an effort to counter the reporting of mainstream news outlets on his administration, Trump has shifted the way the institution of the presidency speaks to the public. Early on, he set up a "Real News" TV program, for example, which airs on his Facebook page and promises the "News of the Week"—its credibility has been called into question not least because it features his daughter-in-law, Laura Trump, as the lead newscaster. But President Trump's most evident innovation is his use of his personal Twitter account, @realDonaldTrump. Unlike his predecessors, Trump came into office as an active social media user, and has defended his continued use of the platforms: "My use of social media is not Presidential," he wrote in one tweet, "it's MODERN DAY PRESIDENTIAL. Make America Great Again!"

President Trump's tweeting has altered the way media monitor the executive branch. Fact-checkers have been added to newsrooms to confirm, in near-real time, the statements coming from the president and his senior staff. And beyond asking their newsrooms to prioritize fact-checking, many media outlets have added staff reporters to the White House beat. The journalists typically start their day at six in the morning, as the president often tweets before he begins work in the Oval Office. Reporters continue to monitor the president's account through the night, as he has been known to tweet at all hours. The president's social media postings frequently reflect the content of the TV programs he is known to watch, such as *Hannity* on Fox News

at 10pm, with host Sean Hannity, or the *Fox & Friends* morning show beginning at 6am. The timing of his tweets is driven by strategic considerations as well: His late night and early morning tweets lead the news cycle of the day, giving him the opportunity to set the terms of the day's conversation.

The president uses social media to do more than post his opinions or break news; he has been dismissive of the press's First Amendment protections and the constitutional reasons for a free press. Trump has charged that the news media is "the enemy of the American People!" In the fall of 2017, during a meeting with Canadian Prime Minister Justin Trudeau (2015–present), he complained to a group assembled in the Oval Office that included reporters: "It's frankly disgusting the way the press is able to write whatever they want to write." In his war against the media, Trump deploys bellicose language: He has not only called mainstream media outlets "fake," but also "disgusting and corrupt," "dumb," "dying," "failing," "garbage," "incompetent," "irrelevant," "nasty," "scum," "sick," a "total disaster" and "worthless." Such epithets are hard to counter in the lightning-fast social media space, but because they are liked and retweeted and made into memes, they are even more difficult to ignore. As Trump tweeted six months into his presidency: "The Fake News Media hates when I use what has turned out to be my very powerful Social Media—over 100 million people! I can go around them."

Trump has also repeatedly used the bully pulpit of the presidency to limit journalists' access to the halls of power—for example, shutting down access to the State Department—and to directly threaten media outlets, as with a tweet recommending that the Senate Intelligence Committee look into network news, or another that threatened the licenses of TV networks. While neither the Federal Communications Commission nor Senate committees are under the direct control of the president, Trump's tweets challenging First Amendment protections

or stating falsehoods as facts regularly receive tens of thousands of likes and replies and retweets each. Such social media feedback spreads the president's messages further and faster than corrections can keep up, while confirming for the White House that such tactics are effective.

Yet it's no longer just the president who is undermining media's role in U.S. democracy; the media are themselves complicit. For example, news programs, especially on cable TV, showcase their on-contract partisan commentators over the academic and other experts who formerly provided the bulk of context and analysis. Investigative reporter Raquel Rutledge noted the consequence in a November 2016 *Nieman Reports* article: Journalistic "bias, both actual (which plenty of data support) as well as perceived, is pummeling us and jeopardizes the stability of our democracy." Further, a 2017 Pew Research poll found that while three quarters of Democrats (76%) said the freedom of the press to criticize politicians is very important to maintaining a strong democracy, only half of Republicans (49%) said the same. According to a recent study from the John S. and James L. Knight Foundation, roughly two out of five high school students (44%) across the U.S. believe that the "First Amendment goes too far in the rights it protects."

Why these attacks against the media and this ambivalence about the First Amendment? It's politics. "Mr. Trump has discovered the benefits of making the opposition scream," wrote Amherst College professor Javier Corrales, in an October 2017 opinion piece in *The New York Times*. "A result is that Mr. Trump successfully transforms the targets of his hate, and those who come to their defense, into an even more extreme image of what the president's base already despises." In short, "the more he disparages people and institutions of repute, the more his core will feel satisfied politically." But what's lost for the country in Trump's media attacks is the Founding Fathers' deeply reasoned argument for why freedom of the press is fundamental for a democracy.

Foreign policy in the Internet age

> "Social media has become diplomacy's significant other.
> It has gone from being an afterthought to being the very first thought of world leaders and governments across the globe, as audiences flock to their Twitter newsfeeds for the latest news and statements." — Burson-Marsteller, Twiplomacy study (2017)

Media, and especially social media, exponentially extend the reach of a brand and its message. Savvy actors recognize that the truly cost-effective way to get their message out is to let their own audiences do most of the work. News and messages trend — they go viral — when an audience passes the story on, when the public retweets it, posts it on Facebook, likes it on YouTube, rejiggers it so the algorithms of Google privilege it in searches. Industry seeks to have its products go viral — the latest smart phone, the newest single from a pop star, the most recent fashion trend. Everyone wants the public's attention — including presidents and government ministries.

Twitter — more so than Facebook, YouTube, Instagram and Snapchat — has become the platform of choice for foreign ministries and heads of state and government to get their policy messages out to the public, as well as to talk to their counterparts in other countries. According to Burson-Marsteller's 2017 Twiplomacy study, 178 countries have Twitter accounts belonging to their heads of state and government and/or foreign ministers. With the exception of German Chancellor Angela Merkel (2005–present), all of the Group of Seven (G-7) leaders have a personal Twitter account. Yet for all of Twitter's appeal, most heads of state and government, their ministries and their embassies have been cautious about using social media platforms for statecraft; they are wary of how social media effectively circumvent the norms and subtleties of traditional diplomacy. Twitter is a blunt instrument, well-suited to declarations; it does not encourage or sustain nuanced, diplomatic conversations.

President Trump uses Twitter more than other world leaders, in part because his goal is less to forge relationships than to attract attention for himself. In an April 2017 interview with the *Financial Times,* President Trump argued that not only did he owe his election to social media, but that in fact social media gave him an unparalleled platform for his policies both at home and abroad. "Without the tweets, I wouldn't be here," the president noted. "I have over 100 million [followers] between Facebook, Twitter, Instagram. Over 100 million. I don't have to go to the fake media."

During a June 2017 press conference, a reporter asked then-White

---

Case study: North Korea

Today the world watches as salvos of messages from Twitter ricochet around the web. Take a look at one extended exchange in late summer 2017, initiated by President Donald Trump, and spurred on by political talk shows on TV and radio.

■ **August 8, 2017:** While visiting the Trump National Golf Club, in Bedminster, New Jersey, the president made a few unscripted remarks in advance of a briefing on the opioid crisis. If North Korea makes "any more threats to the United States," he said to the cameras, "[t]hey will be met with fire and fury like the world has never seen."

■ **August 9, 2017:** *Fox & Friends* tweeted out the president's video soundbite. That, in turn, caught the president's attention. He followed up from his personal @realDonaldTrump account: "My first order as President was to renovate and modernize our nuclear arsenal. It is now far stronger and more powerful than ever before…Hopefully we will never have to use this power, but there will never be a time that we are not the most powerful nation in the world!" North Korea responded with an announcement that it was considering launching a strike of four intermediate-range ballistic missiles that would create "an enveloping fire" around the U.S. territory of Guam in the western Pacific Ocean.

■ **August 11, 2017:** President Trump tweeted his reaction to North Korea: "Military solutions are now fully in place, locked and loaded, should North Korea act unwisely. Hopefully Kim Jong Un will find another path!"

■ **September 23, 2017:** Following a global meeting of leaders at the United Nations (UN), Trump took an even more bellicose stance. "Just heard Foreign Minister of North Korea speak at U.N.," Trump tweeted. "If he echoes thoughts of Little Rocket Man [Kim Jong Un], they won't be around much longer!"

■ **September 24, 2017:** North Korea's Foreign Minister Ri Yong Ho called the president's tweet "a declaration of war," and threatened that North Korea would shoot down U.S. warplanes even if they were not in the country's airspace. Ri warned that Trump's statements suggesting that the U.S. would eradicate North Korea and its leaders made it "inevitable" that North Korea would strike the U.S. mainland.

■ **September 25, 2017:** In a front-page article summarizing the back and forth, *The New York Times* wrote that Ri's warning "escalated the invective-laced exchanges with Mr. Trump and appeared to further preclude the possibility of a diplomatic exit from the biggest foreign crisis the administration has faced."

White House Press Secretary Sean Spicer delivers the press briefing in the James S. Brady Press Briefing Room of the White House on June 2, 2017. (CHERISS MAY/NURPHOTO/GETTY IMAGES)

House Press Secretary Sean Spicer if President Trump's tweets were considered official White House statements. Spicer responded: "The president is president of the United States, so they are considered official statements by the president of the United States." With that affirmation, the world came to understand that Twitter was the official public voice of President Trump. Yet his shoot-from-the-hip style on social media has alarmed both his opposition and his political allies.

The political establishment finds it disconcerting that the president's statements on Twitter and elsewhere are not always factually accurate. Even those within the Trump White House have been startled by his tendency to lash out publicly online at anyone he perceives as opposing his agenda, including GOP leaders and members of his own administration. He has criticized Republican Senate Majority Leader Mitch McConnell, for instance, as well as his own State Department for engaging in diplomacy with North Korea. "I told Rex Tillerson, our wonderful Secretary of State, that he is wasting his time trying to negotiate with Little Rocket Man [North Korean dictator Kim Jong Un]..." he tweeted. "...Save your energy Rex, we'll do what has to be done!"

In a sharp criticism of President Trump, Republican Senator Bob Corker, chairman of the Senate Foreign Relations Committee, expressed his concerns: "I don't think [Trump] appreciates that when the president of the United States speaks and says the things that he does, the impact that it has around the world...I know he has hurt—in several instances—he's hurt us [the U.S.] as it relates to negotiations that were underway by tweeting things out...[H]e doesn't realize that we could be heading towards World War III with the kind of comments that he's making."

Emergency services personnel at the scene of the tube explosion at Parsons Green Underground Station on September 15, 2017, in London, England. (JACK TAYLOR/ GETTY IMAGES)

On the international level, President Trump's unfiltered use of social media has ratcheted up tensions. Take, for instance, his his three early morning tweets in response to a September 2017 improvised explosive device (IED) bombing on the London Underground that injured 30 people. "Another attack in London by a loser terrorist," he wrote. "These are sick and demented people who were in the sights of Scotland Yard [the headquarters for the London Metropolitan Police Service]. Must be proactive!" Six minutes later, he tweeted again: "Loser terrorists must be dealt with in a much tougher manner. The internet is their main recruitment tool which we must cut off & use better!" After another six minutes, he wrote: "The travel ban into the United States [referring to the president's effort to ban entry into the U.S. for people from predominantly Muslim countries] should be far larger, tougher and more specific—but stupidly, that would not be politically correct!"

Reaction in Britain to the tweets was swift. A Metropolitan Police source told the British online newspaper *The Independent* that President Trump's first tweet was "just speculation." British Prime Minister Theresa May (2016–present) pointedly remarked in an interview, "I never think it's helpful for anybody to speculate on what is an ongoing investigation." Former Conservative Member of Parliament Ben Howlett tweeted that "it is highly unhelpful/ dangerous and inappropriate for an ally to make announcements that share intelligence and undermine investigations." *The Telegraph* questioned "whether Mr Trump had received a briefing before making his claims, in which case he leaked British intelligence, or if he jumped to a conclusion without evidence about who was behind the attack." Many others leapt on the president's call for a "far larger, tougher" travel ban in the U.S., criticizing it as a premature assumption about the origins of the perpetrator, given that no suspect had yet been identified.

U.S. policy implications and questions for the future

"[It's] a free press that has distinguished us from other countries. We must stop those who try to silence dissent by silencing an institution whose job is to give voice to dissent." —Dana Priest, Pulitzer Prize-winning reporter, *The Washington Post*

If one weighs U.S. foreign policy successes over the centuries, the greatest is arguably the "export" of the right to a free press and free expression. "Our liberty depends on the freedom of the press," Thomas Jefferson wrote in 1786, "and that cannot be limited without being lost." The Founding Fathers so strongly believed in the principles of free speech and a free press that they codified those rights into the U.S. Constitution, even though the revolutionary leaders themselves faced harsh attacks from the press. President George Washington (1789–97) was "extremely affected by the attacks made and kept up on him in the public papers," as Thomas Jefferson wrote to James Madison. "I think he feels those things more than any person I ever yet met with." As Washington himself explained to his friend Gouverneur Morris, (also a signatory to the Articles of Confederation and the U.S. Constitution), however, the value of a free press and free speech outweighed any suffering he might have endured:

From the complexion of some of our News-papers Foreigners would be led to believe that inveterate political dissentions existed among us, and that we are on the very verge of disunion; but the fact is otherwise—the great body of the people now feel the advantages of the General Government, and would not, I am persuaded, do any thing that should destroy it; but this kind of representations is an evil wch [sic] must be placed in opposition to the infinite benefits resulting from a free Press…

In a 2012 study of constitutions adopted from 1946 to 2006 in 188 countries, 97% include the right of freedom of the press or expression or both. According to Christina Murray, director of the Bingham Centre for the Rule of Law, "there's seldom a constitution-making process in the democratic world that isn't informed by the fundamental principles that inform the U.S. Constitution." Yet Murray, who has advised a dozen countries on the drafting and revision of their constitutions, notes that the U.S. Constitution is aging. It is the oldest written national constitution still in force anywhere in the world, and other countries are looking to newer legal documents as they draft their own constitutions.

If the U.S. still wants to be the world's leading democracy, its government needs to continue to uphold the rights and standards of the First Amendment. *The New Yorker* reported that "[l]aws and institutions designed for liberal democracy can be deployed to restrict media freedom. That's what modern-day autocrats do. Vladimir Putin has used economic instruments against the press, from hostile takeovers of media companies to libel suits that have bankrupted journalists and entire news outlets…Trump is testing the potential of these strategies." In the 2017 annual World Press Freedom Index from Reporters Sans Frontières (RSF), an international organization which evaluates the world's nations on press freedom, the U.S. slipped from 41st to 43rd place. "It's really important to remind the people that the press is reporting for them," said Margaux Ewen, RSF's advocacy and communications director.

In 1961, only three months after his inauguration, President John F. Kennedy (1961–63) gave an address to the American Newspaper Publishers Association. He articulated concerns that remain resonant across the years. Kennedy called for the press to give "greater coverage and analysis of international news—for it is no longer far away and foreign but close at hand and local." He also called for "greater attention to improved understanding of the news as well as improved transmission." Government, he said, "must meet its obligation to provide [Americans] with the fullest possible information outside the narrowest limits of national security." Further, "without debate, without criticism, no administration and no country can succeed—and no republic can survive. That is why our press was protected by the First Amendment—the only business in America specifically protected by the Constitution."

Almost 60 years after that address, it has become clear that media—especially social media—can exacerbate the anti-democratic forces at work in today's world. In our 21st century, we want media to play a positive role in international affairs. To bring that to pass, we must address the following questions: How can the news media better serve the public? How can media, across platforms and types, improve connections to family, friends, community, nation and the world? How can media—even social media, AI technologies and algorithms—better support democratic principles and civil society? Finally, we must ask what we ourselves can do to bring that future into being. "Ask not what your country can do for you—ask what you can do for your country."

President John Kennedy addresses the annual dinner of the Bureau of Advertising of the American Newspaper Publishers Association at the Waldorf-Astoria hotel in New York on April 27, 1961. (AP PHOTO)

discussion questions

1. President Donald Trump's use of Twitter has transformed the way that high-level government officials communicate with the public. Should tweets from the president's personal Twitter account be considered official White House statements? Given that social media provide a direct line of communication between officials and the public, what should be the role of the news media in reporting on Washington?

2. Examine the role of social media in the democratic process. In what ways is the new media landscape consistent with and/or discordant with First Amendment principles?

3. Has President Donald Trump's vocal criticism of mainstream news media outlets as "fake" and "dishonest" changed the way those outlets themselves operate? What effects have the president's tactics had on the media landscape?

4. The Founding Fathers believed that government must be held accountable to its citizens, and they passed the First Amendment to that end. The constitutional right to a free press established the mechanism that many call the Fourth Estate: an investigative "watchdog" media to oversee the executive, legislative and judicial branches of government. What are good recent examples, in your estimation, of mainstream media playing this watchdog role? What are media able to accomplish in this respect that other institutions are not?

5. What recent national security stories or stories about the political processes of other countries do you think media have overlooked? Why do you think those stories have been ignored? Conversely, what foreign policy stories do you think have been over-covered? Why do you think that has been the case?

6. How does the mainstream media's 24/7 coverage of terrorism and other crises in the international arena affect the way listeners, viewers and readers comprehend and respond to those crises? Do terrorists "weaponize" the media? In what ways?

suggested readings

Aday, Sean, "The US Media, Foreign Policy, and Public Support for War," in **The Oxford Handbook of Political Communication**. 23 pp. New York: Oxford University Press, July 2017. Available free online: <http://www.oxfordhandbooks.com/view/10.1093/oxfordhb/9780199793471.001.0001/oxfordhb-9780199793471-e-025?print=pdf>. This report analyzes the relationship between news coverage and foreign policy, with an emphasis on how the U.S. media covers war and other crises.

Hale, Scott, Margetts, Helen, Peter, John, and Yasseri, Taha, **Political Turbulence: How Social Media Shape Collective Action**. 304 pp. Princeton, NJ: Princeton University Press, 2015. This book analyzes data from the Internet and real world events to study the capacity of social media to drive collective action.

Moeller, Susan D., **Packaging Terrorism: Co-opting the News for Politics and Profit**. 240 pp. Hoboken, NJ: Wiley-Blackwell, 2008. Moeller examines and assesses how the U.S. media has covered international terrorism since the 9/11 terrorist attacks.

Osnos, Evan, Remnick, David, and Yaffa, Joshua, "Trump, Putin, and the New Cold War." **The New Yorker**, March 6, 2017. Available free online: <https://www.newyorker.com/magazine/2017/03/06/trump-putin-and-the-new-cold-war>. This long-form article analyzes Russia's interference in the U.S. 2016 presidential election and discusses what this means for future U.S.-Russia relations.

Segal, Adam, **The Hacked World Order: How Nations Fight, Trade, Maneuver, and Manipulate in the Digital Age**. 320 pp. New York: PublicAffairs, 2016. This account traces transformations in geopolitics and cyberwarfare, underscoring that cybersecurity is more often than not in the hands of private enterprise and the technological sector rather than governments.

——, "Trump the Truth: Free Expression in the President's First 100 Days." 55 pp. **PEN America**, April 27, 2017. This report by the nonprofit PEN America assesses how President Donald Trump's first 100 days in office have threatened freedom of speech and freedom of the press.

Don't forget: Ballots start on page 105!

To access web links to these readings, as well as links to additional, shorter readings and suggested web sites,

GO TO www.greatdecisions.org

and click on the topic under Resources, on the right-hand side of the page

Turkey: a partner in crisis

by Ömer Taşpinar

A Turkish commando stands in front of the Turkish flag on Hisar Mountain, in Hakkari, Turkey, on December 31, 2016. Turkish commandos play an active role in fighting against Kurdish militants in the eastern provinces. (ÖZKAN BILGIN/ANADOLU AGENCY/GETTY IMAGES)

O f all North Atlantic Treaty Organization (NATO) allies, Turkey by far represents the most daunting challenge for the administration of U.S. President Donald Trump. In the wake of a failed military coup in July 2016—a chaotic affair that caused over 270 deaths—the autocratic trend in Turkey took a turn for the worse. More than a year later, massive purges, not only in the military and civilian bureaucracy, but also in academia, non-governmental organizations and the media, have left little of a once-praised democratic model for the Islamic world.

Despite these draconian measures and the introduction of emergency law, the security situation remains tense. Both the worsening of the deeply rooted Kurdish conflict and frequent attacks by the Islamic State (ISIS) terrorist organization (to be discussed) represent existential threats. The once thriving economy is also on life support, with unsustainable public spending. Foreign investment, tourism revenues and consumer confidence are down. Who is to blame for all this? As of July 2017, an overwhelming 72% of the Turkish population pointed to the U.S. as their country's *number one* security threat, when asked to consider a list of eight issues that included Russia, China and ISIS.

For seasoned U.S. policymakers, domestic problems in Turkey and downturns in the bilateral relationship are not new. In their eyes, Turkey has always presented major chal-

ÖMER TAŞPINAR *is a professor at the National War College and a non-resident senior fellow at the Brookings Institution. He is the author of two books:* Kurdish Nationalism and Political Islam in Turkey: Kemalist Identity in Transition *(Routledge, 2005) and* Winning Turkey: How America, Europe and Turkey Can Revive a Fading Partnership *(Brookings Press, 2008) with Philip Gordon. His research focuses on the Middle East, Europe, Muslim minorities in the West, radicalization and global political economy.*

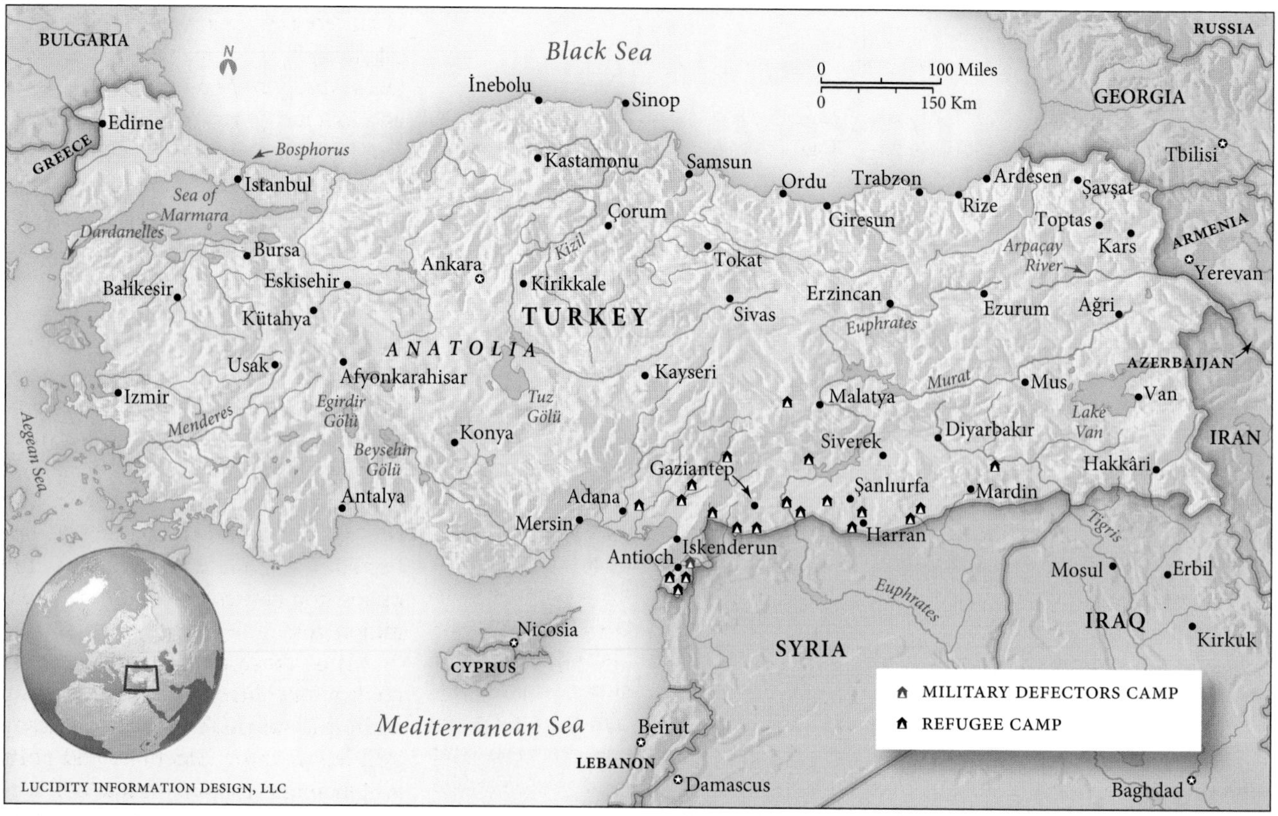

The map shows Turkey and surrounding regions.

BULGARIA	Black Sea
RUSSIA	GEORGIA
İnebolu, Sinop, Kastamonu, Samsun	
Edirne, GREECE	Ordu, Trabzon, Ardesen, Şavşat, Tbilisi
Bosphorus, Istanbul	Giresun, Rize, Toptas
Sea of Marmara, Dardanelles, Bursa	Çorum, ARMENIA, Kars, Yerevan
Balıkesir, Eskisehir, Ankara, Kirikkale	Tokat, Erzincan, Ezurum, Ağrı
Kütahya, TURKEY, Sivas	AZERBAIJAN
Uşak, ANATOLIA, Afyonkarahisar, Kayseri	Malatya, Mus, Van
Izmir, Menderes, Egirdir Gölü, Tuz Gölü	Siverek, Diyarbakır, Lake Van, IRAN
Beysehir Gölü, Konya	Gaziantep, Şanlıurfa, Hakkâri
Antalya, Adana, Mersin	Mardin
Antioch, Iskenderun, Harran	Mosul, Erbil
Nicosia, CYPRUS	IRAQ, Kirkuk
Mediterranean Sea, Beirut	SYRIA
LEBANON, Damascus	Baghdad

⌂ MILITARY DEFECTORS CAMP
⌂ REFUGEE CAMP

LUCIDITY INFORMATION DESIGN, LLC

lenges and great opportunities. The old joke "Brazil is the country of the future, and always will be" seems to apply to Turkey even more aptly, except that Turkey is in a crucial geostrategic position for the U.S. Ankara is Washington's military partner in Asia Minor, where the Middle East, the Caucasus, Ukraine, Russia and the Balkans converge to create formidable security challenges. The NATO ally shares important borders with Syria, Iraq and Iran (on Turkey's south) and with Georgia, Russia and Ukraine (on its north). Turkey is also critically located for efforts to reduce Europe's energy dependence on Russia. It is itself dependent on Moscow for energy, but pipelines under construction will transform the country into an east-west corridor, assuring European access to the oil and natural gas resources of Azerbaijan and Central Asia.

There is more to Turkey's signifi-

cance for Washington than where it sits geostrategically. In this age of a worsening "clash of civilizations" between Islam and the West, Turkey symbolically represents the most institutionally Westernized Muslim country in the world. It is the only Muslim member of NATO and an "eternal" candidate to the European Union (EU). It has a seat at the Group of 20 (G-20) and the Organization for Economic Cooperation and Development (OECD), and despite all of its human rights violations and growing illiberalism over the last few years, it is still the most democratic and secular country in the Islamic world. Turkey also has a vibrant entrepre-

(PARESH/ *THE KHALEEJ TIMES*, DUBAI, UAE/ ©CARTOONARTS INTERNATIONAL/THE NEW YORK TIMES SYNDICATE)

neurial capitalist system that depends on export-led growth and productivity, a young population of 80 million and a growing middle class. It is a generous country when it comes to opening its borders to refugees, and has welcomed some 3 million Syrians fleeing the civil war in their country.

All these dynamics prove Turkey to be a study in paradox. Great potential is combined with equally far-reaching dysfunction. As the astonishing poll about anti-Americanism clearly indicates, Turkish politics tend to disappoint U.S. administrations that come to the table with high expectations for cooperation. The George W. Bush administration (2001–09) discovered this the hard way in 2003: Turkey was the only NATO neighbor of Iraq with a major U.S. military base; its cooperation was crucial for U.S. plans to invade. Nevertheless, after almost a year of contentious negotiations and billions of dollars in financial incentives, Turkish legislators rejected at the last minute the motion opening their territory to U.S. military forces. Then, as now, overwhelmingly negative public opinion about the U.S. played a critical role.

!

Before you read, download the companion **Glossary** that includes definitions and a guide to acronyms and abbreviations used in the article. Go to **www.great decisions.org** and select a topic in the Resources section on the right-hand side of the page.

Anti-Americanism and Turkish democracy

That a vast majority of Turks currently see their NATO ally as enemy number one is highly disturbing for a country that would normally be considered part of the "Western club." Turks today have more favorable views of Russia and China than of the U.S., and anti-Americanism often scores higher in Turkey than in Pakistan or the average in the Arab world. Such opinion poll numbers matter greatly. Unlike most parts of the Middle East, Turkey has a political system wherein elections determine who governs. What makes mass resentment against the U.S. highly consequential is the combination of the ballot box with raw populism.

Given its current authoritarian trend, it is sometimes easy to forget that Turkey is the oldest secular democracy in the Islamic world. Despite several military interventions, political power in Turkey has changed hands through democratic elections more than a dozen times since the inception of multi-party politics in 1946. What people think—who they blame for problems—is therefore of critical importance for the leader of the country, Recep Tayyip Erdoğan, who is a master at winning elections. Erdoğan came to power as Turkey's prime minister from 2003 to 2014 and has served as president ever since. He is a Machiavellian populist who often fuels and exploits anti-Americanism and complains to U.S. politicians about the consequences of their policies. On April 16, 2017, Erdoğan narrowly won a crucial referendum by mobilizing his supporters with an aggressively anti-EU and anti-American nationalist discourse.

In the last five years, Erdoğan has consolidated his hegemony over all aspects of Turkish politics by challenging most norms of liberal democracy. He shows no respect for the rule of law, the independence of the media or the separation of powers between the executive, legislative and judicial branches of government. As a skillful politician who easily connects with masses in large rallies, he above all believes in majoritarian, electoral democracy. Since his legitimacy depends on the ballot box, his biggest fear is to lose at the polls as he almost did a few months ago. The fact that he won the April 2017 referendum with a very narrow margin—putting an end to the parliamentary system and establishing a presidential regime with no real checks and balances—once again demonstrated the importance of public opinion and elections in Turkey.

It is essential to note that elections under Erdoğan's regime are free but not fair. People have the freedom to vote for opposition parties, but don't have access to an independent media. The opposition lacks effective platforms to mobilize its voters because freedom of expression and assembly is highly arbitrary. Dissenting voices face legal and political obstacles. But elections still take place, and despite complaints of partial fraud and ballot stuffing, the opposition grudgingly accepts their outcomes.

At the same time, electoral politics remains the only hope for democratic change in Turkey. Erdoğan knows that his unexpectedly slim victory in April 2017 exposed his vulnerability. In spite of his repressive tactics against the free media and a draconian emergency law that severely curbed freedom of speech and assembly, he barely managed to win 51% of the votes. Worse, he lost in almost all urban centers, including his stronghold Istanbul. In that sense, the April 2017 referendum confirmed a negative trend for his tarnished brand, the opening salvoes of which came in the June 2015 general elections, when Erdoğan's ruling Justice and Development Party (AKP) lost its parliamentary majority for the first time since it came to power in November 2002. Erdoğan recovered ground from that loss a few months later in the November 2015 "repeat" elections, after the opposition parties failed to form a coalition government.

All of these recent developments confirm one thing: Despite worsening authoritarianism, Turkish democracy still has a pulse. Elections and polls will therefore continue to matter greatly, perhaps even more so under the new presidential system. Erdoğan knows he needs to win the 2019 presidential election. The newly established two-round majoritarian system will force his opponents to unite as they did for the April 2017 referendum. As the economy shows signs of weakness, Erdoğan

Turkish President Recep Tayyip Erdoğan (R) and his wife Emine Erdoğan (L) flash the four-finger "Rabia sign" during a campaign rally for the "yes" vote in a constitutional referendum in Istanbul. The vote narrowly passed on April 16, 2017. (OZAN KOSE/AFP/GETTY IMAGES)

will have to rely more and more on nationalist populism. This will make anti-Americanism a very useful commodity.

Recent developments have seriously aggravated Turkish anti-Americanism. In May 2017, the Trump administration, as part of the fight against ISIS in Syria, decided to arm the forces associated with the Kurdish Syrian Democratic Union Party (PYD). In the eyes of most Turks, the PYD is part of the Kurdish Workers' Party (PKK), an outlawed militant group whose fight for autonomy is centered in Turkey's southeast. Ankara considers the PKK a terrorist organization, and has been fighting it since the 1980s. The two groups, the PKK and the PYD, are indeed closely linked (the PKK is the parent organization of the PYD), but unlike the PKK, the PYD has no claims over Turkey and represents the most effective fighting force against ISIS in Syria.

Despite growing numbers of ISIS terrorist attacks in Turkey, most Turks consider the PKK, and now the U.S., as the more urgent security threat. Turkish authorities regularly voice their concern that U.S. military equipment provided to the PYD will end up in the hands of PKK terrorists fighting the Turkish army. Ever distrustful of Western intentions, Turkish officials see a burgeoning strategic partnership between Washington and the Syrian Kurds it links to the PKK. U.S. reassurances that the partnership with the Kurds is just temporary and tactical fail to convince suspicious Turkish minds. Washington, on the other hand, has its own complaints about Ankara's Syria policy, grounded in Turkey's active support for radical Islamist groups in Syria fighting the Kurds and the regime in the Syrian capital Damascus. These dynamics create a tense relationship between the two NATO allies.

The 2016 coup attempt is fueling even more anti-Americanism. At the political level, there is a clear sense that the event offered Erdoğan a convenient excuse to go after all his adversaries. Hundreds of journalists and thousands of political opponents are now behind bars without due process, often on the grounds of supporting the religious and social movement led by U.S.-based Muslim cleric Fethullah Gülen. Europeans and Americans don't subscribe to Erdoğan's narrative that casts Gülen as the "terrorist" mastermind behind the coup. The Trump administration refuses to extradite Gülen in the absence of concrete evidence, fueling frustration and conspiracies in Ankara. Erdoğan supporters, as well as secularist circles that always suspected Gülen had U.S. support, believe in U.S. complicity in the coup. All this creates a nationalist resentment against Washington that transcends domestic political divisions.

Diverging agendas, diverging interests

There are two fundamental problems that have exacerbated tensions between Ankara and Washington since the demise of the Soviet Union in 1991. First and foremost is the absence of a common enemy. In the post-Soviet regional and global order, Turkey and the U.S. no longer share an existential threat perception. "Terrorism" is a generic concept and doesn't provide the sense of urgency, direction or discipline that containing, deterring and defeating the Soviet Union did during the Cold War. Moreover, as previously mentioned, the U.S. and Turkey strongly differ on whom they identify as terrorists: For Ankara, the top priority is combating ethnic terrorism in the form of Kurdish nationalism and separatism; for Washington, it is fighting ideological terrorism in the form of jihadist violent extremism.

The second issue irritating relations is that, as a byproduct of the post-Soviet order, the center of gravity for the U.S.-Turkey relationship shifted from Eurasia to a much more difficult region: the Middle East. Turkey's relevance for the U.S. increasingly became its southern borders with the Arab and Persian world and its role in the region as a democratic model. The U.S.' new threat perception became "rogue states" like Iran, Iraq and Syria, all of which happen to share borders with Turkey. Turkey's growing importance in the Middle East created an organizational problem in the way U.S. bureaucracy thinks about Turkey, and Washington was ill-prepared for this shift.

As former Ambassador to Turkey Mark Parris has argued:

For reasons of self-definition and Cold War logic, Turkey is considered a European nation. It is therefore assigned, for purposes of policy development and implementation, to the subdivisions responsible for Europe: the European Bureau (EUR) at the State Department; the European Command (EUCOM) at the Pentagon; the Directorate for Europe at the National Security Council (NSC), etc. Since the end of the Cold War, however, and progressively since the 1990–91 Gulf War and 9/11, the most serious issues in U.S.-Turkish relations—and virtually all of the controversial ones—have arisen in areas outside 'Europe.' The majority, in fact, stem from developments in areas which in Washington are the responsibility of offices dealing with the Middle East: the Bureau for Near East Affairs (NEA) at State; Central Command (CENTCOM) at the Pentagon; the Near East and South Asia Directorate at NSC.

Given this bureaucratic dilemma, U.S. officials who focus on Turkey are often experts on Western Europe, NATO, Russia, the EU and the Mediterranean. With high expectations and habits established during the Cold War, they tend to look at Turkey as a member of the transatlantic alliance and a Western state. Their disappointment is therefore much greater when Turkey acts in defiance of transatlantic and Western norms. Similarly, there is a tendency to see any deviation from these norms as Islamization.

Although the importance of political Islam in Erdoğan's agenda should not be fully dismissed, growing nationalism and frustration with the U.S. and

Europe present the real threats to Turkey's Western and democratic orientation today. Instead of overstating the role of political Islam, a more nuanced reading of Turkey's geopolitical direction requires looking at the intersection of the three main strategic visions behind Turkish foreign policy: Kemalism, Neo-Ottomanism and, more recently, "Turkish Gaullism"—understood as a hybrid of Kemalism and Neo-Ottomanism. As we will see, these three distinct ideological frameworks share a critical common denominator: the primacy of Turkish nationalism.

In principle, Kemalism—named after Mustafa Kemal Atatürk, who founded the Turkish Republic in 1923—favors strong relations with the West at the expense of the Islamic word. Under Atatürk's leadership, the Turkish Republic undertook ambitious Westernizing cultural reforms. Atatürk disposed of the caliphate, the Arabic alphabet, Islamic education and all reminders of the Ottoman political legacy. The country adopted Western legal codes, the Latin alphabet, the Western calendar, Western holidays and Western dress codes. A new education system glorified pre-Islamic Turkic civilizations, and many Arabic and Persian words were purged to create an "authentically" Turkish vocabulary. Even the Arabic *azan*, the Islamic call to prayer, was translated into modern Turkish and recited in Turkish until Atatürk's party lost power in 1950.

The Kemalist "civilizing mission," as it is sometimes called, was strongly committed to assuming a progressive, secularist position against reactionary Islamist enemies. Yet Westernization failed to win the hearts and minds of the devout masses in the Anatolian countryside. The overwhelming majority of the population felt detached from the social and cultural engineering taking place in the new capital Ankara. The military, the government bureaucracy and the urban bourgeoisie adapted most readily to Westernization, creating a widening cultural gap between the Kemalist elites and the rural periphery.

Behind the façade of rapid Westernization, Kemalist elites always had

ambiguous feelings about the West and maintained a sense of nationalist resentment. After all, it was Western imperialism that carved up the Ottoman Empire. The role that British and French imperialism played during the agonizingly slow centuries of Ottoman decline proved difficult to forget. As a result, national sovereignty and independence became sacrosanct concepts for Kemalists, who adopted an authoritarian nation-building agenda. In the subsequent decades, whenever the West pressured Turkey for democratic reforms—particularly on the Kurdish question—Kemalists would turn increasingly insular, anti-Western and conspiratorial.

In the 1980s and 1990s, as the Cold War came to an end, Turkey faced rapidly changing geopolitical dynamics in its immediate geography. The rise of Kurdish nationalism and Islamist politics at home, combined with wars in the Balkans, Caucasus and Middle East, forced the country to come to terms with its own "identity" problems and Ottoman legacy. Turkish liberals and conservatives began voicing the need for a "post-Kemalist" consensus in domestic and foreign politics. In their eyes, Kemalism suppressed Islamist and Kurdish politics while neglecting Turkey's relations with its historic zones of influence in the regions cited above.

Turkish soldier and statesman Mustaf Kemal Atatürk with his recent and unveiled bride, Latifeh Hanoum, at Tashankaia, near Ankara, Februrary 1923. (CPA MEDIA—PICTURES FROM HISTORY / THE GRANGER COLLECTION)

Neo-Ottomanism was born in this post-Cold War context. It developed first under the leadership of Turgut Özal (prime minister, 1983–89, and then president, 1989–93), who pursued an activist foreign policy in the Middle East and tried to promote some accommodation with Kurdish nationalists at home. Later, with stronger Islamist overtones, Neo-Ottomanism came to be associated with the AKP as a proj-

People participate in a march to celebrate the life of modern Turkey's founder Mustafa Kemal Atatürk during festivities on May 19, 2016, in Istanbul, Turkey. Despite security warnings about possible terrorist attacks by ISIS, people gathered across the country to commemorate the start of Turkey's War of Independence. (CHRIS MCGRATH/GETTY IMAGES)

ect seeking "soft power" projection in formerly Ottoman territories.

Naturally, Kemalism and Neo-Ottomanism had significant differences in domestic and foreign policy. They particularly diverged in their approach to the Kurdish question, Islamic identity and regional engagement. Kemalists—especially in the military establishment—insisted on maintaining hardline anti-Kurdish policies, militant secularism against Islamic symbols and a prudent foreign policy based on realistic national security priorities. Neo-Ottomanism, on the other hand, favored multicultural accommodation with the Kurds, a place for Islamic identity in domestic and foreign policy, and an activist-idealist foreign policy in search of conflict resolution and mediation in the Middle East, the Balkans and beyond.

Despite such differences, Kemalist and Neo-Ottoman strategic visions have something crucial in common: patriotic pride and the primacy of "Turkish" national and security interests. Thus, Kemalism and Neo-Ottomanism share a similar understanding of sovereignty and independence vis-à-vis the West. Both camps express their nationalist frustration with and resentment against European double standards and Turcophobia as Turkey gets second-class treatment in its quest for EU membership. They also share a similar narrative of victimhood in regard to U.S. military interventions in the Middle East and Western support for the Kurdish cause in both Turkey and Syria. Anti-American, anti-EU, anti-NATO and anti-imperialist feelings form the reactionary foundation of this coalition.

In the post-coup-attempt environment of today's Turkey, this peculiar alliance has gained even more visibility. Neo-Ottomanism, represented by Erdoğan and the AKP, and Kemalist Eurasianism, represented by ultra-nationalist and ultra-secularist officers in the army, are strongly in favor of improving strategic ties with Russia, China and Iran, as well as with the Shanghai Cooperation Organization (SCO), a Eurasian security alliance. The West (NATO and the EU) is increasingly seen as supportive of Kurdish nationalism and the Gülen movement.

This perception has become the most important driver of anti-Americanism in the last couple of years.

Given growing similarities between Kemalists and Neo-Ottomans, it is important to employ a different political vocabulary—one that captures this new dynamic in Turkish foreign policy. "Turkish Gaullism" provides a useful conceptual framework that transcends the fallacy of "pro-Western" secular Kemalism versus "anti-Western" Islamist Neo-Ottomanism. The two camps are united by Turkish nationalism and the pursuit of sovereign independence from the West. As Erdoğan's AKP and Kemalist-Eurasianist military circles continue to converge, Turkish foreign policy will not be increasingly Islamist, but rather much more nationalist, defiant, independent and self-centered—in short, a Turkish variant of French Gaullism.

As with French President Charles de Gaulle's (1958–69) anti-American and anti-NATO policies in the 1960s, a Gaullist Turkey may very well decide in the long run to question the overall logic of its partnership with Washington, and to leave the military structure of NATO. Ankara's recent decision to purchase a Russian missile defense system is a step in this Gaullist direction. NATO seriously objects to the purchase of the S-400 system, as it would not be interoperable with the equipment used by other alliance members. Erdoğan announced in September 2017 that Turkey had signed the missile deal, and confirmed that payment had been made for the weapons.

Similarly, a Gaullist Turkey may decide to wait no longer for an elusive EU membership, and instead to seek global relevance and solidarity in institutions like the SCO, to which Erdoğan often alludes. Such a step is not so farfetched for a Gaullist Turkey in search of full independence, full sovereignty, strategic leverage and, most importantly, "national prestige, glory and grandeur." This quest could also lead Turkey to opt for its own "force de frappe"—a nuclear deterrent—and its own realpolitik based on partnership with countries such as Russia, Iran, China and India.

Growing anti-Americanism at home, rapprochement with Russia and Iran, frustration with the EU, Washington's decision to arm Syrian Kurds and a worsening domestic war against the PKK are all factors that will contribute to the growth of Turkish Gaullism. To be sure, no analogy is perfect. Erdoğan is no de Gaulle and Turkey is not France. But Turkey's evolution under Erdoğan toward an "imperial presidency" is reminiscent of the way de Gaulle established the Fifth Republic and became the most important French leader since Napoleon. As we will see in the following sections, Erdoğan has similar ambitions and has already become the most influential Turkish leader since Atatürk.

Turkey's evolution under Erdoğan and Gülen

Erdoğan began his political career in the youth wing of the Islamist Welfare Party. His mentor at the time was Turkey's first Islamist prime minister, Necmettin Erbakan (1996–97). Just a year into his term, Erbakan was ousted by the secularist Kemalist military, and later banned from politics altogether. Erdoğan would go on to rise from the ranks and become the charismatic and effective mayor of Istanbul in 1994. Like his mentor, he became a victim of military interference in politics. He was imprisoned for four months in 1999, charged with inciting religious violence for reciting a poem with Islamist undertones.

Prison changed Erdoğan. When he established the AKP in 2001 with fellow reform-minded religious conservatives such as Abdullah Gül, he was determined to put political Islam behind him by adopting a pro-EU vision based on "conservative democracy." After he came to power in 2003 as prime minister, Erdoğan and his party also set out to revamp civil-military relations. The secularist military intervention against the Welfare Party convinced most of the younger and more pragmatic politicians within the movement to defend liberal democracy (rather than political Islam) against Kemalist authoritarianism. After having participated in democratic politics for over three decades, Turkey's Islamist movement had already learned to temper its views in order to make electoral gains. The red lines established by the secular system and enforced by the generals also helped to moderate political Islam. The support of a devout, entrepreneurial base in the heartland of Anatolia (known as the "Anatolian tigers") proved crucial in helping the AKP shed its Islamist tendencies and rebrand itself as a pro-market and pro-Western conservative democratic party.

Despite efforts to prove its newly acquired moderate credentials, in the eyes of the staunchly secularist army, the AKP shared the same long-term objective with Fethullah Gülen: to topple the secular regime founded by Atatürk. Erdoğan and Gülen were suspect in the eyes of the top military brass for nurturing hidden Islamist agendas behind a façade of "moderate Islam" admired by naïve Westerners. Gülen's movement was known for investing in education, interfaith dialogue, the media and private economic enterprise. It traditionally enjoyed good relations with most political parties and had growing numbers of followers and graduates in the civilian and security bureaucracy. In the late 1990s, as the military clamped down on political Islam, Gülen came to be seen in Kemalist circles as a duplicitous and dangerous cleric. His relations with the military were not helped by a secret sermon in which he encouraged a group of followers to quietly pursue careers in government until the time was "ripe." Fearing persecution, Gülen left Turkey for Pennsylvania in 1999, the same year Erdoğan served his sentence. He has remained in the U.S. ever since.

Turkey's rapid evolution in the last 20 years is largely a product of a formidable alliance between the AKP and Fethullah Gülen's movement. From 2003 to 2012, the two groups worked together to reshape civil-military re-

A Turkish protester holds up a placard with pictures of Turkish Prime Minister Recep Tayyip Erdoğan (L) and the United States-based Turkish cleric Fethullah Gülen, reading "We will cast them down" during a demonstration against corruption in the Kadikoy district of Istanbul on December 25, 2013. (BULENT KILIC/AFP/GETTY IMAGES)

lations in Turkey, stripping away the authority of the secularist Kemalist military. Normally Gülen preferred to work with centrist parties with no clear Islamist agenda. (Hence, he always kept his distance from Erbakan's Welfare Party.) Things changed when Erdoğan's AKP entered the Turkish political scene as a center-right party repudiating its Islamist past. Erdoğan remained highly concerned about another coup by the military. He needed loyal civil servants with pious backgrounds to serve his new party and to protect him from ultra-secularists.

The Gülen movement had already established a presence in the intelligence, security and judicial bureaucracies and was happy to provide the human capital the AKP needed to run the government. In return, the Gülenists required a powerful governing political party to protect and support their movement. The AKP's brand of conservativism and moderate Islam was ideally placed to help promote Gülen's ambitions to spread Turkey's ethno-religious "soft power" with modern, state-of-the-art international schools, while empowering his political base in Turkey by infiltrating more government positions.

The Turkish military was the biggest loser from this marriage of con-

venience. In 2007, the generals tried hard but ultimately failed to challenge Erdoğan's choice for the presidency, then-Foreign Minister Abdullah Gül. Erdoğan pushed back and called for early elections, which the AKP won by a landslide, launching Gül into the presidency. Shortly after the AKP's electoral victory, the Kemalist establishment once again challenged Erdoğan, this time with the help of secularist allies in the judicial branch. The AKP narrowly survived a "judicial coup" attempt in 2008 when the Constitutional Court decided by only one vote not to shut down the governing party.

In the wake of these two attempts to challenge Erdoğan, a day of reckoning between the powerful AKP and the weakened Kemalist political system became unavoidable. Shortly after the judicial coup failed, the AKP-Gülen alliance launched an investigation that prosecuted alleged coup-plotters within the army. Between 2008 and 2011, the AKP sidelined and debilitated Turkey's once very powerful military in great part thanks to Gülenist prosecutors and informants within the security establishment. (It later became clear that some of the evidence charging Kemalist military officers was fabricated.) By 2011, civilian supremacy over the military was firmly established and Erdoğan had consolidated power. In the eyes of domestic and Western liberal supporters of the AKP, it was now time to truly move Turkey toward a post-Kemalist liberal democracy. A new constitution was being drafted; autocratic politics, military coups and political instability seemed to be in the past. By 2012, there was still some merit to the argument that Turkey was a source of inspiration at the vanguard of the democratic wave in the Middle East known as the "Arab Spring."

The unraveling of these democratic hopes came swiftly. By 2014, when Erdoğan took over the presidency, the so-called "Turkish democratic model"

was no more. The country had turned increasingly authoritarian and unstable under the same leader who had once received so much adulation. Relations with the EU and the U.S. were deadlocked, authoritarianism was rampant and an unprecedented peace process with the Kurds was at the brink of collapse. The brutal suppression of the young "Gezi movement" protesters across the country during the summer of 2013 (to be discussed) and major corruption scandals the same year exposed the negative face of Turkey under Erdoğan. 2013 was also the year the Gülen-AKP alliance turned fratricidal. Losing the Kemalist military as a common enemy proved fatal: In July

2016, Turkey faced the unthinkable as allegedly Gülenist elements within the military staged an anti-AKP coup that narrowly failed.

Today, the positive image of a democratic, prosperous and powerful Turkey has been replaced by one of chaos, authoritarianism, systemic corruption, terrorist attacks and a major downturn in relations with the transatlantic community. Yet Erdoğan remains highly popular among significant segments of Turkish society. His rising political profile and hegemony go hand in hand with the polarization of Turkish politics. In the meantime, all checks and balances to what increasingly looks like elected autocracy are vanishing.

The road to authoritarianism

In the West, Erdoğan has the dismal image of an Islamist autocrat destroying Turkey's democracy. Unsurprisingly, then, one can detect a sense of nostalgia for what existed before his hegemony. According to a common Western narrative, Turkey had a liberal and secular past under Kemalism that has been lost under Erdoğan. The problem with this account is twofold. First, it tends to overlook the early achievements of the AKP. Second, it is based on the false assumption of a golden age of liberal democracy in Turkish political history.

For a while, it looked like Erdoğan would truly transform Turkey into a

more liberal and democratic country. Soon after coming to power in 2002, the AKP passed an impressive series of reforms to harmonize the judicial system, civil-military relations and human rights practices with European norms. The EU began accession negotiations with Turkey in 2005, rewarding the AKP's democratic reforms and Ankara's positive pro-unification approach in Cyprus (which has been divided since Turkey invaded the north in 1974 in response to a military coup backed by Greece).

The AKP efforts were not confined to democratization. After the economic

crisis of 2001, the party also managed to get the Turkish economy back on track by following guidelines from the International Monetary Fund's (IMF) stabilization program. The crisis was the worst in Turkish economic history and the culmination of the "lost decade" of the 1990s when political instability, war with the PKK and chronic high inflation plagued Turkey's democracy and economic performance. The AKP's electoral victory in November 2002 came in great part because the Turkish electorate was ready for a fresh start. Between 2003 and 2008, the Turkish economy grew by an average of 7.5%. Lower inflation and lower interest rates led to a major increase in domestic consumption. Thanks to a disciplined privatization program, the Turkish economy began to attract unprecedented amounts of foreign direct investment. The average per capita income nearly tripled, from $2,800 in 2001 to around $8,500 in 2010, exceeding that of some new EU members such as Bulgaria and Romania.

As a result of its ever-expanding grassroots network, the AKP was also able to provide much-needed social and economic services to its poorer constituencies. The AKP government made health care and housing credits more accessible, distributed food, increased grants for students and im-

A family hurries to board a truck bound for shelter for Syrian Kurdish refugees in Yumurtalik, Turkey, September 29, 2014. More Syrian refugees have sought shelter in Turkey than in any other country. (BRYAN DENTON/THE NEW YORK TIMES/REDUX PICTURES)

proved the infrastructure of poorer urban districts. Despite its Islamist image, it prioritized promotion of minority rights for non-Muslims. From the perspective of Western partners, the AKP's Turkey seemed to embody a rare compatibility between Islamic tradition, secularism and good governance. Turkey's domestic democratic reforms and its mediation efforts between Israel and Syria received high praise. Though disappointed with Ankara over Iraq, the Bush administration still considered Turkey a model for the "freedom agenda" it supported in the Middle East.

By 2009, after having won two consecutive elections (in 2002 and 2007), Erdoğan took positive steps toward tackling Turkey's most daunting democratic challenge: the Kurdish question. Secret negotiations with the PKK and its jailed leader, Abdullah Öcalan, began despite objections from nationalist circles and the military. The peace process collapsed in 2014, but these were still bold initiatives that no other Turkish political party had dared to undertake in the long and bloody history of the ethnic conflict. As late as 2012, U.S. President Barack Obama (2009–17) saw Erdoğan as a friend with whom he established a regular line of communication about developments in the region.

In retrospect, it is clear that the Turkish model began to unravel in the summer of 2013, when a group of young environmentalists occupied Gezi Park in Istanbul's Taksim Square. What had started as a protest movement against plans to replace the park with a shopping center turned into a much larger social movement after the police brutally evicted the young activists. Anti-government demonstrations mushroomed across Turkey as the police continued the crackdown. In a few days, more than 8,000 people were injured and at least five killed. Obviously, the Gezi movement was about much more than the environment. In the eyes of the urban, young, diverse and largely middle-class protesters, the real problem was Erdoğan's increasing authoritarianism and conservatism.

The protests came on top of already

Turkish police disperse anti-government protestors with water cannons during a protest near the entrance of Taksim Square on July 20, 2013, in Istanbul. (GURCAN OZTURK/AFP/GETTY IMAGES)

serious concerns about restrictions on freedom of expression, and Erdoğan's tendency to read into his successive election victories the right to intervene in the private lives of citizens in the name of morality. His conservative views—that all those who consume alcohol are alcoholics, that every family should have three children or that co-ed dormitories should be banned, for instance—touched a societal nerve. Taken together with actions curbing freedom of expression and information, self-censorship in the media and regulations limiting the sale of alcoholic beverages, they built a social reaction, at least among progressive and liberal segments of Turkish society. Such concerns, and the violent response to the protests, played a crucial role in the realization that the public sphere in Turkey was being suffocated. The limits of media freedom were exposed when mainstream TV channels, fearing governmental reprisal, chose not to cover the protests. In reaction to such repres-

sion, more and more ordinary citizens came out from their homes and workplaces in solidarity with demonstrators.

Some Western media hastily, and wrongly, proclaimed the events a "Turkish Spring," making sensationalist comparisons between Taksim Square in Istanbul and Tahrir Square in Cairo (associated with the 2011 Egyptian Revolution). The Arab revolutions between 2010 and 2012 were massive uprisings against entrenched dictatorships. Erdoğan, in contrast, was an elected populist who kept winning democratic elections. The scale and cause of Arab revolutions had little in common with the liberal agenda of Turkish protesters. The way Erdoğan reacted to the protests, however, resembled the discourse of Middle Eastern autocrats. His conspiratorial approach—identifying American neo-conservatives, Israel, the U.S. news outlet CNN and even Germany as foreign agitators—left many wondering whether he was losing touch with reality.

Illiberal legacies

Erdoğan's depiction in Western circles as an elected autocrat is well deserved. Problematic, however, is the assumption that Turkish politics was much more liberal and democratic before him. In fact, Turkish politicians have always been patriarchal figures functioning in the shadow of an intru-

sive military. The generals considered themselves the real owners and guardians of the Kemalist system. They intervened four times—in 1960, 1971, 1980 and 1997—following the inception of electoral democracy in 1946, and each time caused considerable damage to democracy. Most importantly, the rule of law—the bedrock of a liberal system—has always been tenuous and arbitrary in the country. In liberal democracies, the judiciary's main role is to protect individual rights and liberties. But Turkey inherited an Ottoman legacy of a centralized state where public order and national security are paramount. Well before Erdoğan came to power, the Kemalist ideology jealously protected the Republic from nefarious societal forces—Islamic reactionaries and Kurdish dissent—and in doing so, limited individual rights and freedoms.

The Turkish secular system also has its own illiberal peculiarities resembling the French model of Jacobin laicism. The Jacobins—the most prominent political group in the 18th-century French Revolution—had an anti-clerical disdain for religion. As in Jacobin France, Turkish secularism is based not on "freedom of religion" but rather on the need for "freedom from religion." The ban on the religious headscarf that is still practiced in French public schools today was the norm in Turkey's public sector and education system until the AKP changed the regulations in 2013. Kemalist secularism has always jealously controlled Islam by incorporating religious personnel, education and sermons into the bureaucratic machinery of the state. Not surprisingly, the AKP and Erdoğan have made no attempt to change this aspect of the Turkish system; they are now exploiting it to their benefit.

Turkish secularism is problematic in a different aspect as well: It is not neutral toward different faith groups. In continuity with Ottoman tradition, the modern Turkish state recognizes only the Sunni branch of Islam and often discriminates against other Muslim groups as well as all non-Muslims. Arguably, the multicultural Ottoman Empire was more "tolerant" of non-Muslims, who were regularly employed in diplomacy during the 19th century. Modern, secular Turkey has no non-Muslim diplomats. Non-Muslims and the Alevi Muslim minority (a branch of Islam closer to the Shi'a tradition) have no legal recourse when the state discriminates against them.

The conundrum of illiberal democracy in Turkey is historically compounded by secularist social engineering and nation-building. As previously discussed, the Kemalist Republic wanted to establish a secular state, not a liberal democracy. The ambitious cultural reforms undertaken by Atatürk barely infiltrated Turkish society at large and worsened the elitist dynamics that were clearly reflected in Atatürk's Republican People's Party (CHP) slogan from the 1920s: "For the People, Despite the People." As a result, the Kemalist system turned out not only to be illiberal, but also undemocratic and distrustful of society at large. While a semblance of democracy began with free elections in 1950, the army maintained its supremacy until relatively recently when Erdoğan and his Gülenist allies finally ended the system of military guardianship. As the army was sidelined, Turkey had a chance, perhaps for the first time in its modern history, to establish a liberal democracy with a new civilian constitution. It soon became clear, however, that liberal democracy had no real popular constituency. The political culture and governmental structure of the country proved deeply patriarchal and autocratic.

Despite essentialist predictions, the Turkish model under the AKP did not come to an end because of a clash between Islam and secularism. The real conflict has proved to be between liberalism and a majoritarian understanding of populist democracy. Erdoğan has a tendency to reduce democracy to elections. History will probably remember him as populist agent of change who failed to liberalize and democratize Turkey. Thanks to Erdoğan, the Kemalist model

of Turkish authoritarianism, in which military and bureaucratic elites called the shots, is now replaced by a democratically elected populist authoritarianism. In some ways, this is the story of a transition from the "tyranny of the minority" to the "tyranny of the majority."

In short, there is remarkable continuity between the AKP and the Kemalist state tradition. In addition to authoritarianism, the two also share a nationalist distrust of external forces and a patriarchal view of Turkish society. Not surprisingly, such dynamics leave no room for a liberal philosophy aimed at defending civil society and individuals from abusive state power. Turkey's small liberal democratic segment is squeezed between the populist-conservative AKP that believes in electoral democracy but not liberalism, and the Kemalist opposition that wants to protect the nationalist-secular system, often at the expense of democracy.

Finally, in analyzing illiberal legacies, it is important not to overstate the role of political Islam. Erdoğan has not been winning election after election since 2002 because the masses are strongly behind his Islamist message. According to polls, consumer confidence and improvements in social and economic services are much better predictors of the AKP's electoral success. Erdoğan may very well lose elections if the economy falters. He has not yet been tested by a long-term recession. The Kurdish question, resentment against the U.S. and the EU, national pride and economic interests create common cause in a way that political Islam does not. This is why an angry anti-Western nativism will continue to be part of Erdoğan's discourse.

A turning point with the U.S.

What can the U.S. and the EU do to stop Turkey's downward spiral toward autocracy? The West, especially in its current state of transatlantic division, does not have the strategic vision and political capacity to change Turkey's direction. Given its understandable reluctance to offer membership to an increasingly illiberal country, the EU

has no leverage over Ankara. The EU's primary objective is to maintain a basic working relationship because Turkey is the most effective bulwark against massive refugee flows from Syria. Providing financial rewards to Ankara in order to stem this flow is surely not a long-term strategy. What's more, after Britain's vote to leave the EU (Brexit), Ankara lost its most vocal advocate for membership. Neither Germany nor France wants to see Turkey as a full member. Sooner or later, Turkey and the EU will have to decide whether it makes sense to continue to pretend that full membership is feasible.

The U.S. approach to Turkey remains more or less the same as it has been since the early days of the Cold War: to maintain a security partnership driven by geostrategic concerns. Continuity in this partnership was traditionally made possible thanks to the belief that the two countries, as fellow democracies, shared the same strategic objectives and often the same values, whatever tactical differences might be present. Today, however, both actors are questioning the validity of these assumptions. U.S. support for Kurdish fighters in Syria, as well as Turkey's rapprochement with Russia and its growing authoritarianism and anti-Americanism, are challenging the fundamentals of the partnership in unprecedented ways.

The two countries clearly diverge in their strategic objectives, national interests and top priorities not only in Syria but also in other parts of the Middle East, such as Israel, Egypt and Iran. Turkey has now become the first NATO member to purchase a Russian missile defense system despite objections and warnings from Washington. Already deteriorating U.S.-Turkey relations reached a nadir in October 2017, when the U.S. stopped issuing visas at its missions in Turkey following the arrest of two U.S. consular staff, both Turkish nationals. Turkey retaliated in kind by suspending visa services for U.S. citizens. It seems like the Trump administration will still engage in damage control with Turkey in order to maintain access to military bases. Yet it is clear that Washington has no interest in democracy promotion. After all, President Trump has expressed a level of admiration for strongmen such as Erdoğan, Russian President Vladimir Putin and Philippine President Rodrigo Duterte.

Perhaps most importantly, Turkish politics is in uncharted waters as a result of the institutional collapse of

People gather in protest outside the Silivri Courthouse during the ongoing trial of journalists from the Cumhuriyet newspaper on September 11, 2017, in Istanbul, Turkey. Seventeen journalists and managers of the Cumhuriyet newspaper are facing trial on charges of aiding a terrorist organization, and Turkish prosecutors are seeking up to 43 years in jail for staff from the paper, including some of Turkey's best-known journalists. Established in 1924, it is one of the country's few remaining opposition newspapers. (CHRIS MCGRATH/GETTY IMAGES)

the military after the failed 2016 coup attempt. The event was a truly seismic affair that deeply traumatized the Turkish army and its relations with the U.S. Almost half of the generals and admirals have been purged and most of these dismissed officers had strong pro-NATO credentials. It will take years for the Turkish military to recover from this unprecedented shake-up. It is important to remember that the Turkish army and the Pentagon have traditionally been the linchpins of a security-heavy bilateral relationship. Today, the Turkish military establishment is in disarray and the Pentagon is no longer advocating a strong U.S. partnership with Erdoğan. In that sense, the natural constituencies supporting strategic relations are no longer vocal.

As these disturbing dynamics clearly show, there is no shortage of problems in the bilateral relationship. Gülen's presence in the U.S. and Washington's support for Syrian Kurds have now become intractable problems and existential security risks for Ankara. Add to these challenges Turkey's current rapprochement with Russia and Iran in Syria, the deadlock in Turkey-EU relations, and the decision to purchase the S-400 Russian missile defense system and you have the disturbing scenario of

a Turkish pivot to Eurasia. These trends should give pause to anyone who is optimistic about Turkey's place within the transatlantic alliance. Resentment toward both the EU and the U.S. has reached levels that make a break up with the transatlantic community not only probable but realistic. Given a Gaullist Turkey seeking Eurasian alternatives to NATO, Donald Trump may become the first U.S. president to face the once unthinkable question: "Who lost Turkey?"

Turkey exports mainly to Western markets and most of its foreign direct investment comes from the West. It has simply come too far in its integration with the global economy to turn into a dictatorship isolated from the West. But since neither Washington nor Brussels seems to have much leverage with Erdoğan, nothing will matter more than Turkey's own internal dynamics when it comes to stopping the slide toward populist dictatorship. There is a glimmer of hope here because Erdoğan needs a strong economy to win elections, and this requires a modicum of good governance. Turkish democracy still has a pulse. The best the EU and Washington can do is to closely monitor the next elections. If elections are rigged, Turkey will be lost.

discussion questions

1. The U.S. has long lauded Turkey as a "model" of secular democracy in the Islamic world. As President Recep Tayyip Erdoğan and his party continue to consolidate power, a common Western narrative has attributed the fall of the Turkish democratic model to a clash between Islam and secularism. What are the limits to this understanding of Turkish democracy? How influential a role does religion play in modern Turkish politics, society and national ideology?

2. Since the Cold War, the U.S. has maintained bases in Turkey and considers the NATO member a crucial ally in the fight against Islamist extremism. In May 2017, the Trump administration decided to arm the Syrian Kurds—a group the Turkish government considers terrorists—in order to ensure victory over ISIS. How will this policy affect the long-standing alliance between the U.S. and Turkey?

3. While Turkey has been a long-standing ally of the U.S., the majority of Turks now express strong anti-American sentiment. What are some of the main factors behind this shift in public opinion?

4. What explains Turkey's interest in strengthening strategic ties with countries like Russia, Iran and China? What consequences does Turkey's pursuit of Eurasian alternatives to NATO hold for relations between Turkey, the U.S. and the transatlantic community?

5. What is at stake for Turkish citizens in the face of an increasingly "illiberal" democracy? What can the U.S. do to encourage Turkish democracy? What *should* it do?

6. What is the relationship between Erdoğan's domestic and geopolitical goals? What does Turkey stand to gain and what does it stand to lose in the international arena as a result of the authoritarian trend under Erdoğan?

Don't forget: Ballots start on page 105!

suggested readings

Aydintaşbaş, Asli and Kirişci, Kemal, "The United States and Turkey. Friends, Family, or Only Interests?" 30 pp. **Brookings Institution**, April 2017. Available free online: <https://www.brookings.edu/wp-content/uploads/2017/04/aydintasbas-kirisci_united-states-and-turkey.pdf>. Part of the Brookings Institution's Turkey Project, launched in 2004, this report charts dilemmas affecting the downturn in U.S.-Turkish relations and seeks to outline a new plan of action for the two countries to cooperate on a world stage marred by uncertainty.

Cagaptay, Soner, **The Rise of Turkey: The Twenty-First Century's First Muslim Power**. 184 pp. Sterling, VA: Potomac Books, February 1, 2014. Written as a travelogue, this book charts how Erdoğan and the AKP have transformed Turkey both domestically and internationally, de-secularizing the state and fortifying the country's economic and diplomatic prowess.

Gordon, Philip H. and Taşpinar, Ömer, **Winning Turkey: How America, Europe, and Turkey Can Revive a Fading Partnership**. 115 pp. Washington, D.C.: Brookings Institution Press, November 1, 2009. In light of contemporary challenges to U.S., European and Turkish relations, this book advocates for renewed Western support to promote liberalism and democracy in Turkey, commitment to EU membership for Turkey and deals to resolve longstanding regional turmoil between Turkey and the Kurds, Armenia and Cyprus.

Obama, Barack, "Remarks By President Obama To The Turkish Parliament." **The White House Office of the Press Secretary**, April 6, 2009. Available free online: <https://obamawhitehouse.archives.gov/the-press-office/remarks-president-obama-turkish-parliament>. On his first overseas trip as president, Obama visited Ankara and spoke to the Turkish Parliament, reiterating critical ties between the two countries and praising Turkey for its model democracy.

———, "Remarks by President Trump and President Erdoğan of Turkey in Joint Statement." **The White House Office of the Press Secretary**, May 16, 2017. Available free online: <https://www.whitehouse.gov/the-press-office/2017/05/16/remarks-president-trump-and-president-erdogan-turkey-joint-statement>. Facing rising tensions after the Trump administration agreed to arm the Kurds in Syria, Trump and Erdoğan speak at a joint press conference during the Turkish president's first visit to the White House since 2002.

Taşpinar, Ömer, "An Uneven Fit? The 'Turkish Model' and the Arab World." **Brookings Institution**, August 2003. Available free online: <https://www.brookings.edu/wp-content/uploads/2016/06/taspinar20030801.pdf>. This report considers the limitations to the predominant idea in the West that Turkey's secular democracy is a model for the Islamic world and that Erdoğan's Justice and Development Party (AKP) provides an opportunity to strengthen that model.

Yaman, Alev, "The Gezi Park Protests: The Impact on Freedom of Expression in Turkey." **English PEN**, March 2014. Available free online: <https://www.englishpen.org/wp-content/uploads/2014/03/PEN_Gezi_Park_Protests.pdf>. This report documents the human rights violations during the summer 2013 Gezi Park protests in Istanbul, calling on the Turkish authorities to respect freedom of expression and advocating for legislative and media reform in the country.

To access web links to these readings, as well as links to additional, shorter readings and suggested web sites,

GO TO www.greatdecisions.org

and click on the topic under Resources, on the right-hand side of the page

U.S. global engagement and the military

by Gordon Adams

A member of the U.S. Army during the International Commemorative Ceremony of the Allied Forces Landing in Normandy in the presence of U.S. Army veterans and troops, and representatives of the French State and the eight allied countries (Belgium, Canada, Denmark, United States, Great Britain, Norway, Netherlands, Poland), that took place at Utah Beach, Manche, France. June 6, 2017, was the 73rd anniversary of the D-Day landings, which saw 156,000 troops from the Allied countries, including the United Kingdom and the United States, join forces to launch an audacious attack on the beaches of Normandy. (ARTUR WIDAK/NURPHOTO/GETTY IMAGES)

Since the end of the World War II (WWII) in 1945, the U.S. has positioned itself as the leader of the international order, the country responsible for the safety and security of the global economic and security "rules of the road." The U.S. economy has been seen as the strongest in the world. Its democratic and free market values have been described as a model, worthy of global emulation, and its power and preeminence have been underwritten by the possession of the world's most powerful military.

Today, a fundamental "rebalancing" of the global order is under way. In the face of major shifts in the distribution of power and clear challenges to its supremacy, the U.S.'s global leadership is in doubt. Economic shifts, the erosion of the democratic/free market model, and the "rebalancing" of power—including military power—among nations pose major dilemmas for U.S. policymakers and the public.

How should the U.S. redefine its global engagement, its national security needs, and the role and missions of its military in this changing world? Four frequently debated strategic visions for U.S. national security policy and for the U.S. military offer competing answers. These are: unilateral preeminence, multilateral leadership, unilateral restraint and assertive nationalism. Each has a very different implication for U.S. policy, for the institutions of U.S. statecraft—particularly the military—and for the future of the U.S. global role.

GORDON ADAMS *is Professor Emeritus of International Relations at the School of International Service, American University, and a Distinguished Fellow at the Stimson Center in Washington, DC. He is co-author of* Buying National Security: How America Plans and Pays for its Global Role and Safety at Home *(Routledge, 2010) and co-editor of* Mission Creep: The Militarization of U.S. Foreign Policy? *(Georgetown University Press, 2014).*

The times they are a'changin': a rebalancing world

For decades, policymakers in Washington have characterized the U.S. as the inevitable leader of the global system and the guarantor of stability and security. The U.S. has been seen, to quote former Secretary of State Madeleine Albright (1997–2001), as an "exceptional" and "indispensable" nation. Today, U.S. leadership is in doubt as global power relationships "rebalance." The evidence for this is clear. As *Financial Times* writer and foreign policy analyst Gideon Rachman puts it:

The West's centuries-long domination of world affairs is now coming to a close…The central theme of international affairs that emerged during the [Barack Obama administration (2009–17)] and that will shape the world for decades to come, is the steadily eroding power of the West to dominate global politics.

Recent events seem to confirm this outlook. No country appears able to restore peace and stability in Syria, U.S.-Russia relations have deteriorated and the European Union is fractured by the British vote to leave (Brexit). But the underlying rebalancing of power has been in progress for some time, as can be seen in the decline in relative U.S. economic power, the rise of authoritarian governance around the globe, growing challenges to U.S. power in different regions and even signs of the erosion of U.S. military preeminence. As the U.S. National Intelligence Council (NIC) put it in 2012: "[W]ith the rapid rise of other countries, the 'unipolar moment' is over and Pax Americana—the era of American ascendancy in international politics that began in 1945—is fast winding down."

The global economy

The size, health, and capabilities of the U.S. economy have been seen as the

source of its diplomatic and military strength since 1945. Yet today, no one nation can claim to dominate the global economy, which is larger and more interconnected as different players rise. The U.S. is a debtor nation today and corporations that were once identifiably American are increasingly independent, global actors. China's economy is as large as that of the U.S., in terms of purchasing power parity (PPP) and will surpass the U.S. in absolute size within the next decade. Nations in the "Global South" produce half of the world's economic product, and nearly half of global trade—both major increases since 1980. This rapid evolution has major implications for U.S. leadership and military power. The NIC predicts that by 2030, Asia as a whole "will have surpassed North America and Europe combined in terms of global power, based upon [gross domestic product (GDP)], population size, military spending, and technological investment."

'Soft power'

The core U.S. values of democracy and free markets (part of what Harvard analyst and former policymaker Joseph Nye calls "soft power") are no longer on the march. The tidal wave of democracy, which was expected to spread around the world with the end of the Cold War, has receded, with a turn toward authoritarian government in Russia, Hungary, Turkey, Thailand and the Philippines. The democratic uprisings of the so-called Arab Spring are but a memory in every Middle Eastern country but Tunisia. The failure of U.S. efforts to bring democracy to Iraq and Afghanistan make it clear that regime change carried out by U.S. military intervention does not guarantee democracy. *Financial Times* writer Edward Luce notes that 25 democracies have essentially failed since 2000. The idea that "democracy and free markets" form the ultimate model for economic success faces growing competition from a more authoritarian governance and economic management model, on the rise in Asia particularly.

Rebalancing: others rise

These economic and cultural trends contribute to a rebalancing of political and diplomatic power around the globe. This trend is most clear in Asia, part of what Rachman has called the "easternization" of the global system. Growing Chinese economic and military power is evident in behavior by Beijing that is altering the Asia-Pacific power balance. Already the key player in that region, China is also increasingly involved in Middle East politics, with growing imports of oil and natural gas, and in Africa, where it became the leading trading partner in 2010. Reflecting its assertive role, China has created new multilateral investment institutions and programs, including the Shanghai Cooperation Organization, the Asian Infrastructure Investment Bank (with 57 members, including not only India, Iran and Russia, but such U.S. allies as Turkey, Britain, France and Germany), and its "Belt and Road" development initiative.

China's rise is not unique; it is part of what analyst Fareed Zakaria has called "the rise of the rest." Take Turkey, a North Atlantic Treaty Organization (NATO) ally, which, under an increasingly authoritarian system, refused to allow the U.S. to use its territory for the 2003 invasion of Iraq, has taken an independent stance on military operations in Syria, opposes U.S. support for the Kurds fighting the Islamic State (ISIS) terrorist organization in Syria and is purchasing military systems from Russia. Pakistan, once a close U.S. ally, has rebalanced by drawing closer to China. Brazil and Mexico engage regimes like Cuba and Venezuela, despite U.S. opposition. South Africa plays a key role in conflict resolution and political change in Africa. India is growing rapidly as a regional diplomatic power in the Indo-Pacific region. Russia has expanded its influence not only to countries once part of the Soviet Union, but into the Middle East as well.

This rebalancing dynamic extends to the Middle East, where U.S. influ-

---

! Before you read, download the companion **Glossary** that includes definitions and a guide to acronyms and abbreviations used in the article. Go to **www.greatdecisions.org** and select a topic in the Resources section on the right-hand side of the page.

ence has declined as Iranian influence has grown in Syria, Iraq and Lebanon. Saudi Arabia is responding to this challenge, expanding its regional security relationships, conducting military operations in Yemen and expanding a military relationship with Russia. As Palestinian-American scholar Rami Khouri describes it:

The political dynamics of the Middle East have been totally upended. To try and discern what is going on in the region today one has to look first to Russia, Ankara, Tehran, Tel Aviv, and the Dahieh of southern Beirut, with secondary attention to Abu Dhabi, Riyadh, Cairo, and Doha, and only occasional fleeting glances to Washington and Brussels.

Military rebalancing

U.S. officials have begun to recognize that global rebalancing poses new dilemmas for leadership and military pre-eminence. As then-Deputy Secretary of Defense Robert Work (2014–17) said in 2015: "[A]mong the most significant challenges in this 25 years, and one in my view, that promises to be the most stressing…is the reemergence of great power competition."

Military power is the one remaining index of global power where the U.S. appears to retain dominance. Since the 1950s, the U.S. has had the only military that can deploy forces on a global basis, fly military aircraft to every corner of the Earth and sail its navy into all of the world's oceans at the same time. It is the only military that has global logistics, basing infrastructure, transportation, communications and intelligence. It has a large, credible nuclear deterrent force at sea, on land and in the air.

It also has deep, extensive relationships with other militaries, through U.S. arms sales and security assistance programs that were first created in the 1950s. For decades, the U.S. has been the principal arms supplier—through grants and sales—to the rest of the world. In 2014, the U.S. accounted for just over half of all the arms sales agreements in the world, or more than $36 billion. In addition, U.S. security assistance programs have had a more

View of U.S troops as they march through a village, South Korea, 1951. (CARL MYDANS/THE LIFE PICTURE COLLECTION/GETTY IMAGES)

than $25 billion annual budget for the past decade.

U.S. global military dominance may be, in part, illusory. U.S. military operations since the Korean War have not been marked by an unbroken string of successes. The Korean War (1950–53) was a military stalemate; the Vietnam War (1955–75) an unqualified failure. While the first U.S. war in the Persian Gulf in 1991 fully achieved the goal of driving the Iraqi military out of Kuwait, the 2003 invasion of Iraq led to a quagmire, as U.S. forces found it difficult to deal with the insurgency that succeeded the ouster of Iraqi dictator Saddam Hussein (1979–2003). U.S. military operations in Afghanistan from 2001 to the present removed the Taliban (the ruling Islamic fundamentalist faction) from power, but the ability of the force to prevent its return and provide security continues to be in doubt. Seven decades of U.S. arms sales, budget subsidies and training have had some successes (in Greece, Japan, Turkey and South Korea, for instance) and some more questionable outcomes (Pakistan, Iran). Despite decades of investment in the military capabilities of other countries, including, in recent years, more than $115 billion of equipment and training for the security forces of Iraq and Afghanistan, the results have been less than success-

ful. As political scientists Steven Weber and Bruce Jentleson put it: "[I]n today's world military superiority has not been the handmaiden of strategic success."

Moreover, economic and diplomatic rebalancing are increasingly accompanied by changes in the global military power balance itself. While allied military spending in Europe declined after the end of the Cold War, in the era of difficulties with Russia and a less certain U.S. commitment to NATO, there are emerging signs of a Franco-German effort to define a more capable, trans-European defense capability that could operate independently in support of European security goals.

Similarly, in the Middle East, the once close military cooperation between the U.S. and Turkey, Egypt, Saudi Arabia and Israel has begun to transform, with only the Israeli military connection fully secure today. As Turkey reshapes its political role in the region, it has begun to expand its security cooperation with other countries, including Russia, China and even Iran. Iranian security forces have expanded their training and military cooperation activities in Iraq, Syria and Lebanon. Saudi Arabia had the world's fourth largest defense budget in 2016, behind the U.S., China and Russia, and, though Saudi cooperation with the U.S. remains significant, Riyadh has begun to independently assert its own regional military power in both Syria and Yemen.

Military rebalancing is most clearly progressing in Asia. As Rachman puts it: "While Western military spending is going down, an arms race of historic proportions is under way in Asia." China has shifted its strategic and military focus toward acquiring a blue-water navy, developing missile systems that can strike U.S. navy vessels at long range from the shore, island-building to assert sovereignty in the South China Sea and expanding its military presence at even greater range by constructing a military base in Djibouti, East Africa. Meanwhile, India is rapidly increasing its defense budgets, military missions and capabilities, with an eye to developing a larger, regionally significant

force. These moves have led other Asia-Pacific countries—Australia, Japan, Indonesia, Malaysia, Vietnam and the Philippines—to expand their militaries as well.

Military rebalancing, both globally and regionally, is gradually undermining the notion that a dominant U.S. military can ensure stability and compliance with the "rules" of the changing global system. Future regional security regimes may be defined less by the U.S. than by the countries in a particular region. As American University analyst Amitav Acharya puts it, "a key transition in the emerging world order could be that regional orders become less geared toward serving America's power and purpose and are more reflective of the interests and identities of the local actors."

The erosion of U.S. global primacy

and leadership may have begun shortly after the unipolar era arrived following the collapse of the Soviet Union in 1989–91. The emerging global system is quite interconnected, but it is no longer dominated by the U.S. economy, U.S. diplomatic power, or even, necessarily, by its military power. As Rachman puts it: "[T]he relative decline of U.S. economic and political power—allied to the much more rapid decline of European power—is encouraging rival nations to explore whether the United States can be challenged and whether, in this new world, there are also new strategic and ideological alternatives to the paths promoted in Washington and Brussels." The rebalancing of the globe has major implications for future U.S. strategy, particularly for the role of U.S. military power.

Strategic visions for U.S. engagement and the military

Not surprisingly, there is a growing debate over the future direction of U.S. national security policy and the role and structure of U.S. military forces in executing that policy. This debate can be sorted into four visions of U.S. strategy: unilateral preeminence, multilateral leadership, unilateral restraint and assertive nationalism. These visions differ significantly on the role they think the U.S. should play in the global system and on future directions for the U.S. military.

Strategic vision one: unilateral preeminence

The unilateral preeminence vision advocates a national security strategy that would restore U.S. leadership, putting U.S. military capabilities at the center of policy. In this view, advocated by neoconservatives, the end of the Cold War left the U.S. in a unipolar moment, positioning it as the hegemon of the global system, with a moral duty to lead. As neoconservative thinkers William Kristol and Robert Kagan put it in 1996, "American hegemony is the only reliable defense against a breakdown of peace and international order. The appropriate goal of American foreign policy, therefore,

is to preserve that hegemony as far into the future as possible."

President George W. Bush's (2001–09) 2001 National Security Strategy laid out unilateral preeminence's three core missions for the military: 1) to ensure safety, openness, and rules-based behavior in the "global commons" (space, air and sea); 2) to ensure the U.S. retains global military dominance; and 3) to support the expansion of democracy and free markets, including via military intervention. The U.S. must be prepared to act unilaterally to meet these objectives.

These themes were echoed in the 2010 independent panel that (with significant neoconservative input) reviewed the Defense Department's Quadrennial Defense Review:

U.S. defense strategy for the near and long term must continue to shape the international environment to advance U.S. interests, maintain the capability to respond to the full spectrum of threats, and prepare for the threats and dangers of tomorrow…the United States can and will continue to play a leading role in world affairs and can and will defend its homeland; guarantee access to global commerce, freedom

of the seas, international airspace, and space; and maintain a balance of power in Europe and Asia that protects America—all while preserving the peace and sustaining a climate conducive to global economic growth.

This vision continues to be advocated today. Neoconservative defense analyst Tom Donnelly of the American Enterprise Institute (AEI) argued in 2016 that it was urgent to restore U.S. military power and leadership:

America's deteriorating international position requires an urgent reinvestment in and expansion of U.S. military forces [which has] only been underscored by events in the interim. In East Asia, in Europe, and especially in the Middle East, a congeries [sic] of adversary states and terrorist groups is destroying the post-Cold War order. What was, not long ago, an extraordinarily peaceful, prosperous, and free world is slipping into chaos.

To restore U.S. global leadership, AEI would assign four key missions to the U.S. military: 1) defend the U.S. homeland; 2) ensure access to the global commons (space, air, sea, cyberspace); 3) ensure the balance of power in Eurasia; and 4) "preserve the international order." U.S. forces would return to the "front lines" from which they have been withdrawn, restoring the military balance in Europe (against Russia), the Middle East (against Iran) and Asia (against China), creating what AEI calls a "three theatre capability."

AEI proposes a larger military force. The active-duty Army would increase to 600,000 from the current goal of 450,000; the Navy would grow from 282 ships to 346 (adding two new aircraft carriers to the current ten); the Marine Corps would grow from 175,000 to over 200,000; and the Air Force would grow to over 1,200 fighter aircraft (including a restart of F-22 production, which ended in 2012). These forces would be deployed forward, including two new aircraft wings and two Marine forward groups in the Pacific region, an additional 25,000 Army forces (on top of the existing 75,000) and a Marine ready group in Europe. It would further increase the ground Army presence in the Middle East (currently 26,000 in Afghanistan, Syria and Iraq) and deploy a new F-22 Air Force wing to that region.

The Navy would have more carriers and surrounding ships to ensure a constant presence in all of the world's oceans. Special Operations Forces (counter-insurgency and counterterrorism forces) would also grow from the current 68,000, and the U.S. would continue to plan for military occupations in fragile states. In addition, the AEI proposal would modernize the entire U.S. strategic nuclear arsenal—land-based and sea-based missiles (and submarines), and the strategic bomber force—while adding new tactical missile programs, such as a nuclear cruise missile.

Overall, the unilateral preeminence strategy would add more than $1 trillion to currently projected defense spending of $5.7 trillion between fiscal year 2018 and fiscal year 2027. The sale of U.S. military equipment and active U.S. security assistance would be key elements of ensuring U.S. superiority and influence. The invasions of Afghanistan (2001) and Iraq (2003)—actions driven by this vision—were followed with sig-

nificant investments in equipment and training for the security forces of both countries. At the same time, the Defense Department expanded its security assistance programs globally, as part of what the Bush administration called the Global War on Terror. In this view, security assistance ensures that the U.S. has influence over the strategy and military decisions of recipient countries, and also has partner militaries with which it can operate on the battlefield.

For neoconservatives, the military is the key to U.S. preeminence and leadership. Diplomacy is given less attention. Many neoconservatives see the State Department as ineffective compared to the military. Defense analyst Thomas Barnett, for example, describes State as "a seriously ossified culture…[It] has developed the negative skill set of always being able to tell you why the change America seeks abroad is simply too hard to achieve, and then doing its best to fulfill that prophecy." The Pentagon, by contrast, is seen as having the capacity to carry out both military operations and security assistance and nation-building administrative tasks. Therefore, unilateral preeminence favors strengthening these latter capabilities at the Defense Department, rather than at the State Department.

The strength of the unilateral preeminence vision is that it appears to

provide an opportunity to reassert U.S. leadership and stave off risks for U.S. security in a rebalancing world. Such risks include: international and regional chaos, a growth in terrorism, and threats to the U.S. and its people. Expanding military dominance would underwrite strong U.S. leadership and the promotion of American values, and ensure a stable, peaceful world. As analyst Bret Stephens put it in 2015: "We live under [Pax Americana] not because it is easy or costless, but because the alternatives have all proved wanting or illusory. The alternative to Pax Americana—the only alternative—is global disorder."

Critics of this vision argue that it is doomed to meet failure and blow-back in a rebalancing world. Its implementation in Iraq and Afghanistan was costly to U.S. leadership and credibility, and may in fact have stimulated some of the political and military rebalancing now taking place. Today, few countries welcome U.S. hegemony or military preeminence. Expanding and deploying forces in an effort to ensure dominance could lead to even more rebalancing.

Strategic vision two: multilateral leadership

A national security vision focusing on multilateral leadership has been the central thrust of U.S. foreign and

The U.S. Navy Blue Angels fly over graduation ceremonies at the U.S. Naval Academy, May 26, 2017, in Annapolis, MD. U.S. Vice President Mike Pence delivered the commencement address for the graduation ceremony. (WIN MCNAMEE/GETTY IMAGES)

national security policy since the end of the WWII and the presidency of Harry Truman (1945–53). This vision is sometimes called "liberal hegemony," "liberal internationalism" (associated with President Woodrow Wilson (1913–21), or "liberal interventionism" (in the post-Cold War era). While this vision has variants that lean more conservative or more liberal, in all cases the U.S. is seen as the center of global events—an "exceptional" and "indispensable" leader.

President Obama's Secretary of Defense Ash Carter emphasized the core role of U.S. military strength in this strategy: "It's evident that America is still, today, the world's foremost leader, partner and underwriter of stability and security in every region across the globe—as we have been since the end of World War II." In this view, America's post-World War II leadership, military strength and economic power saved Western Europe from communism; deterred the Soviet Union from invading Europe and spreading its sphere of influence over less developed countries; brought prosperity and growth to the global economy; and, through global military deployments, ensured that the global commons remained open and secure for everyone. A multilateral leadership position asserts that in the absence of U.S. leadership, U.S. interests and the stability of the system are at risk. As former Secretary of State Hillary Clinton (2009–13) put it in 2016: "If America doesn't lead, we leave a vacuum—and that will either cause chaos, or other countries will rush in to fill the void…. [T]rust me, the choices they make will not be to our benefit."

Multilateral leadership emphasizes alliances, international institutions, and diplomacy, as well as the promotion of democratic and free market values. But U.S. global leadership also depends on having a strong, globally deployed military, available to intervene for both national security and humanitarian aims. Two elements, however, clearly distinguish the military role in this strategy from that espoused by unilateral preeminence. First, its advocates are committed to the idea that U.S. na-

Hillary Clinton, former secretary of state and 2016 Democratic presidential candidate, delivers a national security speech at Balboa Park in San Diego, CA, on, June 2, 2016. (TROY HARVEY/BLOOMBERG/GETTY IMAGES)

tional security interests are best served through multilateral military action. Virtually all presidents since 1945 have emphasized the importance of military alliances like NATO in dealing with regional conflicts. In the post-Cold War era, President George H.W. Bush (1989–93) built a coalition to force the Iraqi military out of Kuwait in 1991. President Obama crafted a multilateral coalition to remove the dictator Muammar Qaddafi (1969–2011) from power in Libya, and argued more broadly that "multilateralism regulates hubris."

Second, in this vision, the military needs to coordinate closely with the non-military tools of U.S. statecraft. Secretary of State Clinton called this concept "smart power," and explained it as involving "the full range of tools at our disposal—diplomatic, economic, military, political, legal and cultural—picking the right tool or combination of tools for each situation. With smart power, diplomacy will be the vanguard of our foreign policy." Former Republican National Security Council staffer Peter Feaver agrees, arguing that "military might is most effective when combined with the 'softer' tools of development assistance, foreign aid, and knowledge of foreign societies and cultures."

While the military mission in this strategy is not preeminence, U.S. forces are seen as having a central role in

overall global engagement. Indeed, administrations have repeatedly had recourse to military force as the key tool of engagement, from conflicts in Korea, Vietnam, Iraq and Afghanistan, to numerous smaller interventions in such countries as the Dominican Republic, El Salvador, Cambodia, Kuwait, the Balkans and Libya, as well as widespread deployments of U.S. forces to combat terrorist organizations over the past 70 years.

In a rebalancing world, the military continues to be a major focus of the multilateral leadership strategy. Recent think tank analyses consistent with this vision pay particular attention to perceived challenges to U.S. military strength and threats to national security. A 2016 Center for Strategic and International Studies proposal for increasing the size of the military described Russian and Chinese "creeping aggression" (referring to recent Russian military actions) and "grey zone aggression" (China) as threats to global security requiring military planning in response. The think tank studies also worried about North Korean and Iranian "provocations," attacks by terrorist organizations, as well as broader issues of "political instability and unrest" among allies and "partners," the "collapse of key states" and "challenges to the rules-based system."

In the face of these broad, global concerns, multilateral leadership advocates today would give the military a wide range of missions, including defending the U.S., providing a "stabilizing presence abroad," projecting power against forces that would deny access to the U.S. (generally a reference to China), deterring and defeating regional aggression, preventing another country from blocking access to the global commons, and carrying out humanitarian and disaster relief.

Multilateral leadership advocates are less ambitious than neoconservatives about required changes to the U.S. military. Military budgets, in this view, would rise between $100 and $400 billion above the current projection of $5.7 trillion. By and large, they would continue or only slightly increase the size of the Army and the Marines. Some argue for a significant expansion of the Navy—to 346 ships—to deal with an expanded naval mission, especially in the Pacific. The Air Force would receive slightly more tactical fighter aircraft than its current force of roughly 1,100. This strategy also includes modernizing the U.S. nuclear arsenal, particularly bombers and nuclear-armed submarines, though it does not advocate the development of new tactical nuclear weapons.

Expanded arms sales and global security assistance are integral in this vision. The Obama administration accelerated arms sales, especially to Middle Eastern countries, and continued the Bush administration's security assistance programs in that region, as well as global programs in Africa and Asia. Such programs are seen as an effective way to strengthen allied security forces, rather than have the U.S. deploy its own forces and risk "blowback."

Multilateral leadership emphasizes using all the tools of statecraft including a powerful military. Its familiarity, apparent reasonableness and bi-partisan character, displayed over the last 70 years, are some of its greatest strengths.

In a rebalancing world, however, this vision may be increasingly inconsistent with global power realities. Unsuccessful military and security assistance outcomes have diminished the role of the U.S. as the global security provider. The growing economic, political and military power of other nations raises questions about the extent to which they will accept the "rules" of a U.S.-dominated international system going forward. As military analyst Barry Posen puts it, multilateral leadership "will likely precipitate more [balancing] as the relative power advantage enjoyed by the United States wanes and others feel more capable of tilting against the United States."

Strategic vision three: unilateral restraint

The third vision for U.S. global engagement is unilateral restraint. Its advocates reject the notion that the U.S. has an "exceptional" or "indispens-able" role to play in global security. They argue that unilateral primacy and multinational leadership strategies and military interventions have been counterproductive and will prove even more so if they continue in a rebalancing world. Advocates of restraint maintain that U.S. conventional and nuclear capabilities are sufficiently overwhelming so as to make ground combat unlikely. These capabilities guarantee the U.S. a level of security that cannot be seriously threatened, even in the case of a smaller U.S. military.

In this vision, security provision is and should be a regional responsibility. As retired U.S. ambassador Chas Freemen stated:

The United States needs to return to respecting the views of regional powers about the appropriate response to regional threats, resisting the impulse to substitute military campaign plans made in Washington for strategies conceived by those with the greatest stake in their success…The need for restraint extends to refraining from expansive rhetoric about our values or attempting to compel others to conform to them.

Restraint advocates reject the label of "isolationism." Instead, they argue that their position is one of engagement, but without the assumption that the U.S. should be responsible for global security and leadership in every case. As political scientists Harvey Sapolsky and Eugene Gholz note, "[r]estraint does not mean retreating from history, but merely ending U.S. efforts to try to manage it. Restraint would rebalance global responsibilities among America and its allies, match our foreign objectives to our abilities, and put domestic needs first."

A restraint policy might well continue or even encourage partnership with other allies and emphasize diplomacy and foreign assistance. Such partnerships would avoid military intrusion and nation-building.

Restraint advocates focus specific attention on the role of the U.S. military, and believe its missions should exclude large, on-shore deployments. They argue that the active deployment of U.S. military forces has been counterproductive, particularly in the Middle East. For many, such as analysts Barry Posen and John Mearsheimer, the core mission of the military should be "offshore balancing." U.S. military presence offshore, they argue, can have a deterrent impact on the strategic and military decisions of other countries, particularly adversaries. Others expand this set of missions to include nuclear deterrence, and military presence offshore in Asia to balance Chinese capabilities. In principle, U.S. counterterrorism military missions would be the responsibility of the coun-

This aerial photo taken on January 2, 2017, shows a Chinese navy formation, including the aircraft carrier Liaoning (C), during military drills in the South China Sea. The aircraft carrier is one of the latest steps in the years-long build-up of China's military, as Beijing seeks greater global power to match its economic might and asserts itself more aggressively in its own backyard. (STR/AFP/GETTY IMAGES)

tries in a given region, with some outside support.

As Cato Institute analyst Ben Friedman puts it:

[Restraint] reflect[s] a preference to take advantage of our nation's geopolitical fortune by staying aloof from conflicts. When U.S. forces go to war, they should come from home bases by air or sea and avoid lingering in occupation. We have the luxury to commence wars on our schedule while those we defend man the front line.

Since U.S. forces would remain globally dominant, but would no longer be responsible for fighting insurgents or providing internal security in other regions, they could be smaller and less forward deployed. The restraint vision would therefore eliminate most U.S. overseas bases and much of the U.S. security assistance programs and arms sales. Since allies would have ground forces of their own in key regions (Europe and Korea, e.g.) ground war involving U.S. forces would be unlikely; hence, the Army and Marines could be smaller, with a larger share in the reserves. Special operations forces could shrink as regional countries assumed greater responsibility for security and U.S. military training missions de-

clined. The Air Force could be reduced as requirements to deploy ground forces declined and fighter technology improved, allowing the same missions to be performed by fewer aircraft.

The Navy would be smaller, but not shrink as much as the ground forces. It would patrol on a reduced basis, surging to clear sea lanes if necessary. This would allow the number of U.S. aircraft carriers to shrink to eight (from the current 11). Offshore balancing would prioritize naval forces deployed in the Pacific to counteract China and provide some reassurance to other countries in the region. Naval aircraft based on carriers could carry out many of the missions the Air Force must do today from a distance, which would allow reductions in the size of the Air Force. Most restraint advocates envision a robust strategic nuclear deterrent based solely on undersea ballistic missile submarines, scrapping land-based missiles as vulnerable and unnecessary, and converting the bomber force to conventional missions. Proponents of restraint argue that the resulting military force would remain more capable and advanced than any other military in the world. It would cost nearly $1 trillion less than the currently projected $5.7 trillion in mili-

tary budgets over the next ten years.

The restraint vision combines a recognition of U.S. global military superiority with an acknowledgment of the political, economic and military rebalancing taking place around the globe. It eschews American exceptionalism and the notion that the U.S. is an indispensable contributor to global, or especially regional, security. It would leave counterterrorism and counter-insurgency operations to regional powers, with U.S. support if necessary. A world in which the U.S. shows military restraint could turn out to be more orderly. As Amitav Acharya puts it: "A key transition in the emerging world order could be that regional orders become less geared toward serving America's power and purpose and are more reflective of the interests and identities of the local actors."

The weakness of this vision is simply that it has been untested over the past 70 years. It is unclear if other countries would rise to the occasion, organize themselves to provide regional security and develop the necessary capabilities. Conflict could increase, rather than decline. A rising major power like China could disrupt the system and challenge the security of its neighbors in a context where the U.S. had not hedged with enough military power to respond.

Strategic vision four: assertive nationalism

The last vision for the U.S. global role is assertive nationalism, captured in President Donald Trump's slogan "America First" (a catchphrase that, as we shall see, has deeper roots than its association with the current president). In this vision, priority is given to defending and promoting U.S. interests, over and against any other nation's interests. As National Security Advisor H.R. McMaster and Council of Economic Advisers Chair Gary Cohn put it: "[T]he world is not a 'global community' but an arena where nations, nongovernmental actors, and businesses engage and compete for advantage."

Assertive nationalists see the U.S. as neither the exceptional nation, nor the indispensable international leader.

The U.S. should deal with other nations on the basis of a realistic assessment of national interests, with no judgment about internal politics, including when it comes to engaging such authoritarian regimes as Turkey, Russia, China or the Philippines. Assertive nationalism is firmly unilateral, not multilateral, and takes a dim view of promoting democracy or military nation-building. A larger, unequivocally dominant U.S. military is central to this vision, with significantly less attention paid to the non-military tools of statecraft.

For the assertive nationalist, unilateral primacy and multilateral leadership strategies have in the past committed the U.S. to actions and agreements that do not benefit the U.S. Proponents

point to military alliances whose members "free ride" on U.S. military capabilities, as well as trade and climate accords that cause manufacturing job losses in the U.S., and immigration policies that threaten security and jobs at home. An assertive nationalist strategy would correct these imbalances, defend U.S. security and leave regional security to other countries.

Although this vision focuses on economic and immigration issues, it is also critical of security agreements, including NATO ("free riders"); the Joint Comprehensive Plan of Action between Iran, Russia, Europe and the U.S., regulating Iran's nuclear program; and previous efforts to negotiate away North Korea's nuclear program. In sum, as an anonymously authored article in the *Claremont Review of Books* in September 2016, put it, "America First" is a policy of "secure borders, economic nationalism, [and] interests-based foreign policy"—one that would lead to "less foreign intervention, less trade, and more immigration restrictions."

Although the missions of the U.S. military would shrink according to this vision, the force itself would grow. As the Trump defense budget request argued in 2017, a strong military is needed "to protect the security of the United States" and "pursue peace through strength." Although details are not available, the missions of this force would appear to include defeating ISIS in the Middle East and dealing with "the rise of advanced potential adversaries, the spread of destructive technology, and the expansion of terrorism." The budget request advocates a significant military buildup. The plan would expand the ground forces (Army and Marines), build up to roughly 350 ships in the Navy and add at least 100 fighter aircraft to the Air Force. The budget would grow at least 10% above the current defense plan, and easily as much as the unilateral preeminence military budget, over the next ten years.

Many current missions would continue under this expanded force. U.S. special operations forces would continue to battle terrorist organizations; the Navy would continue global operations. Increased arms sales would become a priority in part because of their contribution to U.S. manufacturing exports. Security assistance programs, particularly direct military-to-military ties, might be an important feature of an assertive nationalist vision, as the expanded funding for these efforts in the Trump defense budget suggests.

By contrast, diplomatic capabilities would take a hard hit. The 2018 budget request seeks a reduction of nearly 30% in diplomacy and foreign assistance programs, and a significant reduction of more than 10% in the State Department workforce. Office of Management and Budget Director Mick Mulvaney made it clear that in this vision, military capabilities take the lead in protecting U.S. interests abroad. "[T]his administration intends to change course from a soft power budget to a hard power budget," he said. "And that's a message that our adversaries and our allies alike should take."

The strength of the assertive nationalist vision lies in its resonance with the American public, many of whom are unhappy about the decline of manufacturing employment, illegal immigration into the U.S., and long military deployments in the Middle East and Afghanistan. The military buildup may also reflect public reaction to global rebalancing, which seems to diminish U.S. global standing. For its supporters, assertive nationalism represents a return to a realistic, self-interested tradition in U.S. foreign policy, an end to others taking advantage of the U.S., a larger and stronger military force, and fewer overseas interventions. The weakness of this vision may lie in the contradiction between the assertion of U.S. military preeminence and the rebalancing that is underway. U.S. messaging that multilateral security (and economic) arrangements are not beneficial, in conjunction with the expansion of military capabilities, could accelerate the rebalancing trend, particularly by Russia and China.

Choosing a course

U.S. national security and military policies are at a crossroads, facing rapid global change and power rebalancing. These changes challenge the assumptions about U.S. leadership that have characterized the international system for 70 years. The options that face U.S. policymakers are higher-risk than in the past. A unilateral preeminence strategy with a significantly larger military could restore U.S. power, or it could accelerate the rebalancing already taking place. A multilateral leadership approach, relying in part on active use of the military, could continue to serve the U.S., or it could prove outdated and counterproductive. Practicing unilateral restraint and "offshore balancing" might be realistic, welcomed globally, or it might simply put U.S. interests at risk. Assertive nationalism, with significant military expansion, could strike the right balance between U.S. commitments and national interests, or it might accelerate global rebalancing to the detriment of U.S. interests. Whatever course policymakers choose, it will have major consequences for the future of the U.S. role on the global stage.

Donald Trump, 2016 Republican presidential candidate, waves during a rally aboard the battleship USS Iowa in San Pedro, Los Angeles, CA, while wearing a red baseball cap with his campaign slogan, "Make America Great Again." (VISIONS OF AMERICA/UIG/GETTY IMAGES)

discussion questions

1. Since the end of World War II, U.S. foreign and national security policies have been characterized by a bipartisan vision of multilateral leadership and a willingness to intervene militarily abroad. What are the limits to this strategy today and how will these limits influence the future of U.S. military engagement in a "rebalancing world"?

2. In general, what are the pros and cons of an interventionist policy versus a policy of restraint? How might countries outside the transatlantic community view these policies differently than Americans?

3. What does the expanding military and diplomatic presence of countries like China, Russia and Iran on the global stage mean for U.S. national security and military policy?

4. Looking back at the history of U.S. military engagement since the end of World War II, what are some instances of U.S. military intervention abroad that you believe should not have been undertaken? Can you think of situations where the U.S. should have intervened militarily and did not?

5. How does the Trump administration's "America First" policy outlook assess and seek to revise the role of the U.S. military abroad?

6. What might declining U.S. soft power (diplomacy and foreign aid) and increasing hard power (military size and strength) mean for the global balance of power and the protection of U.S. interests? In your opinion, how should soft power and hard power be balanced to best protect and secure U.S. interests?

suggested readings

Acharya, Amitav, "After Liberal Hegemony: The Advent of a Multiplex World Order," **Ethics and International Affairs**. 14 pp. September 2017. Available free online: <https://www.ethicsandinternationalaffairs.org/2017/multiplex-world-order/>. Acharya describes a "multiplex world" characterized by a network of various international orders in which certain elements of the liberal order persist, and offers suggestions for making the transition to this complex system.

Donnelly, Thomas and Kagan, Frederick W., **Ground Truth: The Future of U.S. Land Power**. 164 pp. Washington, D.C.: AEI Press, 2008. This book urges policymakers to address the long overdue need for a rejuvenation of U.S. ground forces in terms of size, training and modernization—issues that the authors claim are inherent to the U.S. military's capabilities and hegemony.

Freeman, Chas W., Jr., "The End of the American Empire," **Remarks to East Bay Citizens for Peace, the Barrington Congregational Church, and the American Friends Service Committee**. April 4, 2016. Available free online: <http://chasfreeman.net/the-end-of-the-american-empire/>. In this speech, former U.S. Ambassador Chas Freeman describes what he calls the "end of the American empire" and argues for a position of restraint in U.S. foreign policy.

———, **Global Trends 2030: Alternative Worlds**. The National Intelligence Council, Office of the Director of National Intelligence. 160 pp. December 2012. Available free online: <https://www.dni.gov/files/documents/GlobalTrends_2030.pdf>. This report by the National Intelligence Council questions how the geopolitical landscape will evolve in the years leading up to 2030.

McMaster, H.R. and Cohn, Gary D., "America First Doesn't Mean America Alone," **The Wall Street Journal**, May 10, 2017. This op-ed by National Security Adviser H.R. McMaster and Director of the National Economic Council Gary Cohn outlines the "America First" vision for U.S. foreign policy and national security.

O'Rourke, Ronald and Moodie, Michael, **US Role in the World: Background and Issues for Congress**. 95 pp. Washington, D.C.: Congressional Research Service, October 10, 2017. Available free online: <https://fas.org/sgp/crs/row/R44891.pdf>. This report presents potential issues facing Congress in light of questions about the U.S.'s traditional global leadership role under the Trump administration.

Rachman, Gideon, **Easternization: Asia's Rise and America's Decline From Obama to Trump and Beyond**. 336 pp. New York: Other Press, 2017. Gideon Rachman analyzes the rise of Asia and the decline of the West, offering advice for how to navigate an uncertain future in international relations.

Don't forget: Ballots start on page 105!

To access web links to these readings, as well as links to additional, shorter readings and suggested web sites,

GO TO www.greatdecisions.org

and click on the topic under Resources, on the right-hand side of the page

South Africa's fragile democracy

by Sean Jacobs

Members of the Economic Freedom Fighters (EFF) march on August 08, 2017, in Pretoria, South Africa. South African President Jacob Zuma was facing a vote of no confidence in parliament, which he narrowly survived. In the hours before the vote, a series of coordinated protests across South Africa demanded Zuma's removal. (ALET PRETORIUS/GALLO IMAGES/GETTY IMAGES)

South Africa's young democracy, at one point considered the most robust in Africa, now faces all kinds of stresses, much of them self-inflicted. The ruling African National Congress (ANC) party enjoyed comfortable majorities in five general elections since 1994, following independence from white minority rule and the end of the system of institutionalized racial segregation known as apartheid. The expectation was that subsequent ANC leaders would build on the example of the country's first democratic president, Nelson Mandela (1994–99), who was one of the most popular and respected world figures of the 20th century.

South Africa's transition to a new national ethos based on human rights, coupled with strong institutions and a robust civil society, has represented hope for deeply divided societies around the world. South Africans themselves have often thought of their political system and economic development as exceptional, to be spared the crises of their neighbors and fellows on the African continent. Today, with Mandela dead, most black South Africans still economically deprived and the ANC riven by factions that undermine its ability to govern effectively, many wonder about the direction South Africa is heading.

The ANC's dominance—especially amongst black voters—is evaporating ahead of elections scheduled for 2019. The ANC may still win the election, but its legitimacy has

SEAN JACOBS *is an associate professor of international affairs at The New School in New York City. A native of Cape Town, he previously worked as a political researcher at the Institute for Democracy in South Africa and held fellowships at Harvard and New York University. He founded the website Africa is a Country.*

largely been eroded. It doesn't help that the party failed to successfully make the transition from a liberation movement to a modern political party. Despite public insistences to the contrary, the ANC is still largely a hierarchical, secretive organization that operates like it is in exile, discouraging internal democracy and debate. Political office is now largely associated with business opportunities and wealth accumulation. In some provinces, most notably KwaZulu-Natal on the eastern coast, rivalries within the party have turned violent. Between January 2016 and mid-September 2017, at least 35 people were murdered in political violence related to ANC rivalries in Kwazulu-Natal. The ANC itself counted 80 of its political representatives killed between 2011 and 2017. At one men's hostel in Durban, the largest city in the province, 89 people were murdered between March 2014 and July 2017 in political violence. No arrests have been made.

Much of the ANC's decline is being experienced under the current president, Jacob Zuma. In power since 2009, he faces 783 corruption charges and maintains questionable alliances with businessmen. The ANC's long-held alliances with trade unions, via the Congress of South African Trade Unions (COSATU), and the South African Communist Party (SACP)—which together manage the social and economic demands of the poor and black working classes and canvas for the ANC during elections—are now under stress. Voters are turned off by the graft and conspicuous consumption associated with ANC leaders. Whites still control the bulk of the country's wealth, and inequality amongst blacks has increased. More than a quarter of South Africans, mostly black, are out of work and more than half are poor. By 2011, there were 1.9 million shacks or informal dwellings in South Africa.

Before you read, download the companion **Glossary** that includes definitions and a guide to acronyms and abbreviations used in the article. Go to **www.great decisions.org** and select a topic in the Resources section on the right-hand side of the page.

A number of smaller parties, including breakaways from the ANC, like the Economic Freedom Fighters (EFF), upstage the ANC and challenge its hegemony. They have gained seats in both national parliament and city governments in the most important metropolitan councils (known as "metros"), and represent opposition to the dominant party in street protests and in the media. In the last series of local elections, in August 2016, the ANC lost majority control of three important metros that it had controlled since the first post-apartheid local elections in 1995. These metros now belong to the the Democratic Alliance (DA), a party that, despite its roots in white liberalism, increasingly appeals to black voters. In Nelson Mandela Bay (Port Elizabeth), a traditional ANC stronghold, the DA, with the aid of smaller parties, ousted the ANC. In Johannesburg, the DA won 45% of the vote, the largest share. With help from the EFF, the DA took over the council. The DA now governs South Africa's capital, Pretoria (also known as Tshwane).

Protests against the government are widespread; they mostly revolve around poor or non-existent service delivery or the negative effects of the government's mostly market-friendly policies. Most protest movements date back to the early 2000s, when demonstrations took place over access to electricity, affordable housing, education, water meters and, crucially, AIDS. Protests are usually met with violence by the police and private security hired by the government. In the most serious case, the police murdered 34 striking miners in Marikana, in the country's northwest, in broad daylight in August 2012. The workers, abandoned by an ANC-aligned trade union, had gone on an illegal strike over wages and working conditions. The government made a show of engaging a public commission to investigate the killings, but no minister, including the country's current Deputy President Cyril Ramaphosa (2014–present)—at the time, non-executive director at the multinational that owned the mine—or high ranking police officials were held accountable.

The Marikana massacre served as a catalyst for the formation of the EFF party and the growth of independent trade unions outside COSATU. It also indirectly inspired protests in 2015 and 2016 by mostly black students on university campuses over racist symbols, class curriculums and free public higher education. The student protests represent the most dramatic recent political development in South Africa, and signal the potential for democratic politics for the black majority—especially among black middle class people—beyond the ANC and its alliance partners.

As for the country's engagement with the rest of the continent, under Mandela and his successor, Thabo Mbeki (1999–2008), the new (post-apartheid) South Africa built a reputation mediating conflicts (in the Democratic Republic of Congo, Zimbabwe, Kenya in 2007 and Côte d'Ivoire). They steered political and economic agendas through a vision of "African Renaissance," promoting Africa's social, economic and political development and an African identity, as well as through an economic program initiated by the African Union (AU) called the New Partnership for Africa's Development (NEPAD). These programs were the brainchildren of President Mbeki, who maintained a profile as a mediator and elder statesman, intervening in conflicts or supervising election monitoring elsewhere on the continent, once he stepped down as president.

By contrast, President Zuma's administration is more inward looking, although his wife and former foreign minister Nkosazana Dlamini-Zuma headed the AU between 2012 and 2017. While Mandela desired an ethical foreign policy for South Africa, the country's present rulers are largely silent on political abuses and rigged elections by fellow AU members. Relations with other African countries are soured by periodic xenophobic violence aimed exclusively at migrants and refugees from elsewhere in Africa. More than 5 million migrants and refugees have entered and settled in South Africa since 1994. Most have settled in black townships, where rents are affordable but locals resent their presence. Xenophobic violence is egged on by political leaders who blame foreigners for high crime rates, though no evidence exists to support such claims. These political leaders include some of Zuma's ministers and the DA mayor of Johannesburg. More significant has been the xenophobic utterances of the Zulu King, Goodwill Zwelithini, who has a claim over about 10 million potential subjects. Zwelithini has referred to immigrants and refugees as, among other things, "rats" and "lice."

Relations with the world's traditional superpowers, particularly the U.S., were cordial, though critical, under Mandela and Mbeki. Mandela had an excellent rapport with President Bill Clinton (1993–2001), and at one point President George W. Bush (2001–09) referred to Mbeki as the U.S.'s "point man" in Africa. Long after he had retired from office, Mandela was still admired by U.S. leaders: President Barack Obama (2009–17) wrote a foreword to Mandela's autobiographical book, *Conversations with Myself*. But Mbeki's AIDS denialism soured relations with the U.S., as did South African opposition to the U.S.-led North Atlantic Treaty Organization (NATO) intervention in Libya and the government's general preference for political rather than military solutions to conflicts.

Under President Zuma, ANC officials, with very little evidence, have accused the U.S. of meddling in South African politics. While South Africa has remained a key plank of U.S. foreign policy on the continent, the U.S.'s priorities in Africa have shifted mostly to combating terrorism and meeting U.S. energy needs. This focuses U.S. attention on West, Central and East African states. In a surprise move, however, U.S. President Donald Trump's first telephone calls to African leaders from the White House were made to Zuma and to Nigerian President Muhammadu Buhari (2015–present). (On the other hand, the head of Egypt's military regime was the first African leader Trump met in person.)

In the meantime, South Africa, like

President George W. Bush (R) is greeted by South African President Thabo Mbeki (L) as Secretary of State Condoleezza Rice and National Security Adviser Stephen Hadley look on during a meeting of the United Nations Security Council on Africa, September 25, 2007, at UN headquarters. (CHARLES DHARAPAK/AP PHOTO)

most other African states, is pivoting east toward China and Russia. China is South Africa's largest trading partner. Beijing declared South Africa a "comprehensive strategic partner" in 2010. Trade between the countries now stands

at over $20 billion. Chinese investment in South Africa stands at $13 billion. At least 50% of South Africans think China has a positive influence on their country, according to the research network Afrobarometer. The new South Africa's relationship with China dates to 1998, when the South African government officially switched to the "One China" policy, recognizing the government in Beijing as the official government of all of China (including Taiwan). It was China who invited South Africa to the BRICS (Brazil, Russia, India, China and South Africa) group of major emerging national economies in 2010. Zuma visited China at least four times between 2010 and 2015, accompanied by large business delegations, resulting in lucrative deals with Chinese state corporations and banks. Increasingly, the next generation of South African business and political leaders are also being trained in China. To some extent, the closer relationship reflects China's power, and the Chinese present aid and investment with few conditions, countering Western power blocs.

History matters

It is worth recognizing that South African democracy is little over two decades old. The bulk of the 350-odd years that constitute South African history were characterized by violence, dispossession, land theft and codified racism against blacks. During that time, the main priorities of the central state and local governments were the welfare, security and comfort of whites. This resulted in stark inequalities that persist to this day.

Though Portuguese sailors "discovered" the Cape (en route to India) in the late 1400s, and proceeded to trade with local farmers known as the Khoi, the usual starting point for modern South African history is 1652. In this year, the multinational Dutch East India Company (VOC) established the Cape Colony at the continent's southernmost edge. The VOC set in motion a series of events that still shapes the country's political and economic destiny. The

Dutch expanded into the interior with agriculture and cattle farming. Wars between the Dutch and the Khoi continued intermittently for the next 18 years, as the Khoi were stripped of their lands and commandeered to work on Dutch farms. Large numbers of Khoi were later wiped out by a smallpox epidemic.

To solve the labor shortage, the VOC imported African and Asian slaves from the Portuguese colonies of Mozambique and Angola, as well as the islands of the Indian Ocean, India and, crucially, Indonesia (where the Dutch also had a colony). By the end of the 18th century, the majority of the population of the Cape Colony were slaves. As the Dutch moved inland and some of its personnel demanded land to farm, they clashed with the Xhosa, a set of independent tribes to the east of the colony.

In 1806, the British took control of the Cape after Napoleon's defeat of the Dutch in Europe. The English wasted no time in exerting control over their subjects or annexing territory. They went to war with the Xhosa and the Zulu, finally defeating both by the late 1870s. The British banished political prisoners to Robben Island, off the coast of Cape Town (the same prison where, 100 years later, Nelson Mandela and his comrades would be sent.)

Slavery's impact on South Africa cannot be underestimated: It governed economic, social and political relations for 180 years in the Cape Colony before it was abolished by the British in 1833. It laid the groundwork for agriculture in the region, now known as Western Cape, where even today the farms remain notorious for their poor labor conditions. Most of the people who would later be classified as "coloured" or "mixed" were descendants of slaves, and slavery also left a legacy of patronizing relations between whites and blacks that continues to

govern politics in Western Cape. Finally, slavery laid some of the foundation for apartheid: Not only did the Dutch and British exploit black labor, but the British introduced the first pass laws and brutally policed relations between "the races."

Slavery was also the catalyst for the formation of "Boer," (meaning "farmer") identity. (The Boer would later call themselves "Afrikaners," to make explicit their link to the continent). White employers of the VOC had developed a frontier mentality at the Cape and clashed with the colonial authorities over how they could treat their slaves. When the British abolished slavery, it set off Boer rebellions and, starting in 1835, a "Groot Trek" (Great Trek) of Dutch settlers out of the Cape Colony to territories deeper into modern-day South Africa that were outside of British colonial administration. The departing Boers encroached on and clashed

with the African nations they encountered. They established "Free Boer Republics" in the Free State, Transvaal (also known as the South African Republic) and Natalia.

In 1866, diamonds were discovered at Kimberley, nearly 600 miles to the north of Cape Town. Two decades later, in 1886, gold was discovered around Johannesburg. This precipitated a mineral rush. It also triggered a demand for cheap labor. British colonial authorities intensified tax collection. Aided by chiefs (local Africans co-opted into "indirectly ruling" their subjects), they pushed African men into the mines. In the process, the migrant labor system was born. Black men would travel from the reserves to the mines, where they would be housed for the bulk of the year in hostels on the outskirts of black townships. To this day, this system—which later included manufacture and service industries—defines employ-

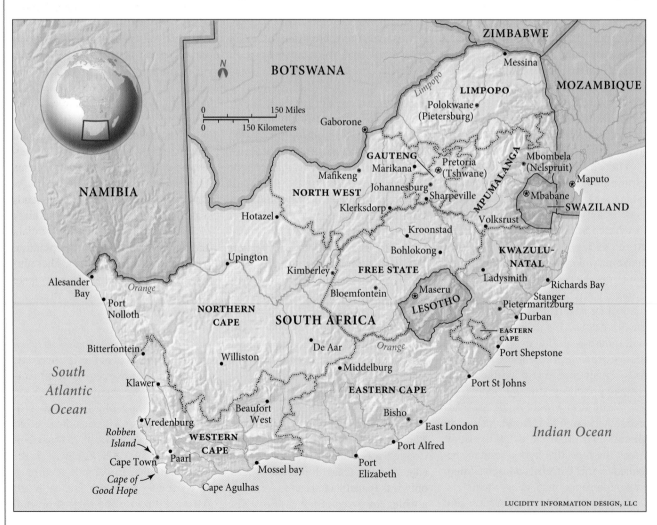

LUCIDITY INFORMATION DESIGN, LLC

ment opportunities for able-bodied men in large parts of the Eastern Cape, South Africa's northern provinces and KwaZulu-Natal.

It was inevitable that the British colonial state (which acted primarily in the interests of mine owners) and Boers would clash over the control of land, minerals and black labor. In the latter half of the 19th century, they fought a series of wars against each other, eventually culminating in the Anglo-Boer War (1899 to 1902) (retroactively known as the South African War, to acknowledge the involvement of blacks as soldiers on both sides). The conflict was quite brutal: British tactics included imprisoning Boer women and children in concentration camps, harsh treatment of Boer war prisoners and large scale destruction of agriculture. Boers' use of guerrilla warfare also garnered attention in Europe and the U.S. Ultimately, the two parties embarked on a protracted peace process that culminated in the establishment of the "Union of South Africa" in 1910. The Union was a self-governing territory within the British Empire, and combined the former British colonies of the Cape, Transvaal, Orange River and Natal with the former Afrikaner independent republics. The country was now organized into four provinces.

The Union marked the formal beginnings of South Africa's present borders. Over the next four decades, joint coalitions of the main factions in white politics would govern South Africa and seek to strengthen the position of white workers and eradicate white poverty, while restricting work opportunities for blacks and stripping them of their limited voting rights (only black men who owned property could vote). Successive Union governments also began to implement residential segregation. Worst of all, blacks were deprived of land rights through a series of acts, most notably the Natives Land Act of 1913, and a slew of amendments in the 1930s. The effect of these laws was that by the start of the World War II (WWII), whites owned 87% of the land, and blacks, who made up two thirds of the population, owned

Circa 1956: A sign common in Johannesburg, South Africa, reading "Caution Beware Of Natives." (EJOR/HULTON ARCHIVE/GETTY IMAGES)

13%. This distribution was unchanged through 1994.

Nevertheless, splits were opening up in white politics. The dominant faction in Afrikaner politics organized into the National Party (NP) and—backed by Afrikaner clergy, academics and media—began to push for a more explicit white supremacist politics. In 1948, the NP won parliamentary elections and introduced apartheid, a series of laws that, for the next 40 years, would govern where black people lived, sent their children to school, worked and travelled, as well as controlling black family relations, and political participation and expression.

Over the next 30 years, large, settled urban and rural black communities were forcibly removed to the outskirts of cities (by the Group Areas Act), and dumped in newly created and inhospitable townships far away from work and from resources like hospitals. Black South Africans living on freehold land in what was deemed "white South Africa" were also uprooted. Blacks were forced to carry pass books, without which they could not be in a city for more than 72 hours (and then only if they had guaranteed work from a white employer). By the mid-1950s,

the government began creating "homelands" (or *bantustans*) for Africans, complete with presidents, parliaments and passports. Every black person was designated a "tribe" or "nation" and would be repatriated "home," whether they had any relation to the assigned place or not.

The homelands ostensibly promoted black "self-government." In truth, they served as labor reservoirs for farms and mines inside white South Africa. One positive legacy of the homelands was their cultivation of a whole class of black politicians, security officials and bureaucrats, all adept at operating within the apartheid system. These individuals would continue to participate in governing the new South Africa.

Resistance and anti-apartheid movements

Black South African resistance was limited to specific nations or ethnicities before the declaration of the Union of South Africa in 1910. In reaction to the Union, the resistance coalesced to form the South African National Natives Congress (SANNC) in 1912, renamed the ANC in 1923.

By the 1920s, some black South Africans had turned to millenarian movements. These movements were mostly inspired by apocalyptic visions from Christian end times prophesies, but their vision was a world in which whites had been defeated. African-Americans were often cast as saviors in these movements. This was the case with Garveyism, named for its founder, Marcus Garvey, a Jamaican immigrant to the U.S., whose Universal Improvement Association became the world's biggest black-led movement in the 1920s. Garvey's message of self-determination initially spoke to the conditions in the Americas and Europe, but also found traction on the African continent, particularly in South Africa. The rise of black-only trade unions and Africanist political strains within the ANC can be partly traced to these Garveyist themes.

Nevertheless, Garvey's black nationalism was less appealing to black South Africa than was the desire for desegregated equality for all. In fact, black South African consciousness was increasingly inspired by the 1917 Russian Revolution. The Communist Party of South Africa (CPSA) was formed in 1921. The Bolshevik ideology proved adaptable to South African conditions in that it promoted class politics in tandem with national self-determination. The Bolsheviks encouraged the CPSA to support black majority rule for South Africa (what became known as the "Native Republic" thesis). In the 1920s, the CPSA endeared itself to the ANC by organizing black workers, and the two groups formed a close partnership. In the 1930s, however, the dominant faction of the ANC discouraged links to the CPSA.

For the first three decades of its existence, the ANC was more interested in deputations and futilely pleading to the government's good conscience than it was in mass struggle. The imposition of apartheid in 1948 roused the ANC from its stasis, and the 1950s were characterized by a joint political program (the "Freedom Charter," adopted in 1955, which rekindled ties to the CPSA) and mass protests against apartheid laws, as well as protests by different opposition groups that united black nationalists,

white communists and colored and Indian civil rights activists.

In the early 1960s, the ANC developed a military wing and declared armed struggle against the NP government, following a police massacre of Africans protesting pass books at Sharpeville (69 people were killed; nearly 200 injured) and an NP ban on the ANC. The government clamped down on the opposition, rounding up activists, forcing large numbers into political exile and charging the most important leaders, including Mandela, with treason, which carried a life sentence in prison. The opposition only recovered in the 1970s, with the emergence of the Black Consciousness Movement (consisting mostly of young black university students calling for exclusively black-led politics) and a strike in Durban in 1973, which gave a boost to organized workers. A nationwide uprising in June 1976 that began with high school students in the Johannesburg township of Soweto gave further impetus to resistance. In 1977, however, police murdered the most important Black Consciousness leader, Steve Biko, and crushed most social movements.

While for its first three decades, apartheid operated more or less from the same script (i.e. overt racism, strict enforcement of its laws), the system "reformed" and reinvented itself over time, including by coopting elements in the black community. By the mid-1970s, it began to accept the reality of black urbanization and trade union rights for black workers. In the early 1980s, it started to experiment with "constitutional reforms," i.e. promising some black "self-government" at the local level, though in practice whites remained in charge. Police and local authorities were also lax in enforcing "petty apartheid," or the myriad local laws upholding the system. For instance, they allowed for "gray areas" (racially mixed residential neighborhoods) in the inner parts of major cities. Through the 1980s, the apartheid government continued to play tough publicly—governing via states of emergency, occupying black townships,

arresting and detaining black political leaders, or, worse, carrying out assassinations by death squads. Privately, it began negotiating with the ANC to fashion a "new deal" for South Africa.

The end of apartheid

By the mid-1980s, apartheid was in perpetual crisis. In 1983, the opposition regrouped, forming the United Democratic Front (UDF). The UDF and CO-SATU, founded two years later, together had the ability to mobilize millions of South Africans for mass marches, rent boycotts, work stoppages, school closures and bus and train strikes on levels not seen before in South Africa. The global context had also changed. The U.S. and United Kingdom (UK) had been long-time supporters of the apartheid government, with rationales shifting from racial solidarity to anticommunism. The end of the Cold War in 1991 removed much of the rationale for that support and these governments now put pressure on the NP to negotiate with the ANC. Multilateral economic, cultural and sporting sanctions also began to have an effect, leaving white South Africans increasingly isolated. At the same time, however, the Soviet Union—one of the ANC's main benefactors in aid, weapons and training—was in crisis, limiting the movement's options.

By the end of the decade, the government began releasing most of Mandela's comrades from prison. In February 1990, President F.W. de Klerk (1989–94) announced in parliament that his government was unbanning the ANC and other liberation movements (banned groups totaled 33). He released Mandela from prison a few days later. What followed were four years of negotiations over the terms of the new South Africa. The negotiations revolved around political institutions; economic systems were off limits.

The "transition" (as negotiations became known) was particularly violent: Nearly 20,000 people were killed in a government-funded proxy war between the Inkatha Freedom Party (IFP) and the UDF/ANC. The IFP advocated for Zulu nationalism, governed one of the homelands and enjoyed some support amongst Zulu migrant workers in the Transvaal (now Gauteng). Mandela publicly accused de Klerk of allowing the violence to continue. In April 1993, Chris Hani, the most popular black leader after Mandela, was murdered by white right-wingers. Hani's death moved the transition forward on two counts: First, Mandela appeared on TV to calm the nation, making him seem presidential long before he was elected to the position; second, the government agreed to an election date: April 27, 1994. Less than two months before the elections, a coalition of white racists (including elements in the apartheid government army and neo-Nazis) along with homeland leaders (the IFP and the homeland governments of Bophuthatswana and Ciskei) threatened to secede from South Africa. These threats came to nothing, partly because of Mandela's appeal across racial and ethnic lines and little public support for the secession. The ANC handily won elections and Mandela became president. The ANC now held majorities in seven of the nine new provincial governments (the NP won the Western Cape and the IFP won KwaZulu-Natal).

The new South Africa

In the first decade of its rule, the new government's main priority was to stabilize the economy and build national consensus. The ANC ruled through a Government of National Unity, which included the NP and IFP in crucial ministries. It set up the Truth and Reconciliation Commission, a restorative justice body which emphasized reconciliation in the aftermath of apartheid, and adopted an economic policy known as the Growth, Employment and Redistribution policy (GEAR), which prioritized growth over redistribution. President Mandela was universally popular. This meant that whatever shortcomings he might have exhibited as a leader (a delay in effecting economic equality or his conciliatory politics concerning the country's apartheid past, e.g.) were less likely to be called out.

Mandela proved a difficult act to follow. His successor, Mbeki, developed a reputation as a technocrat, but his presidency was undermined by a para-

noid, factional style, derided as "imperial." Policy-wise, Mbeki was undone by his "quiet diplomacy" over the political crisis in neighboring Zimbabwe, where Robert Mugabe (prime minister, 1980–87; president, 1987–2017) governed through a mix of repression and empty appeals to anti-imperialism. Domestically, the government's hamhanded response to the AIDS crisis (Mbeki promoted denialist science) frustrated many South Africans. In the end, however, it was his firing of then-Deputy President Jacob Zuma in 2005, over kickbacks from a lucrative state arms deal, that united Mbeki's enemies in the ANC and the trade unions. Not even charges of sexual assault against Zuma (he was accused of raping the daughter of his former Robben Island cellmate) could quell support for him. Zuma became the proxy candidate for all the grievances of Mbeki's critics.

In 2007, at the ANC's national conference (where leaders are selected every five years), Zuma roundly defeated Mbeki, who subsequently resigned. An interim president, Kgalema Motlanthe, served until the next general elections in 2009, when Zuma took the seat. Zuma immediately reversed Mbeki's disastrous AIDS policy. Yet whatever other policy plans he had, they were soon overshadowed by his associations with a wealthy Indian immigrant family, the Guptas, who were accused of being favored for government tenders and of improperly influencing Zuma's cabinet appointments to advance their own business interests.

Above all, Zuma's tenure has exposed more than ever the tensions and emerging splits within the ANC. It has

Supporters climb to every vantage point while awaiting the arrival of Nelson Mandela, in 1994, Lamontville, Natal, South Africa. (IAN BERRY/MAGNUM PHOTOS)

also politicized public institutions like the police, judiciary and intelligence services. These have become arsenals in internal ANC battles over leadership positions and control of the presidency. Though Zuma's faction consolidated its hold over the ANC, purging his enemies from party leadership positions and his cabinet, he remains deeply unpopular. Outside of KwaZulu-Natal, his home province, Zuma is regularly booed (most spectacularly during a memorial service in December 2013 for Mandela in the country's biggest football stadium, and in front of leaders from around the world) or disrupted while performing his duties for the government or the ANC. By September 2017, Zuma's approval rating stood at 20%.

The outlines of postnationalist politics

In the first decade or so of freedom, the ANC could rely on most South African votes based on its record as a triumphant nationalist liberation movement. The 2014 general election, one year after Mandela's death, was probably the last election where this held true. Younger voters have no memory of apartheid and instead associate the

ANC with the failures and broken promises of the post-1994 period. They hold the ANC responsible for its failure to tackle systemic racism (what they call white supremacy) and its legacies (for instance, violent attacks on black farmworkers by white farmworkers and racial outbursts by whites who suffer no consequences), waste in govern-

Confederation of South African Trade Unions (COSATU) members cheer and dance as they march through the streets protesting against corruption on September 27, 2017, in Johannesburg. Thousands of angry South African trade unionists took to the streets across the nation on September 27, demanding the resignation of South African President Jacob Zuma and the institution of a Judicial Enquiry Commission over alleged top-level corruption. (GIANLUIGI GUERCIA/AFP/GETTY IMAGES)

ment and widespread corruption. The demands of young voters, as well as recent protests on university campuses and the emergence of parties like EFF, offer the first outlines of a possible postnationalist politics.

The ANC has always walked a tightrope between its leftist and nationalist impulses. As it began to negotiate with the NP in anticipation of gaining power, the ANC was relatively open to compromise. Initially, it favored a more redistributive economic policy—called the Reconstruction and Development Programme (RDP)—but in 1996 ditched it for GEAR. This signaled the power of pro-business elements in the ANC under Mandela and Mbeki, as well as changes within the ANC. While GEAR includes some social democratic policies—generous welfare provisions for the poor, for instance—overall, it ensures that white businesses thrive, politically-connected businesspeople benefit and a black middle class (now numerically the size of the white minority) grows. When Zuma took power and faced questions over corrupt practices in government, his public rhetoric opportunistically blamed the country's woes on "white monopoly capitalism." He has also promised "radical

socioeconomic transformation." Few South Africans take either claim seriously, with the exception of hardcore ANC supporters in the party's Youth League, in more rural provinces like KwaZulu-Natal, as well as some in the trade unions.

Zuma has unmasked himself as a Zulu traditionalist, and publicly courts ethnic nationalist politics. He is particularly close to the Zulu king, and has also attempted to stage manage who will succeed him as president. Historically, the party's deputy president has been first in line for the top job. But Deputy President Ramaphosa, a billionaire businessman and former mine union organizer, is not favored by the Zuma faction. Instead, Zuma has made it clear that he prefers his former wife, Nkosazana Dlamini-Zuma, who had been out of ANC leadership politics for over a decade.

The SACP, though damaged by its history of support for Zuma, began to openly criticize him after he fired a number of SACP leaders from his cabinet. Meanwhile, COSATU is in disarray over Zuma. The current COSATU president has endorsed Ramaphosa to head the ANC. A number of unions, unhappy over Zuma and their federation's defense

of his excesses, have broken away from COSATU. The country's largest trade union, the National Union of Metalworkers (NUMSA), was expelled from COSATU in 2014 when it announced it would not endorse the ANC in elections. NUMSA played a pivotal role in the establishment of a new independent federation, the South African Federation of Trade Unions (SAFTU), in 2017. SAFTU is now the second largest union federation in the country.

One of Jacob Zuma's key organizers and allies in his rise to the top was then-ANC Youth League President Julius Malema (2008–12). When Malema was expelled from the ANC in 2012, he formed the EFF, taking the League's best organizers and base with him. While the EFF's national electoral strength is limited (it plateaus at about 8% of the national vote), the party strategically intervenes in politics; most notably in the way it stalks Zuma publicly over state corruption and king-making in the local elections. The EFF has problems of its own: Malema has a cult-like following and former party members have accused the organization of a lack of internal democracy. The EFF is certainly taking votes from the ANC, but its leaders insist for now that they see themselves in the opposition benches.

That leaves the DA as the other key electoral player. The DA has governed the Western Cape province and Cape Town for at least a decade. DA propaganda speaks of the Western Cape as the "best governed province." That claim is undermined by the province's reputation as the most unequal and segregated in the country. Cape Town boasts the highest murder rate (it is known as the "murder capital") and gang violence is rampant on the Cape Flats, where most coloured people were forcibly relocated under apartheid. The DA also claims to be the authentic representative of Nelson Mandela's legacy, but struggles with internal racism. When the NP disbanded in the late 1990s, most of its white followers shifted allegiances to the DA. On its own, the DA won't be able to unseat the ANC nationally, though its informal and unexpected "alliance" with the EFF in

Johannesburg's and Tshwane's council elections has emboldened supporters.

More significantly, in August 2017, opposition parties nearly succeeded in unseating Zuma via a parliamentary vote of no confidence, despite the ANC's clear majority in the National Assembly—249 of 400 seats. Zuma survived had five previous such votes since 2009, all public, with ANC members of parliament voting as a block. The latest vote was instead held by secret ballot. At least 26 ANC members voted with the opposition, coming 21 votes short of the 50 needed to unseat Zuma.

Meanwhile, Zuma's supporters plant "fake news" stories about his opponents via Gupta-owned media. Their response to accusations of graft is to defend Zuma (and the Guptas) as standing up to whites who still happen to dominate the economy. At the same time, the ANC increasingly finds common cause with more conservative elements in South Africa, such as traditional leaders, who can significantly impact people's livelihoods in at least five of the nine provinces, and religious moralists, who see connections between Zuma's patriarchal attitude and their submission to divine authority.

Outside of formal party politics, there have been small, independent social movements, such as Reclaim the City, the Social Justice Coalition and Equal Education, agitating for housing, police accountability and education, among other causes. They are mostly concentrated in the bigger cities and have gained some small victories through the courts, but struggle to gain the same national acclaim and momentum as the early-2000s nationwide Treatment Action Campaign that publicly shamed the Mbeki government for AIDS denialism.

Student protests

The most interesting recent political development has been a series of protests by university students over colonial symbols, curricula and, crucially, free public higher education. The students, mostly black, are clear beneficiaries of ANC rule. Their open defiance of the police and of their elders gives a glimpse of what it could look like if the black majority turned on the ANC.

South Africa has 23 public universities, which includes some former technical colleges since upgraded to university status. Students at historically black universities (like Tshwane University of Technology or the University of the Western Cape) had been protesting over fees and outsourcing of service jobs on campuses for a while, but it was protests over symbols at the historically white University of Cape Town, Wits University and Rhodes University that kick-started the student movement.

In March 2015, at University of Cape Town, students protested a prominent statue of Cecil John Rhodes, a divisive colonial figure. At Rhodes University, students objected to the name of the school. Those protests morphed into demands for more diverse faculty and the "decolonization" of curricula to better represent non-white culture in education. By midyear, the protests linked up with trade unions opposing outsourcing on campuses, and by year's end, they demanded a freeze on fee increases, as well as free public higher education. In late October 2015, after students had marched to his office in the capital, Zuma announced there would be no fee increase.

By 2016, the movement stalled as a result of a mix of state repression, universities' use of private security firms and internal tactical and strategic difference amongst student activists. But in the process, the activists invented new political language (for example, a more race-based critique of capitalism supplanting the ANC's more Marxist orientation) and new tactics (their use of social media is particularly innovative and causes are identified by hashtags: #FeesMustFall, #RhodesMustFall). The movement was also distinctive for its attention to the patriarchy and sexual abuse in black movement politics, its open questioning of the hegemony of the ANC and its criticism of how the new South Africa has dealt with racial and class inequality.

The student protests, coupled with the growing appeal of the EFF and the restructuring of the trade union movement away from the ANC, represent an interesting political moment for South Africa. Previously, the most vocal opponents of the ANC government in the public sphere were middle class whites. Now, mobilized young black people, with no memory of apartheid or the ANC's heroic role in that struggle, represent a greater threat to the party's hegemony and, more crucially, the current party-political system.

South Africa's foreign policy

Most assessments of South Africa's modern foreign policy begin with a 1993 speech given by a newly free Nelson Mandela, in which he pledged that "human rights will be the light that guides [South Africa's] foreign affairs." During his tenure, Mandela used a human rights lens to condemn countries that violated these principles. The U.S., in the name of anti-communism, backed the apartheid regime and helped it skirt sanctions (the ANC was largely funded by the Soviet Union). Mandela publicly criticized the U.S.'s human rights record and its expedient relationship with dictators during the Cold War, including with South African racists. Nevertheless, Mandela built a remarkable rapport with President Bill Clinton.

The ANC had its own contradictions, of course. To finance its 1994 electoral campaigns, it took millions of dollars in donations from Indonesia's dictatorship and Libya's autocracy. Nevertheless, Mandela, basking in the afterglow of the struggle against apartheid, insisted his would be a regime guided by human rights. The first test of this approach came just months after he took power. Mandela pleaded with the regime of Nigeria's de facto president (1993–98), General Sani Abacha, to release nine leaders of the ethnic minority Ogoni people held on trumped-up charges over protests against corruption in the oil sector in Nigeria's southeast. Mandela's entreaties fell on deaf ears and General Abacha executed the "Ogoni Nine" in 1995. In response, Mandela pushed for Nigeria's expulsion from the Commonwealth of Nations (the intergovernmental organization of states formerly in the British Empire), and though he succeeded, the execution of the Ogoni leaders was viewed as a humiliation.

The experience led Mandela to shy away from publicly tackling undemocratic leaders and human rights offenders on the continent. Instead, the South African government increasingly took on the role of behind-the-scenes mediator. Mandela's biggest success was convincing besieged military dictator Mobutu Sese Seko (1965–97) to relinquish power and leave Zaire (now the Democratic Republic of Congo).

Mbeki's presidency made a considerable effort to promote regional integration and unification of the continent via his "African Renaissance" rhetoric and NEPAD, which was co-authored by then-powerful presidents in Algeria, Nigeria and Senegal. African Renaissance—Mbeki's vision of a Pan-Africanism for the 21st century—recast South Africa as politically and culturally African. NEPAD, which merged proposals already circulating among African leaders, pushed for the economic integration of Africa, and developed a set of priorities for economic development. When NEPAD was adopted in 2001, it was enthusiastically embraced by the United Nations (UN), funding agencies and major Western powers, thrusting Mbeki into the forefront as a continental leader.

Mbeki's insistence on "African solutions for African problems," and on political instead of legal remedies to political crises, often favored incumbents and despots. His indecisiveness on Robert Mugabe's repressive regime in Zimbabwe could be ascribed to this strategy. There, Mbeki relied on "quiet diplomacy," which favored backchannel meetings to convince Mugabe to run free and fair elections and cease oppressing the opposition. Instead, Mugabe ratcheted up the violence.

The ANC's loyalty to those who had aided it during the antiapartheid struggle also contributed to Mbeki's

approach toward foreign repression and crises. For all his Pan-Africanism, Mbeki never intervened on behalf of African migrants and refugees to South Africa, opting instead to release tepid statements about solidarity while his government deported thousands and left others in legal limbo. In some senses, Mbeki's Pan-Africanism also cleared the way for South African corporations (e.g. retail, mining, telecoms, satellite television and construction) to gain a foothold in markets throughout the rest of the continent.

While President Zuma has dialed back commitments on the continent, it is hard to make out the strategic goal of his foreign policy. In 2016, South Africa criticized the International Criminal Court (ICC) for having it out for African countries (it claims the court singles out African leaders for human rights abuses while Western governments get off), joining a chorus of detractors. South Africa subsequently announced that it would formally withdraw from the court. However, in March 2017, after a South African court declared the government's decision "unconstitutional and invalid," the government reversed its decision.

Critics have accused South Africa of having long abandoned its claim to a foreign policy guided by human rights culture. Within the UN, South Africa has voted with countries who want to water down or reject conventions protecting gay people (South Africa is the only African country that legally protects gay rights, including the right to marry) or to protect freedom of expression online. In June 2015, Sudanese President Omar al Bashir (1993–present) traveled to South Africa to attend an AU summit. Bashir was (and continues to be) wanted by the ICC for human rights abuses and genocide in the Sudanese province of Darfur. As a signatory to the Rome Statute (which established the court), South Africa was obliged to arrest Bashir. Instead, he was allowed to leave the country.

Trade and economic considerations also seem to have guided South Africa's foreign policy under Zuma. Between 2009 and 2014, South Africa denied

the Dalai Lama entry into the country three times so as not to offend China. Meanwhile, the DA has replicated apartheid South Africa's foreign policy. DA leader Mmusi Maimane (2015–present) traveled to Israel to meet Prime Minister Benjamin Netanyahu (2009–present). South Africa had close military—including nuclear—and diplomatic links with Israel during apartheid, while the ANC has been close to the Palestinians. Similarly, in defiance of the government's stance on the "One China" policy, DA Mayor of Tshwane Solly Msimanga (2016–present) traveled to Taiwan at the end of 2016.

U.S.-South Africa relations

Like others on the continent, South Africans have been anxious to get a sense of the new U.S. president's Africa policy. Africa didn't feature into candidate Donald Trump's campaign, though some old tweets about his sons hunting in Zimbabwe resurfaced, and he repeated talking points about South Africa that are popular on social media and favored by expatriate white South Africans.

In January 2017, right after Trump's inauguration, *The New York Times* reported that the president's transition team had submitted a four-page list of Africa-related questions to the State Department. The questions indicated "an overall skepticism about the value of foreign aid, and even about America's security interests, on the world's second largest continent." Long-time Africa specialists in Washington were "alarmed" and noted that the framing and tone of the questions indicated a U.S. withdrawal from development and humanitarian goals, "while at the same time trying to push forward business opportunities across the African continent." None of the questions were specifically about South Africa.

A month later, Trump called Buhari and Zuma (as previously mentioned). The calls focused on combating terror and trade relations. In a short statement, Zuma summarized their discussion as being about "strengthening the already strong bilateral relations between the two countries." Zuma also highlighted the presence of nearly 600 U.S. companies in South Africa. Finally, Zuma and Trump discussed South Africa's peacekeeping role in Africa. Singling out these two countries may suggest that, like his predecessors, Trump understands their role as hegemons on the continent.

In September, during the UN General Assembly, Trump gave a short speech at a lunch with nine African leaders, including Zuma. The speech repeated Trump's broad views on U.S. energy and security concerns in Africa. But it was remembered for all the wrong reasons: It was ridiculed in the media for Trump's mispronunciation of Namibia as "Nambia" and his admission that "I have so many friends going to your countries, trying to get rich... They are spending a lot of money."

South Africa remains one of Africa's most powerful countries. Foreign direct investment by South African businesses in retail, manufacture, telecommunications, television, tourism and mining drive this influence. The presence of South African retail stores like ShopRite, Jet and Pick n Pay, or fast food like Nando's, are its most visible representatives. But it is not all plain sailing. South Africans already have a reputation for being xenophobic. South African investors and businesses can arrive abroad with superiority complexes, inspiring negative reactions by host populations. In some countries, South African investors, many of whom are white, have been accused of arrogance and racism. While media company MultiChoice provides most of the continent with satellite television, this does not necessarily translate to cultural dominance; Nigerian music and film, distributed more informally, are often more influential. More recently, South Africa's political leadership under Zuma has come to be associated less with democratization and more with propping up autocrats. Nevertheless, South Africa's very open and robust political culture, the strength of its accountability institutions and its diversity are still admired on the continent.

South African President Jacob Zuma (C) and South African ruling party African National Congress (ANC) Deputy President Cyril Ramaphosa (L) gesture as they arrive at Orlando Stadium in Soweto on January 8, 2017, for a ceremony marking the ANC's 105th anniversary. (MUJAHID SAFODIEN/AFP/GETTY IMAGES)

South Africa remains the most important regional power in Southern Africa. It exports manufactured goods, including cars and agri-processed goods like wine and fruit, as well as services, to the U.S., unlike most countries on the continent outside North Africa. Approximately 39% of U.S. imports from sub-Saharan Africa were from South Africa and 15% from Angola in 2015, according to the Office of the United States Trade Representative. At the same time, South Africa is the largest market—at 31%—for U.S. exports on the African continent.

U.S. diplomats speak openly about maintaining and deepening this relationship as a bulwark against growing Chinese economic influence on the African continent. In 2015, the African Growth and Opportunity Act (AGOA), which provides tariff-free access for African goods to U.S. markets, was renewed for another ten years. South Africa is one of 39 African countries benefiting from the agreement. There is concern in South Africa that the Trump administration will revisit or roll back agreements like AGOA or President Obama's Power Africa initiative (to increase access to electricity).

As U.S. ambassador to South Africa from 2013 to 2016, Patrick Gaspard did much to build relations and raise the U.S. profile there. South African newspapers in 2016 speculated with disquiet that a senior editor at the rightwing news outlet Breitbart would be the next ambassador under the new administration. Perhaps reflecting Trump's business focus, by mid-2017, speculation centered on a Washington-based businessman, Tony Carroll, with deep connections to Southern Africa. By November 2017, 11 months after Patrick Gaspard left the post, the Trump administration had not yet appointed a replacement.

Currently, the question that will determine the future of South Africa is whether its democratic institutions and norms can withstand the pressures of personalities, individuals and political parties. It remains to be seen whether the ruling elites can persist in a commitment to transforming unequal social and economic systems. The next year or so, especially leading up to the 2019 general elections, will be crucial in assessing the country's ultimate direction. In the meantime, it is clear that the story of the new South Africa continues to compel interest across the world, especially in the U.S. In the early 2000s, the social theorist Paul Gilroy saw South Africa "and its lessons" as "the best hope for a politically realigned world." Some still hold on to that hope.

discussion questions

1. In what historical context was the African National Congress (ANC) party formed? Why is support for the party now eroding?

2. What legacies of apartheid are reflected in the contemporary South African economy, politics and culture?

3. The Trump administration has thus far provided little insight into its intentions for U.S.-Africa relations. What should the Trump administration's foreign policy toward Africa look like? What about policy toward South Africa, specifically?

4. How does the history of the Cold War, and specifically the history of relations between South Africa and the Soviet Union, affect contemporary relations between South Africa and the U.S.?

5. South African President Jacob Zuma has criticized the International Criminal Court (ICC) for acting with bias against African states. In 2015, South Africa announced its intention to withdraw from the ICC, and then formally reversed that decision in 2017. What consequences would leaving the ICC have for South Africa's standing on the international stage? How would its withdrawal affect other African states in the ICC?

6. South Africa has a long history of student protests, dating back to the apartheid era. Considering the student protests that took place in 2015–16, what role might such demonstrations play in South Africa's future?

suggested readings

Bond, Patrick, **Elite Transition: From Apartheid to neoliberalism in South Africa (2nd ed.).** 352 pp. London: Pluto Press, 2014. Bond examines post-apartheid South Africa to survey the complex factors behind failures in the new government to address domestic development.

Feinstein, Andrew, **After the Party: A personal and political journey inside the ANC**. 300 pp. Johannesburg: Jonathan Ball, 2009. In this book, Feinstein, a former African National Congress (ANC) member of South African Parliament, analyzes his party's tenure in power, revealing corrupt practices, the trial of current President Jacob Zuma and South Africa-Zimbabwe relations.

Jacobs, Sean and Johnson, Krista, eds., **The Encyclopedia of South Africa**. 373 pp. Boulder, CO: Lynne Rienner Publishers, 2001. This encyclopedia includes photographs and nearly 300 entries on South African history, politics, economy and culture, including material on apartheid legislation since 1856 and heads of state since 1910.

Mandela, Nelson, **Long Walk to Freedom: The Autobiography of Nelson Mandela (1st paperback ed.).** 656 pp. New York: Back Bay Books, 1995. Mandela, lauded as an international moral and political leader, shares his story—a memoir that spans from his anti-apartheid activism to his 27-year incarceration, and later to his presidency of post-apartheid South Africa.

Msimang, Sisonke, **Always Another Country: A Memoir of Exile and Home**. 352 pp. Johannesburg: Jonathan Ball, 2017. The South African author and activist, born in exile, details her life in Zambia, Kenya and North America, and her eventual return to South Africa at the end of apartheid in the 1990s.

Southall, Roger, **Liberation Movements in Power: Party and State in Southern Africa**. 402 pp. Woodbridge, Suffolk: James Currey, 2013. This book charts the evolution of the African National Congress in South Africa and other progressive groups on the continent, analyzing their transition from liberation movement to governing political party.

Don't forget: Ballots start on page 105!

To access web links to these readings, as well as links to additional, shorter readings and suggested web sites,

GO TO www.greatdecisions.org

and click on the topic under Resources, on the right-hand side of the page

Global health: progress and challenges

by Joshua Michaud

Indonesian Muslim women participate in commemorating World AIDS Day in Medan, Indonesia, December 1, 2016. (XINHUA/ALBERT DAMANIK/GETTY IMAGES)

People around the world now live longer and healthier lives on average than ever before in history. The last several decades have seen remarkable and unmistakable progress across many measures of health and disease. In 1990, 12.7 million children under five years old died, a rate of almost one child for every 10 born. By 2016, that number had been cut in half, to 5.6 million, even with a growing global population. Average global life expectancy grew by seven years between 1990 and 2015, rising from 65 to 72. The world has been successful in slowing some of the deadliest global epidemics and reducing preventable deaths from many causes, even in the poorest regions. In the year 2000, nearly 30 million people were living with HIV/AIDS, most in sub-Saharan Africa. Almost none of them had access to effective treatment. By 2016, however, 53% of those infected with HIV who needed treatment had access. The number of annual deaths from the disease has been halved, from a peak of 1.9 million in 2005 to 1 million in 2016. The death rate from malaria, a parasitic disease transmitted by mosquitoes that is primarily a killer of poor children living in rural areas of Africa and Asia, dropped 60% between 2000 and 2015. Polio, a viral disease that crippled an estimated 350,000 children worldwide in 1988, is now at the brink of eradication with 37 cases of the disease reported in 2016 and only 11 cases through October 2017. There are many other success stories to tell, including declines in deaths in women during pregnancy and childbirth, an expansion of access to vaccines and a subsequent decline in childhood deaths from vaccine-preventable diseases, and reductions in the numbers of chronically undernourished people worldwide.

JOSHUA MICHAUD *is Associate Director for Global Health Policy at the Kaiser Family Foundation, and Adjunct Lecturer at the Johns Hopkins University School of Advanced International Studies where he teaches courses on global health and development.*

Global health's 'golden age'

A number of key factors coincided to drive the historic health gains that have been made over the last few decades. Together, they brought about what some have called a "golden age" for global health. Unprecedented economic growth has helped lift many out of poverty. In 1990, almost half of the population in developing countries lived on less than $1.25 a day. By 2015, this number had dropped to 14%, even as overall population grew. When incomes rise, governments and households alike typically spend more on health. In addition, rising incomes in developing countries usually bring about improvements in broader social and environmental conditions and in services that affect people's health, such as safe water, sanitation, food security and education. We should note that studies indicate the directionality between health and wealth goes both ways: Better health can drive economic growth; at the same time, rising incomes foster conditions for health improvements.

Even so, health is not predetermined by income level. Poverty explains some, but not nearly all, differences in health outcomes. There is a clear correlation between national income and life expectancy but much variation between countries: There are relatively unhealthy rich countries and relatively healthy poor countries. For example, despite the fact that Americans spend a far greater portion of their national income on health care than any other high-income country, the U.S. does poorly on many health indicators, with a lower life expectancy, relatively high infant mortality rates and very unequal population access to health and medical services. Costa Rica has a higher life expectancy than the U.S. even though its per capita income is one fifth that of the U.S. Ethiopia's life ex-pectancy is five years longer than countries with similar levels of development, while in Peru and Niger, life expectancy is about six years longer than expected from looking at its level of development. Clearly, economic growth does not automatically lead to better health. As Nobel Prize-winning economist Angus Deaton wrote in his book *The Great Escape*, "Income—although important both in and of itself and as a component of wellbeing, and often as a facilitator of other aspects of wellbeing—is not the ultimate cause of wellbeing."

If not economic development alone, what explains the progress we have witnessed? Simply put, there has been a virtuous cycle of 1) better knowledge about health and disease; 2) development of technologies and interventions to address causes of ill health; and 3) political and societal support to implement solutions on a grand scale.

Better understanding of health and disease is a first step. Until the late 20th century, our knowledge about which diseases were having significant impacts in developing countries was limited. Even the most basic measures of health status—population size, age distribution and annual births and deaths—were not available in many areas, let alone a sophisticated understanding about the causes of deaths and illnesses. Subsequent national and international surveys and other studies began to allow for more robust understanding. The U.S. Agency for International Development's (USAID) Demographic and Health Surveys, the World Bank's Global Burden of Disease Project (now housed and overseen at the Institute of Health Metrics and Evaluation in Seattle), along with other public health research, have developed metrics for deaths and illnesses. There is room for improvement (health data is still lacking or of poor quality in many locations), but our growing understanding helps target where interventions are most needed.

The second part of the cycle is the development of new health technologies and interventions. Simple, cost-effective tools to address major health issues have been hallmarks of global health practice. Oral rehydration therapy (ORT) is a simple product used to treat severe dehydration, often stemming from diarrheal disease, which is a common killer of children. Developed in India and Bangladesh in the 1960s and 1970s, ORT was being used in more than 80% of communities across the developing world by 1995. This helped drive yearly deaths from diarrhea down 67% from 1979 to 1999. In the 1980s and 1990s, Vitamin A deficiency was found to contribute to childhood mortality and large-scale supplementation programs were implemented in response. Presently, more than 60 countries implement supplementation programs that reach 80% of children in need, saving about 600,000 children's lives a year and preventing many cases of pediatric blindness. Another important technology has been insecticide-treated bed nets for malaria prevention, distribution of which began to be scaled up in the 2000s. New birth control technologies have made family planning (FP) easier and cheaper in many developing countries.

Medicines have been another key technology for global health. In the 1980s and 1990s, scientists began to formulate antimalarial medications from artemisinin, a compound initially identified through study of traditional Chinese medicine texts. Artemisinin-based combination therapies are now the most important first-line treatment for malaria worldwide. Perhaps the most striking example of the life-saving potential of newly developed medicines can be found in the fight against HIV/AIDS. No truly effective options for treatment were available for the first 15 years of the epidemic. Since 1995, many new antiretroviral compounds have been developed and have proven critical in drastically reducing AIDS mortality.

Arguably no technology has had a more profound effect on global health than vaccines. A vaccine (along with a continual cycle of research and innovation supporting its use) was the essential tool in the eradication of smallpox.

Before you read, download the companion **Glossary** that includes definitions and a guide to acronyms and abbreviations used in the article. Go to **www.great decisions.org** and select a topic in the Resources section on the right-hand side of the page.

This terrible disease killed between 300 and 500 million people in the 20th century; its eradication is considered one of the single greatest achievements in public health, and, indeed, in international cooperation writ large. The U.S. recoups the cost of its investment in eradication every 26 days when you count funds saved from not having to vaccinate or provide care for smallpox. The smallpox vaccine alone has saved more lives than could have been saved by eliminating all wars, genocides and famines in the 20th century *combined*. Other vaccines of note include the core set of childhood vaccines established by the World Health Organization (WHO) in the 1970s: measles, diphtheria, tetanus, pertussis, BCG (tuberculosis vaccine) and polio. Their use has been scaled up over time and together these vaccines avert an estimated 2 to 3 million deaths every year. In 1980, only 16% of kids worldwide were vaccinated against measles; by 2016, cover-

age reached 85% and measles has been eliminated in many countries including the entirety of the Americas. Newer vaccines are being introduced globally, even in the poorest countries. Hepatitis B vaccine coverage grew from 3% in 1992 to 84% in 2016, and vaccines for various forms of pneumonia, diarrhea and human papillomavirus (HPV) are in the process of being integrated into routine immunization schedules.

The third component in the virtuous cycle has been the combination of social activism, political leadership and financial commitments to health at the local, national and international levels. In the post-World War II era, there were many notable campaigns for health causes, including the malaria and smallpox eradication campaigns coordinated by the WHO in the 1960s and 1970s, child survival efforts led by the United Nations (UN) Children's Fund (UNICEF) and influential leaders such as Jim Grant (executive director of UNICEF

from 1980 to 1995), and FP and reproductive health programs supported by the UN Population Fund, USAID and others. Even so, it was the response to HIV/AIDS that marked a real turning point and transformed global health efforts into what they are today.

AIDS was first identified in gay men in the U.S. in the early 1980s. It soon became clear that the condition was also affecting men and women in Central Africa, Haiti and elsewhere. Over the subsequent two decades, HIV/AIDS became a truly global pandemic, spreading to tens of millions of people across all continents. The initial societal and political responses to AIDS were, unfortunately, slow, tepid and marred by stigmatization and fear. Faced with a deadly new infectious disease with no cure or treatment, and with governments that demonstrated little sense of urgency, activists in the U.S. pressured health officials to take greater action. This activist approach was adopted in

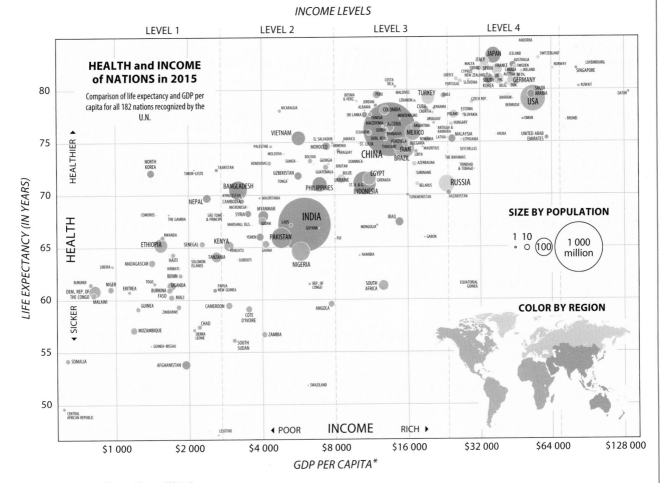

*Dollars adjusted for price differences, PPP 2011)
SOURCES: World Bank (Income); United Nations (Population); IHME GBD-2015 (Life Expectancy); Gapminder.

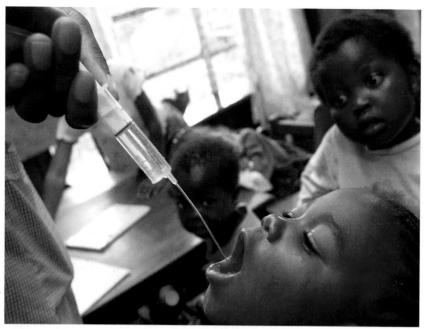

HIV positive children receive liquid AZT as part of their triple drug anti-retroviral (ARV) therapy at Grace Children's Home, an orphanage in Nairobi for HIV/AIDS children, in June 2003. (R.CHALASANI/REPORT DIGITAL-REA/REDUX)

many other countries, and civil society groups helped push for more money and more attention to be directed toward the burgeoning epidemic. These groups were instrumental in forcing governments and pharmaceutical companies to reduce prices on AIDS medications, which dropped from between $10,000 and $15,000 per patient per year in the 1990s, to less than $350 in the 2000s.

Global institutions were initially slow and ineffective in addressing AIDS. The WHO at first mostly ignored the disease as a condition of rich countries, and displayed some of the same prejudice toward the affected as many governments. The WHO's initial Global Program on AIDS (GPA) was founded in 1986. It struggled to find purpose and was seen as ineffective by some as it faced increasing demands and found it difficult to coordinate with the many other burgeoning AIDS programs at other UN and multilateral institutions, such as the World Bank and UNICEF. GPA was eventually shuttered in 1995, and a new UN-wide special agency for AIDS (UNAIDS) was created in 1996. At this point, it had become impossible to ignore the scale of AIDS and the ominous trend lines of the growing epidemic. Politi-

cal leaders began to pay more attention, alarmed by analyses that drew the first links between AIDS and national and international security. The disease came to be viewed not simply as a humanitarian crisis, but as a societal crisis with potentially destabilizing effects across Africa. Worries arose that other countries, like India, China and Russia, would soon experience southern Africa-level rates of the disease. In response, the UN Security Council declared HIV/AIDS a security threat in 2001—the first time a health issue had been the subject of such a declaration.

The combination of activist pressure, alarming epidemiological trends, emerging availability of treatment options and concerns about wider security implications pushed donor countries to address AIDS on a much greater scale. In 2001, UN Secretary General Kofi Annan, supported by many countries, proposed a brand new multilateral funding mechanism to combat AIDS. This eventually became the Global Fund to Fight AIDS, Tuberculosis and Malaria (the Global Fund). The Global Fund has now provided more than $38 billion to affected countries to combat these epidemics. U.S. President George W. Bush (2001–09) surprised many when he used

a 2003 State of the Union speech to declare his intention to commit the U.S. to address AIDS through a new program, the President's Emergency Plan for AIDS Relief (PEPFAR). PEPFAR is now the internationally lauded cornerstone of U.S. support for global health, and has provided over $60 billion to combat HIV/AIDS since 2004.

In parallel with the growing response to HIV/AIDS, many new and notable global health frameworks, actors and approaches were created over the last two decades. The Millennium Development Goals (MDGs) were declared in 2000—eight broad goals for global development that included three goals directly focused on health: MDG 4 (reduce child mortality), MDG 5 (improve maternal health), and MDG 6 (combat HIV/AIDS, malaria and other diseases). These goals served to motivate governments and donors, and set benchmarks to measure progress. (The MDGs were replaced in 2016 by the Sustainable Development Goals.)

Global health became a common theme in high-level political and technical discussions, including the UN General Assembly; the Group of Eight (G-8), G-7 and G-20 meetings; and the World Economic Forum and World Bank annual meetings. A group of private, public and multilateral partners came together to launch the Global Alliance for Vaccines and Immunization (now known as the Gavi Alliance, or simply Gavi) in 2000. Gavi has helped introduce and scale up vaccine use in poor countries, supporting programs that have saved an estimated 9 million children's lives already. After creating PEPFAR, the U.S. government set its sights on malaria, launching the President's Malaria Initiative (PMI) in 2005. Other notable global health programs included new child survival efforts, food security programs and efforts to combat neglected tropical diseases.

The Bill and Melinda Gates Foundation, formally launched in 2000, has been a key entrant into the global health sphere. The former Microsoft CEO and his wife have dedicated much of their time and their fortune to supporting global health, often serving as a catalytic force for new financing, innovation and implementation approaches. Some of the Foundation's priorities have been vaccines (it was instrumental in forming and supporting Gavi), tuberculosis, malaria and other tropical diseases, child survival and FP. The Gates Foundation spends more each year on global health than any government with the exception of the U.S. and Britain; it accounted for almost 8% of all development assistance for health in 2016.

Global efforts have been able to scale up as a result of increased spending on health by donor nations, private philanthropy (such as from the Gates) and domestic governments. The chart below shows the latest estimates for international assistance for global health, which rose from $7 billion in 1990 to over $37 billion in 2016. Domestic resources for health have also been growing. Overall health spending in African Union countries increased more than threefold in ten years, from $30.7 billion in 2001 to $106.6 billion in 2011. UN-AIDS reported in 2016 that the amount of AIDS financing in high-burden countries from domestic sources surpassed that provided by international assistance for the first time that year.

International Assistance For Health Care, 1990-2016

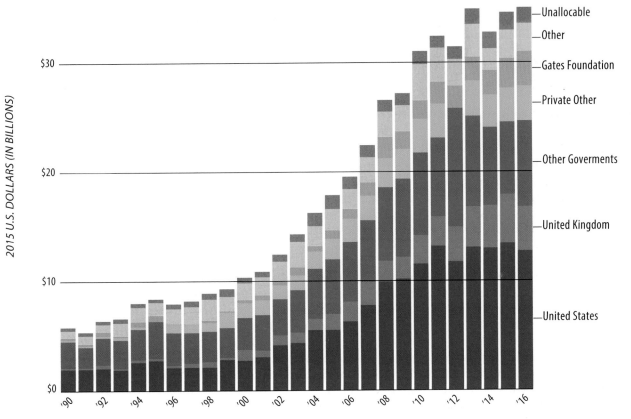

SOURCE: Institute for Health Metrics and Evaluation (IHME) http://ihmeuw.org/42o9

Unfinished business and new challenges

While it is important to recognize the many success stories, now is not the time for the global health community to rest on its laurels. Preventable and curable diseases continue to kill an unconscionable number of people. Cutting childhood deaths by more than half since 1990 is an achievement to celebrate, but some 5.6 million children per year—about 15,000 per day—still die, mostly from preventable causes. More access to treatment has curtailed global deaths from HIV/AIDS, but the number of people newly infected every year is still greater than the number who newly receive treatment, meaning that without further reductions in incidence, the number of people living with the virus will continue to grow. We know from experience that malaria can come roaring back into areas where it has been eliminated if prevention and control measures are eased. Over 800 women a day still die giving birth; most of these deaths are preventable. Such long-standing issues are the "unfinished business" of global health.

At the same time, the world faces a set of new and emerging health challenges. Perhaps foremost is the rise in non-communicable diseases (NCDs), such as cancer, heart disease and diabetes. Cardiovascular disease is now the number one cause of death in all regions of the world except sub-Saharan Africa. Death rates from the most

Epidemics, pandemics and global health security

This year marks the centennial of the deadliest infectious disease pandemic in history, the great influenza of 1918, which infected 500 million people and led to 50 million deaths over the course of 24 months. There is a worry that conditions are ripe for another disease to emerge that could be just as bad—or even worse. Since 1980, we have seen the emergence of many new and deadly diseases, including HIV/AIDS, H5N1 "avi-

Red cross workers, wearing protective suits, carry the body of a person who died from Ebola during a burial with relatives of the victims of the virus, in Monrovia, on January 5, 2015.
(ZOOM DOSSO/AFP/GETTY IMAGES)

an" influenza (1997), severe acute respiratory syndrome (SARS, 2003), H1N1 "swine" influenza (2009), Middle East respiratory syndrome (MERS, 2012), Ebola (2014) and Zika (2016).

It is not by accident that diseases emerge, but rather a consequence of a common set of drivers present in our modern world. Population growth—much of it concentrated in urban areas in developing countries—creates efficient conditions for disease spread. A globalized economy with rapidly increasing trade and transportation links means diseases that emerge in one country can be in any other country within a day. Higher demand for animal protein, changes to agricultural practices and encroachment into previously uninhabited areas lead to more contact between humans and animals. The human-animal link is important because most emerging diseases are of animal origin.

Despite facing outbreak after outbreak, international cooperation to address emerging diseases has a dismal record of accomplishment. As mentioned above, it took international institutions two decades to begin to respond forcefully to HIV/AIDS. During the SARS outbreak, China purposely hid evidence of the disease and initially refused to work with the WHO and international experts. More recently, the international community failed in its early response to the West Africa Ebola epidemic, which ultimately caused 11,000 deaths from a disease that could

common forms of cancer are rising in poor countries while declining in rich ones. Diabetes prevalence more than doubled in sub-Saharan Africa, the Middle East and Southeast Asia between 1980 and 2014, a rate of growth much higher than in Western Europe or North America. Countries with the least capacity to address the rising tide of NCDs are the ones most likely to experience the greatest increases over the next several decades.

When countries make the transition away from high rates of childhood mortality, it is only natural that they begin to confront more diseases of adulthood. Still, there are a number of other factors that are fueling the trend. These present complex challenges for global health. The developing world is adopting unhealthy "Western" lifestyles and diets, with terrible consequences. The top three risk factors contributing to all deaths globally are now high

blood pressure, poor diet and smoking. Being overweight, using alcohol and having high blood glucose (an indicator of diabetes) are also among the top ten health risks worldwide. All of these contribute to rising death and disability from NCDs. A number of inexpensive public health interventions and policies—such as screening for and treating high blood pressure, and eliminating trans fats and reducing sodium levels in food—could save millions of lives from NCDs for little money. Some progress has been made in combatting tobacco use through the Framework Convention on Tobacco Control, a unique public health treaty adopted by many WHO member states, which has in some cases helped reduce the use of tobacco products. Still, in echoes of the early days of HIV, international and national action to broadly tackle NCDs has for the most part been slow and tentative, raising questions

about how (and if) we will turn the tide of these conditions.

Beyond NCDs, there are many other challenges to note. With growing vehicle ownership and poor safety regulations, injuries and deaths from road traffic accidents are a serious health problem. The WHO estimates 90% of all road traffic deaths occur in low- and middle-income countries despite those countries owning only half of all vehicles. Undiagnosed and unchecked depression and other mental health issues are an enormous and growing source of disability: In fact, the WHO estimates depression will be the *number one cause of ill health* in 2030 if current trends continue. Climate change is already negatively affecting people's health by exacerbating existing problems such as malnutrition and transmission of disease, as well as increasing the number of people affected by extreme weather events like heatwaves have been easily contained and prevented with basic public health measures. Back in 2005, 194 countries signed an international agreement [the revised International Health Regulations (IHR)] committing themselves to a set of rules and regulations about how diseases will be detected, reported and managed, and to building a core set of capabilities to prevent, detect and respond to disease outbreaks within a decade. Only one third of countries succeeded in reaching these agreed-upon capacity targets after ten years.

Recognizing these failures, governments, multilateral agencies and other groups have tried to take steps toward building a better global system for addressing epidemic disease threats. Since Ebola, the WHO reorganized and increased funding for its health emergency programs. The World Bank increased spending in this area and in 2017 launched a new Pandemic Emergency Financing Facility intended to provide early, flexible funding for response—something that was not available during Ebola. Governments and international institutions came together in 2014, even before knowledge of the Ebola epidemic, to launch the Global Health Security Agenda, a multi-year partnership designed to mobilize support and provide assistance to help countries build basic public health capacities to address epidemics and bolster compliance with IHR requirements. Over 50 countries have now joined this effort, alongside the WHO, the World Bank, the private sector and civil society. For its part, the U.S. government has ramped up its own spending on global health security from less than $500 million a year before 2014 to several billion in the wake of Ebola, though most of the additional funding is set to expire in 2019 and it is unclear if Congress will continue at this higher level. In 2017, the Gates Foundation, the non-profit biomedical research organization Wellcome Trust, government donors and others launched the Coalition for Epidemic Preparedness Innovations, a public-private partnership designed to spur research and development into vaccines for epidemic-prone diseases.

Despite these positive steps, all agree that major gaps remain and the world is still vulnerable to emerging diseases. In a 2016 report, the U.S. National Academy of Medicine (NAM) estimated that the expected economic costs of future epidemics are on the order of $60 billion a year (to say nothing of the number of lives potentially lost). Yet globally, less than $1 billion a year is spent to address the threat. The NAM report authors state:

A pandemic could kill as many people as a devastating war, yet the resources committed to pandemic prevention and response are a fraction of the resources we commit to security. There are also very few risks that have greater potential for catastrophic economic impact—potentially on the scale of a global financial crisis—but the measures we are taking to avoid another financial crisis are of an entirely different magnitude…This is the neglected dimension of global security.

Only a more proactive, well-financed and sustained effort can keep the world safe from emerging infections and save us from another terrible pandemic like the 1918 influenza.

and hurricanes. The expectation is that these effects will grow with time.

Another troubling issue is the increasing risk posed by emerging epidemic and pandemic diseases in a world that appears unable to prevent or effectively respond to them. One aspect of this threat is the phenomenon of microbes becoming increasingly resistant to common forms of treatment. For example, the number of multi-drug resistant and extensively drug-resistant tuberculosis cases is growing in many parts of the world, and malaria parasites resistant to our last effective treatment options are now spreading across Southeast Asia. Many common bacterial infections are increasingly resistant to antibiotics, raising the specter that we could someday enter a "post-antibiotic era" in which no effective treatment would exist for infections following surgeries or even for simple infected cuts.

Unequal is unhealthy

Why are we facing this dual agenda of combatting old and new global health challenges at the same time? A major reason is that the quality and availability of health care is highly unequal. Rich countries have a relative abundance of medical professionals, hospitals and clinics delivering quality care, while poor countries do not. Globally, the world needs 2.6 million more doctors and 9 million more nurses and midwives, mostly in Africa and Asia, to meet basic health care needs. In addition, many people cannot access health care in times of need due to lack of insurance or other difficulties in paying for care. 40% of people worldwide and 80% of people in poor countries do not have access to healthcare without financial hardship.

We see the effects of this inequality in health outcomes. Life expectancy may have improved on average worldwide, but there remains a massive 34-year gap between the country with the highest (Japan, 84 years in 2015) and the lowest (Sierra Leone, 50 years) life expectancies. A child born in sub-Saharan Africa is over 15 times more likely to die before their fifth birthday than one born in Western Europe. Inequality and poverty worsen the impact of NCDs. Conditions that are manageable in rich countries can be death sentences in poor countries that lack access to proper prevention, care and treatment. Huge inequalities in health exist *within* countries, too. In the U.S. for example, there is a 15-year gap in life expectancy between men living in the richest areas compared with those in the poorest—the same difference in life expectancy seen between the U.S. as a whole and the country of Sudan.

Similar gaps between the richest and poorest are apparent in other populous countries, including China, India, Brazil, Nigeria and Indonesia.

Our success in addressing some diseases has masked much slower progress in building health systems that make quality basic health care available to all those who need it. There has been a decades-long tension in global health between delivering programs targeted to a specific condition (the "vertical" approach) and building up basic health care services (the "horizontal" approach). Since 1980, most programs and funding in global health have been channeled to specific diseases, not primary care systems. We have had great success in addressing polio, HIV, malaria and vaccine-preventable diseases, but relatively little attention and funding have gone to health system capacities. At times, this has distorted health care priorities and quality. Some targeted programs have even drawn health workers and other resources away from countries' public systems into (typically) better paying private positions that support disease-specific efforts. Programs are more cognizant of this issue now and have made adjustments, but the tension still exists between disease-specific and health system approaches in global health.

In one effort to address the long-standing neglect of health systems, we have seen in recent years a growing movement in support of the idea of universal health coverage (UHC). UHC is meant to ensure that no one is excluded from health care for cost reasons, and that every individual has access to a package of quality essential health services. Achieving this ambitious goal will require countries to invest more (and more effectively) in their health systems and social protection. While there has been a strong movement toward UHC, there is little evidence so far that donors are shifting from disease-specific to health systems assistance. In 2015, only about 7% of development assistance for health, or $2.7 billion out of $38 billion in total assistance, was for systems strengthening.

The innovation gap and access to medicines

As described above, much of the success of global health programs has stemmed from research and development (R&D) for prevention and treatment tools like vaccines, drugs and diagnostics. But a major gap exists between health R&D needs in developing countries and the amount spent on addressing those needs. The pharmaceutical and medical device sectors are mostly private and market-driven, meaning that decisions about how and where to invest in R&D are based on an expected return. New drugs or diagnostics for diseases affecting the poor provide little incentive for companies, which leads to market failure. Of the estimated $159 billion spent globally on health R&D by private companies in 2016, only $471 million (<0.3%) was spent on R&D for neglected diseases of the developing world, including malaria, tuberculosis and diarrhea, even though these are responsible for a disproportionate amount of the disease burden there.

As it currently stands, most spending on neglected R&D comes from public (wealthy country governments) and philanthropic sources. In fact, just two sources—the U.S. National Institutes of Health and the Gates Foundation—comprised over half of all funding for such R&D in 2015. The gap in funding has major consequences for the development of relevant products. Less than 5% of 850 therapeutic products newly registered between 2000 and 2011 were for diseases mostly affecting poor countries. A similar market failure impedes the development of new antibiotics. The WHO has even recently said that the world is "running out of antibiotics" and has made a call for increased investments specifically for R&D in this area. To address the gaps, many have advocated for more government and philanthropic funding for neglected R&D, or the adoption of "innovative financing mechanisms" to draw in additional funding and speed develop-

ment. Without a sizeable increase in funding of one form or another, the innovation gap is likely to remain.

Poor countries also face difficulties in accessing already existing medicines. Under current multilateral trading rules, such as the 1994 Trade-Related Aspects of Intellectual Property (IP) Rights (known as the TRIPS agreement), companies that develop pharmaceutical products are provided global patent protection for their innovations with a period of monopoly pricing power to provide a return and offset R&D costs. Patented products, as opposed to generics, are often expensive, which can leave them out of reach of people in poor countries. Advocates have fought for certain flexibilities in IP rules to be recognized for medicines that are critical to address major public health problems, but the flexibilities are not routinely used and often contested when they are.

We have already seen a showdown regarding access to HIV medications, when activists and developing country governments fought pharmaceutical companies for cheaper access to antiretroviral therapies. The next great access to medicines battle might revolve around drugs for NCDs. Following the model pioneered for HIV, some groups have already been successful in negotiating for expanded access to some affordable NCD medicines. For example, two major pharmaceutical companies and the American Cancer Society recently announced a deal to drastically reduce the price of 16 chemotherapy medications for poor countries in Africa. Egypt, a country shouldering a huge burden from Hepatitis C, has recently reached agreement with the maker of a breakthrough Hepatitis C drug to distribute the medicine there at a fraction of its cost in the U.S. Even so, governments and companies continue to fight to maintain strong patent protection for pharmaceutical products, setting up future battles over access and cost.

Social and political challenges

Protesters march by the White House during a rally to support women's health programs and protest the global "gag rule" on March 8, 2017, in Washington, DC. (JUSTIN SULLIVAN/ GETTY IMAGES)

Global health efforts can come up against obstacles when interventions are seen as taboo or clash with cultural or social norms and values. HIV transmission is often concentrated in high-risk groups engaging in behaviors that are stigmatized or even criminalized, including sex work, injection drug use and sex between men. Addressing HIV requires programs that work with and for these groups, a challenging prospect in many countries due to existing social norms and beliefs, if not outright prejudice. FP programs have proven contentious at times as well. Providing access to contraceptives and discussing sex and sexuality can be controversial. FP assistance is a perennial hot-button issue for the U.S. government because policymakers tie these programs to U.S. domestic abortion politics.

Each Republican president since Ronald Reagan (1981–89) has instituted a regulation known as the Mexico City Policy (sometimes called the "global gag rule" by its opponents), which blocks foreign aid to non-governmental organizations that provide information about abortion as part of FP, or that advocate for abortion rights, regardless of whether funding for those services comes from the

U.S. This policy is in addition to the many other U.S. laws that already restrict support for abortion-related activities using U.S. foreign assistance funding. Recently, the Donald Trump administration announced that it was expanding the policy to encompass all global health financing; previous versions of the policy only applied to FP program funding specifically. The details of implementation for the policy are still being determined, and already some organizations have said they will be ending certain activities because of the new policy, raising concerns among some about the policy's future effects on global health.

Yet another challenge is providing access to services in areas of conflict and instability. Ongoing civil wars, insurgencies and other violent conflicts in Afghanistan, Nigeria, Pakistan, South Sudan, Syria, Yemen and elsewhere have significant public health effects, including precipitating outbreaks of diseases such as polio and cholera. Yemen in 2017 experienced the largest cholera epidemic in modern history: Over three quarters of a million people were infected and more than 2,000 died from this entirely preventable disease as a result of the circumstances created by the conflict. Overall direct deaths from conflict and violence have more than doubled in ten years, from 60,000 in 2006 to more than 150,000 in 2016. In Syria, life expectancy dropped by *20 years* over the four years since the start of the conflict there. Conflict interrupts health services and disrupts health systems within a country. It also generates refugees whose health must be addressed.

The recent trend of violence targeting health workers and health facilities is especially troubling. According to data collected by the WHO, from January 2014 through December 2015, there were 594 reported attacks on health care facilities, which resulted in 959 deaths and 1,561 injuries across 19 countries. These attacks are a clear, disturbing violation of the Geneva Conventions and humanitarian law, and therefore represent war crimes of the highest order. Instability and violence are the number one reason why the world has not yet completed eradication of polio, the billion-dollar-a-year effort that was launched 30 years ago. The only two countries never to have interrupted transmission of the disease are Afghanistan and Pakistan. Insurgents there have specifically targeted and killed polio vaccinators, and ongoing instability has made access to polio vaccination difficult and dangerous.

The search for solutions: governance and financing of global health in the next generation

Given the numerous, daunting issues facing global health, it is natural to seek someone or something to lead the charge in completing the unfinished agenda and tackling emerging challenges. In reality, no one agency or

organization can take responsibility for transforming global health to address all these issues.

The WHO might seem a good candidate to lead the charge. After all, the constitution of the WHO states that the agency is empowered to be "the directing and coordinating authority on international health work." It is true that the WHO is important for global health, especially as a source of technical guidance and best practices. As a political body, it is able to convene member states for important multilateral policy discussions. Its advice is heeded in many countries, and its support is usually respected. The reality is, though, that the agency is quite limited in its resources and powers. The WHO is chronically underfunded in relation to its responsibilities, with an annual budget of around $2 billion—equivalent to the budget of the New York City Health Department—and a remit that covers all health everywhere. The U.S. government's annual HIV budget through PEPFAR alone is over two times the total budget for the WHO. In addition, over three quarters of the WHO's budget is earmarked for specific projects by donors, over which the agency has little ability to redirect. This often leaves it hamstrung and inflexible when global health needs and priorities shift quickly.

The WHO is a beast of a bureaucracy, with a headquarters in Geneva, six autonomous regional offices (each with their own directors and budgets) and over 150 country offices and representatives. It has a reputation as an organization where staff placement and promotion are based more on patronage and political considerations than technical competence. It has a spotty—some might say poor—record of accomplishment over the last 30 years. This reputation was further tarnished in the wake of the WHO's universally derided response to the West Africa Ebola outbreak. When major global health crises have emerged, responsibilities often seem to have been moved out of the WHO and into the hands of a different UN system entity (at least temporarily). This occurred, for instance, when the GPA was shuttered and UNAIDS created in 1996, when the UN Influenza Coordinator was created in 2006 and when the UN Ebola Response Coordinator was created in 2014. Steps taken at the WHO to reform since 2012, accelerated following the experience with Ebola, appear to be moving it in a more positive direction. Still, many concerns about the agency remain. Without radical transformation, the WHO will not be in a position to lead major changes in global health.

Another important, long-standing global health institution is the World Bank. Indeed, the Bank has been a larger source of health funding than the WHO since 1994. It occupies a unique position in that it advises and supports ministries of finance, whose decisions are often more consequential for health than those made by ministries of health themselves. For many years, global health proponents criticized the Bank for imposing "structural adjustment" and other policies that drained public funding out of the health sector in developing countries, and for imposing user fees in the health system that effectively barred the poorest and most vulnerable populations from accessing care in some cases. More recently, the Bank has moved away from these controversial policies, and has championed UHC. It has focused an increasing amount of attention and funding on health, especially since Jim Kim, a medical doctor and long-time global health activist and practitioner, became president of the institution in 2012. The Bank is now an important source for and overseer of innovative financing in health, from trust funds and special bond programs, to a newly developed insurance instrument for pandemic response. Even so, health lending still comprises a small portion of the Bank's portfolio and responsibilities, and its comparative advantage lies in its financial and technical capacity and its network of influence and relationships, rather than globally transformative leadership in the health sector.

Donor governments are also important actors in global health. The U.S. government is by far the largest donor to global health programs, and it greatly increased support for global health between 2001 and 2009. However, U.S. support for global health has plateaued since the economic crisis of 2008–09, reflecting a new environment in Washington of fiscal constraint and pressure on the federal budget. Bipartisan support in Congress remains strong for global health, so related programs have avoided cuts seen in other areas of foreign assistance in recent years.

Nevertheless, there are concerns

The new World Health Organization (WHO) director general, Ethiopia's Tedros Adhanom Ghebreyesus (L), reacts after his election, in front of the outgoing director general, China's Margaret Chan, during the World Health Assembly (WHA) on May 23, 2017, in Geneva. (FABRICE COFFRINI/AFP/GETTY IMAGES) about future financing. The Trump administration's most recent budget proposal at the time of writing would cut global health spending by 25%. This would have potentially serious consequences for U.S. programs and the health of the populations served by U.S. assistance. Few believe Congress would enact cuts of that magnitude, but the potential for significant cuts to global health budgets — something that had not seriously been contemplated for more than 10 years — appears to be on the table. Going ahead with such cuts goes against prevailing U.S. public opinion. According to national polling, most Americans (including a majority of Republicans, Independents and Democrats) believe the U.S. should play a major role in improving health for people in developing countries. Americans believe, most of all, that doing so is the morally correct thing to do, over and above diplomatic or national security benefits that might accrue from such efforts. The U.S. remains an important voice and force in global health, though the next few years will indicate whether and how much the country will change its approach.

Other donor nations have also had flat, or even lower, assistance for global health over the last several years, raising concerns about "donor fatigue." Sustained support from national donors through bilateral programs such as PEPFAR and PMI, and multilateral mechanisms such as the Global Fund and Gavi, are especially important to completing the unfinished agenda. Given the trend toward flat or decreasing budgets even for existing programs, few expect major increases in donor assistance for the emerging set of health challenges (for instance, NCDs), or dramatically increased support for R&D for neglected diseases, despite clear needs in these (and other) areas.

In the absence of major increases in foreign assistance funding from governments, global health proponents are increasingly looking to a model that creates partnerships between governments and the private sector to help fill the gaps. Such public-private partnerships (PPPs) have already had a major

Microsoft founder and philanthropist Bill Gates speaks at the Global Alliance for Vaccines and Immunisation (GAVI) conference in London, June 13, 2011. (PAUL HACKETT, POOL/AP PHOTO)

impact in global health: Gavi and the Global Fund, for example, both integrate the private sector into their management structures and bring in private funding along with public funding. The Gates Foundation has been at the center of many of these efforts, including helping to create a number of R&D-focused PPPs looking for innovations to tackle malaria, tuberculosis, NCDs and other conditions. Many welcome the increased presence of private companies. There is a perception that the private sector has a comparative advantage over the public sector when it comes to problem-solving, innovation, management, logistics and communication — and there does seem to be a need in global health in these very areas.

However, there are downsides to an increased private sector role. The addition of more private actors and entities to the already large pool of actors overall makes the management and governance of global health efforts that much more difficult. Further, the interests of the private sector and those of global health do not always align. In fact, there are times when the private sector can actually be an antagonist, with companies standing in the way of achieving global health goals. The clearest example of this is in the area of tobacco: Public health advocates seek restrictions and taxes on tobacco products,

while tobacco companies, corporate lobbyists and governments with strong ties to tobacco companies fight such efforts. The gaze of global health is now turning to other private companies that support so-called "public bads," such as food and beverage companies distributing unhealthy food and drinks, and fast-food chains providing cheap but unhealthy meals to a growing number of people in the developing world. Reconciling the sometimes competing interests between the commercial sector and the public health sector will continue to be a challenge.

The combined efforts of different types of actors will determine wellbeing across nations in the coming decades. Governments in developing countries themselves are going to be essential to financing and overseeing the development of their health systems and the push toward UHC. Prevention saves lives and money, but it can be a notoriously hard sell when budgets are tight, so high level political support will be needed. Civil society will also be critical, and can help advocate for, and monitor the implementation of, effective health policy and interventions at the community, national and international levels. In the end, further success will be the outcome of the same virtuous cycle approach, and of the combined purposeful action of all of these groups.

discussion questions

1. Universal Health Coverage (UHC) is one proposed approach to addressing the long-standing issues and emerging challenges facing global health in the 21st century. What are the arguments for taking a health systems approach as opposed to a disease-specific approach?

2. In 2001, the UN Security Council declared HIV/AIDS a security issue—the first time a health issue was the subject of such a declaration. Why think about global health issues from a security perspective? Should the U.S. Congress continue global health funding at current levels, considering spending was raised from $500 million in 2014 to several billion in the wake of Ebola?

3. The World Health Organization (WHO) was criticized for its ineffective and inefficient response to the Ebola outbreak in West Africa. Consider international organizations concerned with global health issues—the WHO, the UN, the World Bank and others. What are the unique advantages that large multilateral institutions have when it comes to addressing global health? What are their deficiencies?

4. The richest and poorest domestic populations in the United States and elsewhere experience significant gaps in life expectancy. What policies might countries adopt to reduce inequalities in health?

5. While the U.S. remains the top donor to global health policy initiatives worldwide, the Donald Trump administration has proposed major cuts to the global health budget. What would a decline in U.S. funding mean for global health governance?

6. It took a grassroots, civil society movement to transcend stigma and garner a political response to the HIV/AIDS pandemic. Has the global health regime responded adequately to more recent pandemics and epidemics, such as the H1N1 virus, or Zika and Ebola? What roles should governments, multilateral institutions and civil society play to ensure that future epidemics and pandemics are addressed with maximal efficiency on the policy level?

suggested readings

Bollyky, Thomas J., Daniels, Mitchell E., Jr., Donilon, Thomas E. and Tuttle, Christopher M., **The Emerging Global Health Crisis: Noncommunicable Diseases in Low- and Middle-Income Countries**. 114 pp. Council on Foreign Relations Press, December 2014. Available free online: <http://www.cfr.org/diseases-noncommunicable/emerging-global-health-crisis/p33883>. This report looks into the factors behind the burgeoning epidemic of noncommunicable diseases and outlines methods for the U.S. to combat the problem.

Deaton, Angus, **The Great Escape: Health, Wealth, and the Origins of Inequality (Reprint ed.)**. 376 pp. Princeton, NJ: Princeton University Press, 2013. Drawing on hundreds of years of data, Deaton provides a comprehensive overview of links between economic growth and health status, as well as the consequences of ongoing health inequality.

Foege, William H., **House on Fire: The Fight to Eradicate Smallpox (Reprint ed.)**. 240 pp. Berkeley, CA: University of California Press, 2011. Foege, who helped lead the global campaign against smallpox, describes the effort to rid the world of one of the deadliest scourges in human history.

France, David, **How to Survive a Plague: The Inside Story of How Citizens and Science Tamed AIDS (1st ed.)**. 640 pp. New York: Knopf, 2016. Investigative reporter David France tells the story of how a small grassroots movement brought about the global response to the HIV pandemic.

Kidder, Tracy, **Mountains Beyond Mountains: The Quest of Dr. Paul Farmer, a Man Who Would Cure the World (Reprint ed.)**. 332 pp. New York: Random House Trade Paperbacks, 2009. This account is a portrait of global health visionary and physician Paul Farmer and his work to bring quality health care to rural Haiti and other impoverished areas of the world.

McNeil, William H., **Plagues and Peoples**. 368 pp. Norwell, MA: Anchor, 1976. McNeil, a historian, provides a sweeping exploration of the effects that health and disease have had on the course of human history across the globe, from antiquity to modern times.

Oshinsky, David M., **Polio: An American Story (1st ed)**. 368 pp. New York: Oxford University Press, 2006. Oshinsky reviews the efforts to find a vaccine to address polio, one of the most feared public health threats of the 20th century.

Spinney, Laura, **Pale Rider: The Spanish Flu of 1918 and How It Changed the World (1st ed.)**. 352 pp. New York: PublicAffairs, 2017. This book examines the truly global effects of the 1918 influenza pandemic.

Don't forget: Ballots start on page 105!

To access web links to these readings, as well as links to additional, shorter readings and suggested web sites,

GO TO www.greatdecisions.org

and click on the topic under Resources, on the right-hand side of the page

Global Discussion Questions

No decision in foreign policy is made in a vacuum, and the repercussions of any single decision have far-reaching effects across the range of strategic interests on the U.S. policy agenda. This GREAT DECISIONS feature is intended to facilitate the discussion of this year's topics in a global context, to discuss the linkages between the topics and to encourage consideration of the broader impact of decision-making.

1. Consider "China and America" in the context of "U.S. global engagement and the military." China has continued to cooperate with North Korea in trade and other forms of assistance, even as the nuclear threat from Pyongyang mounts and tensions rise between the Trump administration and Kim Jong Un's regime. How can the U.S. balance its relationship with China at the same time that it seeks to rein in North Korea's nuclear and missile programs?

2. Consider "Turkey" in the context of "South Africa's fragile democracy." What are the parallels between the AKP in Turkey and the ANC in South Africa? What do their transitions from political movements to long-standing ruling parties say about how democracy has evolved in each country? As Turkish President Erdoğan and South African President Zuma seek to consolidate control over their respective political systems, what obstacles are they erecting to strong democratic systems?

3. Consider "Global health" in the context of "South Africa's fragile democracy." Protest movements have played a crucial role in inciting political change in South Africa, including in drawing attention to the South African HIV/AIDS crisis. What role does civil society play in addressing global health challenges, not only in South Africa, but elsewhere? In what ways are pandemics and epidemics politicized and how can different actors work to find solutions and enact real change?

4. Consider "Turkey" in the context of "U.S. global engagement and the military." Rapprochement between Turkey and Russia poses a threat to U.S. interests in the Syrian civil war, as does Turkey's support of the Syrian regime and radical Islamist groups fighting the Syrian Kurds. How does the web of interests in this region affect the ability of Turkey and the U.S. to achieve their respective goals? How does the current state of U.S.-Turkey relations affect prospects for improving the humanitarian situation and combatting terrorism in Syria?

5. Consider "Media and foreign policy" in the context of "The waning of Pax Americana?" Today, emerging forms of communication pose new challenges and opportunities for protecting democracy and free speech in the U.S. and around the world. How can new media and technologies assist in bolstering free speech and democratic values? What hand should the government have in the new media landscape?

Questions continue on the next page...

6. Consider "China and America" in the context of "The waning of Pax Americana?" What is the future of the postwar international order and its central institutions (the UN, the EU, the IMF and the World Bank, e.g.) in the face of new multilateral bodies in which China plays a central role (the Asian Infrastructure Investment Bank, the Shanghai Cooperation Organization and the BRICS grouping, e.g.)?

7. Consider "Russia's foreign policy" in the context of "Turkey." Europe's two largest neighbors, Russia and Turkey, are both illiberal democracies. Their proximity to, but exclusion from, the EU creates some opportunities for cooperation (the EU-Turkey refugee deal), but also stirs conflict (Russia's disputed annexation of Crimea and the ongoing conflict in eastern Ukraine). What is at stake for Russian and Turkish national security and regional interests given their geographic proximity to the EU? How are the two countries attempting to counterbalance the EU?

8. Consider "Russia's foreign policy" in the context of "Media and foreign policy." While Russian interference in the 2016 U.S. presidential election was verified in a joint report by the FBI, CIA and NSA, it was also established that the actions in question did not impact electoral results. What strategic goals did the Kremlin accomplish and what are the broader implications of this type of foreign election meddling for U.S. policy on social media regulation and cybersecurity?

9. Consider "Global health" in the context of "The waning of Pax Americana?" Despite global health's "golden age," problems in multilateral organizations create fundamental obstacles to addressing ongoing and newly emerging issues. What reform(s) might be enacted to tackle inefficiencies within the global health regime that obstruct progress? How would the Trump administration's recent budget proposal, which seeks to cut 23% of global health spending, affect the global health landscape?

10. Consider "Russia's foreign policy" in the context of "U.S. global engagement and the military." After Russia annexed the Crimean peninsula in 2014 and began an armed conflict in Ukraine's east, the U.S. and EU have enacted sanctions against Russia in lieu of a direct military response. What questions does Russian aggression in Ukraine raise for NATO, which manages crises and aims to maintain peace and security around the world? What are the pros and cons of sanctions against Russia as opposed to military intervention? What other options might the U.S. have to de-escalate the situation in Ukraine?

For glossaries, additional readings and more, visit
www.GreatDecisions.org

About the balloting process...

Dear Great Decisions Participants,

As you may already know, my name is Dr. Lauren Prather and I have been working with the Foreign Policy Association (FPA) for the last four years on the National Opinion Ballot (NOB). A version of this letter has appeared in previous briefing books, so I'm only writing a quick hello this year.

My research is primarily focused on international relations. I am a faculty member at the School of Global Policy and Strategy at the University of California, San Diego (UCSD) and have research projects on a range of public opinion topics, from foreign aid to climate change to national security issues. I also teach a class on public opinion and foreign policy for my university.

One of the key difficulties in my research is that the public is often uniformed or misinformed about the topics. This is where you come in! The Great Decisions participants continue to be some of the most informed Americans about foreign policy issues, and the NOB is the perfect opportunity to voice those opinions.

The NOB is also one of the only public opinion surveys in the United States that attempts to gather the opinions of the educated public. Thus, it has great value to researchers and policymakers alike. Some of the questions in which researchers are interested include the following:

- Are the opinions of the educated public significantly different from those of the average American?
- How does public opinion about foreign policy change over time?
- How does public opinion on one foreign policy issue relate to public opinion on other foreign policy issues? For example, are people who support U.S. government policies to mitigate climate change more or less willing to support drilling in the Arctic?
- How do different segments of the population, men or women, liberals or conservatives, view foreign policy choices?

In order to answer the types of questions researchers are interested in, such as how do people's opinions change over time, the NOB needs to have certain attributes. We need to have a way to organize the ballots by participant across all topics. That way, we know, for example, how participant #47 responded to the question about climate change mitigation and how he or she responded to the question about drilling, even if those were in different topics in the NOB. Your random ID number is the **only thing** connected to your responses and **never** your e-mail address. In fact, as a researcher, I must receive the approval of my Institutional Review Board by demonstrating that your data will be protected at all times, and that your responses will be both confidential and anonymous.

If you have any questions or comments, I am always happy to respond via e-mail at LPrather@ucsd. edu. To learn more about my research and teaching, you can visit my website at www.laurenprather.org.

Thank you again to everyone who has participated in the NOB over the years. I have learned a tremendous amount about your foreign policy views and it has greatly informed my own research. In the future, I hope to communicate to the scholarly world and policy communities how the educated American public thinks about foreign policy.

Sincerely,

Lauren Prather

2018 National Opinion Ballot

First, we'd like to ask you for some information about your participation in the Great Decisions program. If you are not currently a Great Decisions program member, please skip to the "background" section.

How long have you participated in the Great Decisions program (i.e., attended one or more discussion sessions)?

❏ This is the first year I have participated

❏ I participated in one previous year

❏ I participated in more than one previous year

How did you learn about the Great Decisions Program?

❏ Word of mouth

❏ Local library

❏ Foreign Policy Association website

❏ Promotional brochure

❏ Other organization _____

Where does your Great Decisions group meet?

❏ Private home

❏ Library

❏ Community center

❏ Learning in retirement

❏ Other _____

How many hours, on average, do you spend reading one Great Decisions chapter?

❏ Less than 1 hour

❏ 1–2 hours

❏ 3–4 hours

❏ More than 4 hours

Would you say you have or have not changed your opinion in a fairly significant way as a result of taking part in the Great Decisions program?

❏ Have

❏ Have not

❏ Not sure

Background Section: Next, we'd like to ask you some information about your background.

How strongly do you agree or disagree with the following statement? Although the media often reports about national and international events and developments, this news is seldom as interesting as the things that happen directly in our own community and neighborhood.

❏ Agree strongly

❏ Agree somewhat

❏ Neither agree nor disagree

❏ Disagree somewhat

❏ Disagree strongly

Generally speaking, how interested are you in politics?

❏ Very much interested

❏ Somewhat interested

❏ Not too interested

❏ Not interested at all

Do you think it is best for the future of the United States if the U.S. takes an active role in world affairs or stays out of world affairs?

❏ Takes an active role in world affairs

❏ Stays out of world affairs

How often are you asked for your opinion on foreign policy?

❏ Often

❏ Sometimes

❏ Never

Have you been abroad during the last two years?

❏ Yes

❏ No

Do you know, or are you learning, a foreign language?

❏ Yes

❏ No

Do you have any close friends or family that live in other countries?

❏ Yes

❏ No

Do you donate to any charities that help the poor in other countries?

❏ Yes

❏ No

Generally speaking, do you usually think of yourself as a Republican, a Democrat, an Independent or something else?

❏ Republican

❏ Democrat

❏ Independent

❏ Other _____

With which gender do you most identify?

❏ Male

❏ Female

❏ Transgender male

❏ Transgender female

❏ Gender variant/non-conforming

❏ Other _____

❏ Prefer not to answer

What race do you consider yourself?

❏ White/Caucasian

❏ Black/African American

❏ Hispanic/Latino

❏ Asian American

❏ Native American

❏ Other _____

❏ Prefer not to answer

Were you born in the United States or another country?

❏ United States

❏ Another country

Are you a citizen of the United States, another country, or are you a citizen of both the United States and another country?

❏ United States

❏ Another country

❏ United States and another country

How important is religion in your life?

❏ Very important

❏ Somewhat important

❏ Not too important

❏ Not at all important

What is your age?   _____

Are you currently employed?

❏ Full-time employee

❏ Part-time employee

❏ Self-employed

❏ Unemployed

❏ Retired

❏ Student

❏ Homemaker

What are the first three digits of your zip code? (This will allow us to do a state-by-state breakdown of results.)

_____   _____   _____

Can you give us an estimate of your household income in 2017 before taxes?

❏ Below $30,000

❏ $30,000–$50,000

❏ $50,000–$75,000

❏ $75,000–$100,000

❏ $100,000–$150,000

❏ Over $150,000

❏ Not sure

❏ Prefer not to say

What is the highest level of education you have completed?

❏ Did not graduate from high school

❏ High school graduate

❏ Some college, but no degree (yet)

❏ 2-year college degree

❏ 4-year college degree

❏ Some postgraduate work, but no degree (yet)

❏ Post-graduate degree (MA, MBA, MD, JD, PhD, etc.)

Now we would like to ask you some ballot questions from previous years:

1. From 2016's "Nuclear security": How likely do you think it is that the U.S. will experience a nuclear terrorist attack in the near future?

❏ Very likely

❏ Somewhat likely

❏ Not too likely

❏ Not likely at all

2. From 2015's "The future of Kurdistan": To what extent do you support or oppose the Turkish government's bombing of Kurdish regions in Turkey against militants fighting for independence?

❏ Strongly support

❏ Somewhat support

❏ Neither support nor oppose

❏ Somewhat oppose

❏ Strongly oppose

3. From 2013's "Turkey's challenges": How likely or not do you think it is that Turkey will join the European Union?

❏ Very likely

❏ Somewhat likely

❏ Not too likely

❏ Not likely at all

4. From 2011's "Promoting democracy": In your opinion, which method of promoting democracy is the most appropriate unilateral U.S. strategy?

❏ Diplomacy

❏ Sanctions (includes conditional aid)

❏ Democracy assistance in the form of funding, training, organizing, etc.

❏ Military force

5. From 2011's "Cybersecurity": Which of the following is the most compelling argument for cyberspace governance?

❏ The proliferation of internationalized cybercrime

❏ The incidence of "political" cyber-attacks (e.g. pro-nationalist hackers)

❏ The impact of cyber activity on foreign and military policy

❏ The possibility of a cyber "arms race" in the near future

❏ Other

6. From 2010's "Caucasus": Please indicate whether you agree or disagree with the following statement: U.S. relations with the regional powers, Russia and Turkey, are more important and should have priority over relations with other states in the region.

❏ Strongly agree

❏ Agree

❏ Disagree

❏ Strongly disagree

7. From 2013's "Trade": People debate whether the U.S. government should increase restrictions on imports, keep restrictions on imports at current levels or decrease restrictions on imports. What do you think the U.S. government should do?

❏ Increase restrictions on imports

❏ Keep restrictions on imports at current levels

❏ Decrease restrictions on imports

8. From 2002's "Alone or together: the U.S. and the world": Overall, have organizations such as the World Bank, the International Monetary Fund and the World Trade Organization done more good than harm for poor nations?

❏ More good

❏ More harm

❏ Both equally

9. From 2013's "Defense technology": Do you think the U.S. government should increase, maintain or decrease the amount of money it spends on programs to develop new defense technologies?

❏ Increase the amount

❏ Maintain the current amount

❏ Decrease the amount

10. From 2009's "The global financial crisis and its effects": Which of the following statements best describes the future U.S. role in the world?

❏ The U.S. will remain the dominant power for the next 10 years

❏ The U.S. will remain the dominant power for the foreseeable future

❏ The U.S. is no longer the dominant global power

11. From 2007's "U.S.-China economic relations": In terms of the U.S., do you see China's surging economy as:

❏ A threat, taking jobs from the U.S.

❏ A boon, providing cheap goods to the U.S.

❏ Both

12. From 2007's "Russia and 'Putinism'": Considering the following, do you believe that, as a matter of policy, the U.S. should:

12.1 Actively seek a closer and more stable relationship with Russia?

❑ Yes

❑ No

12.2 Attempt to have friendly relations with the former Russian republics but avoid meddling in Moscow's 'sphere of influence'?

❑ Yes

❑ No

12.3 Make strong efforts to establish close ties to those former Russian republics that could be most use to the U.S. for security reasons or to promote stable access to fossil fuels for the U.S. and its European allies?

❑ Yes

❑ No

13. From 2014's "Syria's Refugee Crisis": In general, do you support or oppose Western countries sending arms and military supplies to anti-government groups in Syria?

❑ Support strongly

❑ Support somewhat

❑ Oppose somewhat

❑ Oppose strongly

❑ Not sure

Topic 1. The waning of Pax Americana?

1. Have you engaged in any of the following activities related to the "Waning of Pax Americana?" topic? Mark all that you have done or mark none of the above.

❑ Read the article on Pax Americana in the 2018 Great Decisions briefing book

❑ Discussed the article on Pax Americana with a Great Decisions discussion group

❑ Discussed the article on Pax Americana with friends and family

❑ Followed news related to Pax Americana

❑ Taken a class in which you learned about issues related to Pax Americana

❑ Have or had a job related to Pax Americana

❑ None of the above

2. How interested would you say you are in issues related to Pax Americana?

❑ Very interested

❑ Somewhat interested

❑ Not too interested

❑ Not at all interested

3. What kind of leadership role should the United States play in the world? Should it be the dominant world leader, play a shared leadership role or not play any leadership role?

❑ Dominant world leader

❑ Shared leadership role

❑ Should not play any leadership role

4. Do you believe that globalization, especially the increasing connections of the U.S. economy with others around the world, is mostly good or mostly bad for the United States?

❑ Mostly good

❑ Mostly bad

5. Which of the following comes closest to your view on international agreements between the United States and other countries?

❑ They mostly benefit the United States

❑ They mostly benefit other countries

❑ They benefit both the United States and other countries

❑ They benefit neither

6. How effective do you think each of the following approaches is to achieving the foreign policy goals of the United States?

6.1. International agreements

❑ Very effective

❑ Somewhat effective

❑ Not too effective

❑ Not effective at all

6.2. Participating in international organizations

❑ Very effective

❑ Somewhat effective

❑ Not too effective

❑ Not effective at all

6.3. Signing free trade agreements with other countries

❏ Very effective

❏ Somewhat effective

❏ Not too effective

❏ Not effective at all

6.4. Economic aid to other countries

❏ Very effective

❏ Somewhat effective

❏ Not too effective

❏ Not effective at all

7. Compared to ten years ago, do you think the United States is more powerful as a world leader today, less powerful as a world leader today or about as powerful a world leader as it was ten years ago?

❏ More powerful

❏ Less powerful

❏ About as powerful

8. Thinking about the future of the U.S., please indicate whether you feel generally optimistic or generally pessimistic about America's role as a global leader in the world.

❏ Generally optimistic

❏ Generally pessimistic

9. Would you like to share any other thoughts with us about the waning of Pax Americana? If so, please use the space below.

. . . .

. . . .

. . . .

. . . .

. . . .

Topic 2. Russia's foreign policy

1. Have you engaged in any of the following activities related to the "Russia's foreign policy" topic? Mark all that you have done or mark none of the above.

❏ Read the article on Russia's foreign policy in the 2018 Great Decisions briefing book

❏ Discussed the article on Russia's foreign policy with a Great Decisions discussion group

❏ Discussed the article on Russia's foreign policy with friends and family

❏ Followed news related to Russia's foreign policy

❏ Taken a class in which you learned about issues related to Russia's foreign policy

❏ Have or had a job related to Russia's foreign policy

❏ Traveled to Russia

❏ None of the above

2. How interested would you say you are in issues related to Russia's foreign policy?

❏ Very interested

❏ Somewhat interested

❏ Not too interested

❏ Not at all interested

3. In general, do you think that Russia's power and influence is a major threat, a minor threat or not a threat to the U.S.?

❏ Major threat

❏ Minor threat

❏ Not a threat

4. Do you think the Russian hacking into the 2016 U.S. elections poses a major threat, a minor threat or no threat at all to future elections in the United States? If you don't think Russia was involved with hacking the 2016 U.S. elections, please say so.

❏ Major threat

❏ Minor threat

❏ No threat

❏ I do not believe Russia was involved with hacking the 2016 U.S. elections

5. If the United States reduces its role on the world stage, how likely do you think it is that Russia will benefit compared to other countries?

❏ Very likely

❏ Somewhat likely

❏ Not too likely

❏ Not likely at all

6. Do you think the government of Russia respects the personal freedoms of its people or do you think the government of Russia does not respect the personal freedoms of its people?

❏ Respects the personal freedoms of its people

❏ Does not respect the personal freedoms of its people

7. Do you consider Russia to be a friend or an enemy of the United States?

❏ Friend

❏ Enemy

8. If Russia got into a serious military conflict with one of its neighboring countries that is a NATO ally of the United States, do you think the United States should or should not use military force to defend that country?

❏ Should use military force

❏ Should not use military force

9. Which of the following poses the greatest immediate threat to the United States: North Korea, Iran, Russia, China or ISIS?

❏ North Korea

❏ Iran

❏ Russia

❏ China

❏ ISIS

10. Would you like to share any other thoughts with us about Russia's foreign policy? If so, please use the space below.

. . . .

. . . .

. . . .

. . . .

Topic 3. China and America

1. Have you engaged in any of the following activities related to the "China and America" topic? Mark all that you have done or mark none of the above.

❏ Read the article on China in the 2018 Great Decisions briefing book

❏ Discussed the article on China with a Great Decisions discussion group

❏ Discussed the article on China with friends and family

❏ Followed news related to China

❏ Taken a class in which you learned about issues related to China

❏ Have or had a job related to China

❏ Traveled to China

❏ None of the above

2. How interested would you say you are in issues related to China?

❏ Very interested

❏ Somewhat interested

❏ Not too interested

❏ Not at all interested

3. Do you think that China's power and influence is a major threat, a minor threat or not a threat to the United States?

❏ Major threat

❏ Minor threat

❏ Not a threat

4. Do you think the government of China respects the personal freedoms of its people or do you think the government of China does not respect the personal freedoms of its people?

❏ Respects the personal freedoms of its people

❏ Does not respect the personal freedoms of its people

5. If the United States reduces its role on the world stage, how likely do you think it is that China will benefit compared to other countries?

❏ Very likely

❏ Somewhat likely

❏ Not too likely

❏ Not likely at all

6. To what extent do you approve or disapprove of the way President Donald Trump is handling U.S. policy toward China?

❏ Strongly approve

❏ Somewhat approve

❏ Somewhat disapprove

❏ Strongly disapprove

7. Which concerns you more about China: its economic strength or its military strength?

❏ Its economic strength

❏ Its military strength

8. Below is a list of things that may be problems for the U.S. For each one, please indicate if you think it is a very serious problem, a somewhat serious problem, not too serious a problem or not a problem at all.

8.1. The loss of U.S. jobs to China
- ❏ Very serious problem
- ❏ Somewhat serious problem
- ❏ Not too serious a problem
- ❏ Not a problem at all

8.2. The U.S. trade deficit with China
- ❏ Very serious problem
- ❏ Somewhat serious problem
- ❏ Not too serious a problem
- ❏ Not a problem at all

8.3. China's policies on human rights
- ❏ Very serious problem
- ❏ Somewhat serious problem
- ❏ Not too serious a problem
- ❏ Not a problem at all

8.4. Tensions between China and Taiwan
- ❏ Very serious problem
- ❏ Somewhat serious problem
- ❏ Not too serious a problem
- ❏ Not a problem at all

8.5. China's impact on the global environment
- ❏ Very serious problem
- ❏ Somewhat serious problem
- ❏ Not too serious a problem
- ❏ Not a problem at all

8.6. The large amount of American debt that is held by China
- ❏ Very serious problem
- ❏ Somewhat serious problem
- ❏ Not too serious a problem
- ❏ Not a problem at all

8.7. Territorial disputes between China and neighboring countries
- ❏ Very serious problem
- ❏ Somewhat serious problem
- ❏ Not too serious a problem
- ❏ Not a problem at all

9. Would you like to share any other thoughts with us about China and America? If so, please use the space below.

. . . .

. . . .

. . . .

. . . .

. . . .

Topic 4. Media and foreign policy

1. Have you engaged in any of the following activities related to the "Media and foreign policy" topic? Mark all that you have done or mark none of the above.
- ❏ Read the article on media and foreign policy in the 2018 Great Decisions briefing book
- ❏ Discussed the article on media and foreign policy with a Great Decisions discussion group
- ❏ Discussed the article on media and foreign policy with friends and family
- ❏ Followed news related to media and foreign policy
- ❏ Taken a class in which you learned about issues related to media and foreign policy
- ❏ Have or had a job related to media and foreign policy
- ❏ None of the above

2. How interested would you say you are in issues related to media and foreign policy?
- ❏ Very interested
- ❏ Somewhat interested
- ❏ Not too interested
- ❏ Not at all interested

3. Overall, do you think the U.S. government is doing enough or not doing enough to protect the government's computer systems from a future cyber-attack?
- ❏ Doing enough
- ❏ Not doing enough

4. How important is it to you that the news media hold public officials accountable?

- ❏ Very important
- ❏ Somewhat important
- ❏ Not so important
- ❏ Not important at all

5. What type of effect are the national news media having on the way things are going in the U.S. these days? A positive effect, a negative effect, a mixed effect, or neither a positive nor a negative effect?

- ❏ Positive
- ❏ Negative
- ❏ Mixed
- ❏ Neither

6. Would you say that the tensions between the Trump administration and the U.S. news media are getting in the way or not getting in the way of Americans' access to important national political news and information?

- ❏ Getting in the way
- ❏ Not getting in the way

7. How often do you get news from social media, such as Facebook or Twitter?

- ❏ Often
- ❏ Sometimes
- ❏ Hardly ever
- ❏ Never

8. How much do you trust information you see on social media, such as Facebook or Twitter?

- ❏ A lot
- ❏ Somewhat
- ❏ Not too much
- ❏ Not at all

9. Would you like to share any other thoughts with us about media and foreign policy? If so, please use the space below.

. . . .

. . . .

. . . .

. . . .

Topic 5. Turkey: a partner in crisis

1. Have you engaged in any of the following activities related to the "Turkey" topic? Mark all that you have done or mark none of the above.

- ❏ Read the article on Turkey in the 2018 Great Decisions briefing book
- ❏ Discussed the article on Turkey with a Great Decisions discussion group
- ❏ Discussed the article on Turkey with friends and family
- ❏ Followed news related to Turkey
- ❏ Taken a class in which you learned about issues related to Turkey
- ❏ Have or had a job related to Turkey
- ❏ Traveled to Turkey
- ❏ None of the above

2. How interested would you say you are in issues related to Turkey?

- ❏ Very interested
- ❏ Somewhat interested
- ❏ Not too interested
- ❏ Not at all interested

3. Do you consider Turkey to be a friend or an enemy of the United States?

- ❏ Friend
- ❏ Enemy

4. Please indicate how you view Turkey's relationship with the United States: Do you consider it a strong ally, somewhat of an ally, somewhat of an enemy or a bitter enemy?

- ❏ Strong ally
- ❏ Somewhat of an ally
- ❏ Somewhat of an enemy
- ❏ A bitter enemy

5. Do you think President Donald Trump considers Turkey to be a friend or an enemy of the United States?

- ❏ Friend
- ❏ Enemy

6. Do you think the United States should or should not have long-term military bases in Turkey?

- ❏ Should have long-term military bases in Turkey
- ❏ Should not have long-term military bases in Turkey

7. To what extent do you approve or disapprove of the way Turkey is handling the Syrian crisis?

- ❏ Strongly approve
- ❏ Somewhat approve
- ❏ Somewhat disapprove
- ❏ Strongly disapprove

8. Do you think the government of Turkey respects the personal freedoms of its people or do you think the government of Turkey does not respect the personal freedoms of its people?

- ❏ Respects the personal freedoms of its people
- ❏ Does not respect the personal freedoms of its people

9. Please indicate whether you strongly agree, somewhat agree, somewhat disagree or strongly disagree with the following statement: Turkey contributes to peace and stability in the Arab world

- ❏ Strongly agree
- ❏ Somewhat agree
- ❏ Somewhat disagree
- ❏ Strongly disagree

10. Would you like to share any other thoughts with us about Turkey? If so, please use the space below.

. . . .

. . . .

. . . .

Topic 6. U.S. global engagement and the military

1. Have you engaged in any of the following activities related to the "U.S. global engagement and the military" topic? Mark all that you have done or mark none of the above.

- ❏ Read the article on U.S. global engagement and the military in the 2018 Great Decisions briefing book
- ❏ Discussed the article on U.S. global engagement and the military with a Great Decisions discussion group
- ❏ Discussed the article on U.S. global engagement and the military with friends and family
- ❏ Followed news related to U.S. global engagement and the military
- ❏ Taken a class in which you learned about issues related to U.S. global engagement and the military
- ❏ Have or had a job related to the military
- ❏ None of the above

2. How interested would you say you are in issues related to U.S. global engagement and the military?

- ❏ Very interested
- ❏ Somewhat interested
- ❏ Not too interested
- ❏ Not at all interested

3. How effective do you think each of the following approaches is to achieving the foreign policy goals of the United States?

3.1. Maintaining existing alliances

- ❏ Very effective
- ❏ Somewhat effective
- ❏ Not too effective
- ❏ Not effective at all

3.2. Maintaining U.S. military superiority

- ❏ Very effective
- ❏ Somewhat effective
- ❏ Not too effective
- ❏ Not effective at all

3.3. Building new alliances with other countries

- ❏ Very effective
- ❏ Somewhat effective
- ❏ Not too effective
- ❏ Not effective at all

3.4. Military intervention

- ❏ Very effective
- ❏ Somewhat effective
- ❏ Not too effective
- ❏ Not effective at all

3.5. Military aid to other countries

- ❏ Very effective
- ❏ Somewhat effective
- ❏ Not too effective
- ❏ Not effective at all

.6. Which of the following comes closest to your view on U.S. security alliances in East Asia?

- ❏ Mostly benefit the U.S.
- ❏ Mostly benefit our allies
- ❏ Benefit both the U.S. and our allies
- ❏ Benefit neither

.7. What about security alliances with countries in Europe?

- ❏ Mostly benefit the U.S.
- ❏ Mostly benefit our allies
- ❏ Benefit both the U.S. and our allies
- ❏ Benefit neither

.8. Finally, what about our security alliances with countries in the Middle East?

- ❏ Mostly benefit the U.S.
- ❏ Mostly benefit our allies
- ❏ Benefit both the U.S. and our allies
- ❏ Benefit neither

. Some people say that NATO is still essential to U.S. security. Others say it is no longer essential. Which of these views is closer to your own?

- ❏ NATO is still essential to U.S. security
- ❏ NATO is no longer essential to U.S. security

. There has been some discussion about circumstances that might justify using U.S. troops in other parts of the world. To what extent would you favor or oppose the use of U.S. troops in the following situations?

.1. To stop or prevent a government from using chemical or biological weapons against its own people

- ❏ Strongly favor
- ❏ Somewhat favor
- ❏ Somewhat oppose
- ❏ Strongly oppose

.2. To deal with humanitarian crises

- ❏ Strongly favor
- ❏ Somewhat favor
- ❏ Somewhat oppose
- ❏ Strongly oppose

.3. To fight against violent Islamic extremist groups in Iraq and Syria

- ❏ Strongly favor
- ❏ Somewhat favor

- ❏ Somewhat oppose
- ❏ Strongly oppose

5.4. If North Korea invaded South Korea

- ❏ Strongly favor
- ❏ Somewhat favor
- ❏ Somewhat oppose
- ❏ Strongly oppose

5.5. If Russia invaded a NATO ally like Latvia, Lithuania or Estonia

- ❏ Strongly favor
- ❏ Somewhat favor
- ❏ Somewhat oppose
- ❏ Strongly oppose

5.6. If China initiated a military conflict with Japan over disputed islands

- ❏ Strongly favor
- ❏ Somewhat favor
- ❏ Somewhat oppose
- ❏ Strongly oppose

5.7. If Russia invaded the rest of Ukraine

- ❏ Strongly favor
- ❏ Somewhat favor
- ❏ Somewhat oppose
- ❏ Strongly oppose

6. Do you think that the U.S. military presence in the following regions should be increased, maintained at its present level or decreased?

6.1. Europe

- ❏ Increased
- ❏ Decreased
- ❏ Maintained at present level

6.2. Asia-Pacific

- ❏ Increased
- ❏ Decreased
- ❏ Maintained at present level

6.3. Middle East

- ❏ Increased
- ❏ Decreased
- ❏ Maintained at present level

6.4. Africa

❏ Increased

❏ Decreased

❏ Maintained at present level

6.5. Latin America

❏ Increased

❏ Decreased

❏ Maintained at present level

7. Would you like to share any other thoughts with us about U.S. global engagement and the military? If so, please use the space below.

. . . .

. . . .

. . . .

. . . .

Topic 7. South Africa's fragile democracy

1. Have you engaged in any of the following activities related to the "South Africa's fragile democracy" topic? Mark all that you have done or mark none of the above.

❏ Read the article on South Africa in the 2018 Great Decisions briefing book

❏ Discussed the article on South Africa with a Great Decisions discussion group

❏ Discussed the article on South Africa with friends and family

❏ Followed news related to South Africa

❏ Taken a class in which you learned about issues related to South Africa

❏ Have or had a job related to South Africa

❏ Traveled to South Africa

❏ None of the above

2. How interested would you say you are in issues related to South Africa?

❏ Very interested

❏ Somewhat interested

❏ Not too interested

❏ Not at all interested

3. Overall, how much of a democracy do you think South Africa is today?

❏ A full democracy

❏ A democracy, but with minor problems

❏ A democracy, but with major problems

4. Do you think South Africa is having a mainly positive or mainly negative influence in the world?

❏ Mainly positive

❏ Mainly negative

5. Do you feel that South Africa is a close ally of the U.S., is friendly but not a close ally, is not friendly but not an enemy, or is unfriendly and is an enemy of the U.S.?

❏ Close ally of the U.S.

❏ Friendly but not a close ally

❏ Not friendly but not an enemy

❏ Unfriendly and is an enemy of the U.S.

6. To what extent would you favor or oppose adding South Africa as a permanent member of the United Nations Security Council?

❏ Strongly favor

❏ Somewhat favor

❏ Somewhat oppose

❏ Strongly oppose

7. Generally, do you think American foreign policy has a positive effect on South Africa or a negative effect, or does American foreign policy have no effect on South Africa?

❏ Positive effect

❏ Negative effect

❏ No effect

8. In making international policy decisions, to what extent do you think the United States takes into account the interests of South Africa: a great deal, a fair amount, not too much or not at all?

❏ A great deal

❏ A fair amount

❏ Not too much

❏ Not at all

9. Would you like to share any other thoughts with us about South Africa's fragile democracy? If so, please use the space below.

. . . .

. . . .

. . . .

Topic 8. Global health: progress and challenges

. Have you engaged in any of the following activities related to
he "Global health" topic? Mark all that you have done or mark
one of the above.

❏ Read the article on global health in the 2018 Great Decisions briefing book

❏ Discussed the article on global health with a Great Decisions discussion group

❏ Discussed the article on global health with friends and family

❏ Followed news related to global health

❏ Taken a class in which you learned about issues related to global health

❏ Have or had a job related to global health

❏ None of the above

. How interested would you say you are in issues related to
global health?

❏ Very interested

❏ Somewhat interested

❏ Not too interested

❏ Not at all interested

. When it comes to efforts to improve health in developing
countries, do you think the U.S. should or should not give money to each of the following?

.1. To international organizations like the Global Fund to Fight
AIDS, Tuberculosis and Malaria

❏ Should give money

❏ Should not give money

.2. To international organizations like the United Nations and
the World Health Organization

❏ Should give money

❏ Should not give money

.3. Directly to U.S.-based non-profits operating programs in
developing countries

❏ Should give money

❏ Should not give money

.4. Directly to local non-profits based in developing countries
and not in the U.S.

❏ Should give money

❏ Should not give money

3.5. Directly to religious or faith-based organizations

❏ Should give money

❏ Should not give money

3.6. Directly to governments in developing countries

❏ Should give money

❏ Should not give money

4. In terms of what the U.S. government could spend on foreign
aid, do you think combating global outbreaks of diseases like
Ebola and Zika should be one of the top priorities, important but
not a top priority or not that important?

❏ One of the top priorities

❏ Important but not a top priority

❏ Not that important

5. To what extent do you agree or disagree that Americans will
be better off if the U.S. government invests in global health
research?

❏ Strongly agree

❏ Somewhat agree

❏ Somewhat disagree

❏ Strongly disagree

6. To what extent do you agree or disagree that it is a moral
obligation for the U.S. government to spend money supporting
global health research?

❏ Strongly agree

❏ Somewhat agree

❏ Somewhat disagree

❏ Strongly disagree

7. To what extent do you agree or disagree with the following
statement? The U.S. government should not spend money on
global health because the problems of global health are just too
big to be solved.

❏ Strongly agree

❏ Somewhat agree

❏ Somewhat disagree

❏ Strongly disagree

8. Would you like to share any other thoughts with us about
global health? If so, please use the space below.

. . . .

. . . .

. . . .

This year, give the student in your life
the gift of knowledge

FPA is pleased to offer Student Membership, at a reduced rate of $50.00. A perfect gift for the budding internationalist in your life, Student Membership includes unlimited free admission to all FPA Associate events, discounts on guest tickets, and a subscription to the Great Decisions Annual Briefing Book.

If you are interested in this special offer, please contact Adam Camiolo, Director of Membership, at membership@fpa.org or at 212-481-8100 ext. 251.

FOREIGN POLICY ASSOCIATION

Become a Member

For nearly a century, members of the Association have played key roles in government, think tanks, academia and the private sector.

As an active participant in the FPA's Great Decisions program, we encourage you to join the community today's foreign policy thought leaders.

Member—$250

Benefits:
- Free admission to all Associate events (includes member's family)
- Discounted admission for all other guests to Associate events
- Complimentary **GREAT DECISIONS** briefing book
- Complimentary issue of FPA's annual ***National Opinion Ballot Report***

Visit us online at

www.fpa.org/membership

Make a Donation

Your support helps the FOREIGN POLICY ASSOCIATION's programs dedicated to global affairs education.

Make a fully tax-deductible contribution to FPA's Annual Fund 2018.

To contribute to the Annual Fund 2018, visit us online at **www.fpa.org** or call the Membership Department at

(800) 628-5754 ext. 333

The generosity of donors who contribute $500 or more is acknowledged in FPA's *Annual Report.*

All financial contributions are tax-deductible to the fullest extent of the law under section 501 (c)(3) of the IRS code.

FPA also offers membership at the SPONSOR MEMBER and PATRON MEMBER levels. To learn more, visit us online at www.fpa.org/membership or call (800) 628-5754 ext. 333.

Return this form by mail to: Foreign Policy Association, 470 Park Avenue South, New York, N.Y. 10016. *Or fax to:* (212) 481-9275.

ORDER ONLINE: WWW.GREATDECISIONS.ORG

OR CALL (800) 477-5836

FOR MEMBERSHIP: WWW.FPA.ORG/MEMBERSHIP

❏ MR.   ❏ MRS.   ❏ MS.   ❏ DR.   ❏ PROF.

NAME _____

ADDRESS _____

_____ **APT/FLOOR** _____

CITY _____ **STATE** _____ **ZIP** _____

TEL _____

E-MAIL _____

❏ AMEX   ❏ VISA   ❏ MC   ❏ DISCOVER
❏ CHECK (ENCLOSED)
  CHECKS SHOULD BE PAYABLE TO FOREIGN POLICY ASSOCIATION.

CARD NO.

☐☐☐☐☐☐☐☐☐☐☐☐☐☐☐☐

SIGNATURE OF CARDHOLDER

☐☐☐☐☐☐☐☐☐☐☐☐☐☐☐☐☐

EXP. DATE (MM/YY)

☐☐☐☐

PRODUCT	QTY	PRICE	COST
GREAT DECISIONS 2018 Briefing Book (FPA31671)		$30	
SPECIAL OFFER TEN PACK SPECIAL GREAT DECISIONS 2018 (FPA31678) *Includes 10% discount		$270	
GREAT DECISIONS TELEVISION SERIES GD ON DVD 2018 (FPA31672)		$40	
GREAT DECISIONS 2018 TEACHER'S PACKET (1 Briefing Book, 1 Teacher's Guide and 1 DVD (FPA 31674) E-MAIL: (REQUIRED) _____		$70	
GREAT DECISIONS CLASSROOM-PACKET (1 Teacher's Packet & 30 Briefing Books (FPA31675) E-MAIL: (REQUIRED) _____		$660	
MEMBERSHIP		$250	
ANNUAL FUND 2017 (ANY AMOUNT)			

For details and shipping charges, call FPA's Sales Department at (800) 477-5836.
Orders mailed to FPA without the shipping charge will be held.

SUBTOTAL $ _____
plus S & H* $ _____
TOTAL $ _____